CW01640531

Profiles in Power

Biography Studies

Editor-in-Chief

Hans Renders (*University of Groningen*)

Editorial Board

Nigel Hamilton (*University of Massachusetts Boston*)
Sigurður Gylfi Magnússon (*University of Iceland*)
Lindie Koorts (*University of the Free State*)

Biography Institute

VOLUME 2

The titles published in this series are listed at *brill.com/bio*

Profiles in Power

Personality, Persona, and the U.S. President

Edited by

Jelte Olthof
Maarten Zwiers

BRILL

LEIDEN | BOSTON

Cover illustration: Presidents' heads in Williamsburg, Virginia. Photograph by Jan Postma.

Library of Congress Cataloging-in-Publication Data

Names: Olthof, Jelte, editor. | Zwiers, Maarten, 1979- editor.
Title: Profiles in power : personality, persona, and the U.S. President / edited by Jelte Olthof, Maarten Zwiers.
Other titles: Personality, persona, and the U.S. President
Description: Leiden ; Boston : Brill, [2020] | Series: Biography studies, 2468-2497 ; volume 2 | Includes bibliographical references and index.
Identifiers: LCCN 2020030421 | ISBN 9789004414440 (hardback) | ISBN 9789004422643 (ebook)
Subjects: LCSH: Presidents–United States–Biography. | Character–Political aspects–United States. | Presidents–United States–Conduct of life. | Executive power–United States–History.
Classification: LCC E176.1 .P9747 2020 | DDC 973.09/9–dc23
LC record available at https://lccn.loc.gov/2020030421

Typeface for the Latin, Greek, and Cyrillic scripts: "Brill". See and download: brill.com/brill-typeface.

ISSN 2468-2497
ISBN 978-90-04-41444-0 (hardback)
ISBN 978-90-04-42264-3 (e-book)

Copyright 2020 by Koninklijke Brill NV, Leiden, The Netherlands.
Koninklijke Brill NV incorporates the imprints Brill, Brill Hes & De Graaf, Brill Nijhoff, Brill Rodopi, Brill Sense, Hotei Publishing, mentis Verlag, Verlag Ferdinand Schöningh and Wilhelm Fink Verlag.
All rights reserved. No part of this publication may be reproduced, translated, stored in a retrieval system, or transmitted in any form or by any means, electronic, mechanical, photocopying, recording or otherwise, without prior written permission from the publisher. Requests for re-use and/or translations must be addressed to Koninklijke Brill NV via brill.com or copyright.com.

This book is printed on acid-free paper and produced in a sustainable manner.

Printed by Printforce, United Kingdom

Contents

Acknowledgements

The editors of this volume would like to thank Hans Renders, professor of History and Biography and director of the Biography Institute at the University of Groningen, the Netherlands. He facilitated the publication of this book and was our main liaison with Brill. We also want to thank the two peer reviewers who critically read the manuscript and offered constructive comments. Their feedback substantially improved the contributions to this volume. Finally, we are grateful to Francis Knikker, assistant editor of History at Brill, and the entire team at VTeX for their help getting the book ready for publication.

Contributors

Kathryn Cramer Brownell
is associate professor of history at Purdue University. Her research and teaching focus on the intersections between media, politics, and popular culture, with a particular emphasis on the American presidency. She is the author of *Showbiz Politics: Hollywood in American Political Life* (University of North Carolina Press, 2014) and serves as a co-editor of the history section of the *Washington Post*, "Made By History."

Arthur Eaton
is a historian and psychologist. He is a member of the Centre for the History of Psychological Disciplines at University College London (UCL), and regularly contributes to *De Groene Amsterdammer* and *NRC*. He sees patients in Heemstede, the Netherlands.

Dario Fazzi
works as senior researcher at the Roosevelt Institute for American Studies and teaches at several Dutch universities. He has published on nuclear culture and policymaking, peace movements, transnational protests, base politics, and transatlantic crossings. He is the author of *Eleanor Roosevelt and the Anti-Nuclear Movement* (Palgrave, 2016).

Keith M. Finley
is assistant professor of history at Southeastern Louisiana University and assistant director of the Center for Southeast Louisiana Studies. He is the author of *Delaying the Dream: Southern Senators and the Fight Against Civil Rights, 1938-1965* (Louisiana State University Press, 2008).

Nigel Hamilton
is senior fellow at the McCormack Graduate School of Policy and Global Studies, UMass Boston. The concluding volume of his "FDR at War" trilogy, *War and Peace: FDR's Final Odyssey, D-Day to Yalta, 1943-1945* was published in 2019.

Robert Mason
is professor of History at the University of Edinburgh. His research is on the United States during the twentieth century, especially American political history of the post-World War II years. He is the author of two books, *Richard Nixon and the Quest for a New Majority* (University of North Carolina Press,

2004) and *The Republican Party and American Politics from Hoover to Reagan* (Cambridge University Press, 2011).

Jelte Olthof

is assistant professor of American Studies at the University of Groningen, where he teaches rhetoric and the U.S. Constitution. His dissertation *Patchwork Republic* traces the rhetorical career of "we the people" in Congressional debates.

Sara Polak

is assistant professor in American Studies at Leiden University (LUCAS). Her research interest is in presidential media and memory-making. Her book *"This Is Roosevelt's World": FDR as an Icon in American Memory* is forthcoming with Johns Hopkins University Press.

Mark Leon de Vries

completed a PhD at Leiden University in 2015 on racial and political terrorism in Louisiana's Red River Valley during Reconstruction. After combining teaching and research for a number of years, he left academia to work full-time in education.

David Zarefsky

is emeritus professor at the Department of Communication of Northwestern University and past president of the National Communication Association and the Rhetoric Society of America. He has published widely on argumentation theory and rhetorical criticism and more recently, on the rhetorical style of Abraham Lincoln.

Maarten Zwiers

is assistant professor of American Studies and History at the University of Groningen. He specializes in rural and southern studies and is the author of *Senator James Eastland: Mississippi's Jim Crow Democrat* (Louisiana State University Press, 2015).

INTRODUCTION

The Personal Presidency

Jelte Olthof and Maarten Zwiers

Donald Trump's victory in the 2016 election and his years in the White House once again demonstrate the central role of personality in presidential campaigns and politics. Trump managed to win the race for the presidency on the basis of his persona and his subsequent administration appeared to rely more on personal whims than on a coherent program for government. Not just the general public, but also Trump's senior staff regularly had trouble to make sense of his deeper motivations. In his controversial book *Fire and Fury*, journalist Michael Wolff described it as "the lasting conundrum of dealing with President Trump: the 'why' of his often baffling behavior."[1] Besides the highly personalistic nature of Trump's politics, critics claimed he personified a broader current in U.S. political culture: a spokesman for the hypercapitalist class that has little regard for minorities, women, the environment, or middle- and lower-class white voters, but which feeds on the fears and anxieties that live amongst these latter two groups. For social activist Naomi Klein, Trump was in fact the embodiment of "the worst of all that [U.S.] culture is capable of, all of it bundled into one human being."[2] From different perspectives, the exploits of the Trump White House thus show the importance of studying the role of individual agency in politics. Besides policy-making, an emphasis on powerful individuals also reveals how one person can represent broader sentiments in U.S. society and how these sentiments can be politically mobilized.

In this light, it is unsurprising that the personal nature of presidential politics can count on renewed scholarly interest. Historian David Bell even concluded that Trump's election marked a resurgence of 'great man theory.' Professional academics like himself, Bell writes, are trained in the social science tradition of the *Annales* school that is hostile to the type of 'histoire evenementielle' the 2016 election represents and prefer to look at "large-scale, long-term,

1 Michael Wolff, *Fire and Fury: Inside the Trump White House* (London: Little, Brown, 2018), 303.

2 Naomi Klein, *No Is Not Enough: Defeating the New Shock Politics* (London: Allen Lane, 2017), 123.

© KONINKLIJKE BRILL NV, LEIDEN, 2020 | DOI:10.1163/9789004422643_002

impersonal forces." Trump's election, in his view, forms a watershed moment because unlike his predecessors, Trump will not respect established traditions or abide by the advice of his staff, fellow Republicans, or the bureaucracy. Bell concludes: "Trump has the potential to become the most powerful president in American history. And he is one of the most radically unpredictable men ever elected to that office (…) Donald Trump's personality could assume, difficult as it is to apply these words to him, world-historical importance."[3]

One of the aims of this volume is to demonstrate that the influence of the personal on the political holds true not just for Trump, but for all presidents before him – recognizing, of course, the expanded powers of the modern presidency. At the same time, presidents are constrained by the structure in which they operate, including the choices their predecessors made. While Bell's assessment about Trump's world historical significance may be an exaggeration spurred by the dramatic moment, this in itself proves the formative role of contemporary events on our thinking and actions. Moreover, scholars of the United States presidency have not suddenly started to realize this. Two decades ago, for example, professors Stephen Skowronek and Douglas Hoekstra crossed swords about so-called "executive determinism" in accounting for presidential politics in the pages of the *Presidential Studies Quarterly*.[4] Far from rousing historians from a structuralist dream, then, Trump's election has rather reignited the debate about the relative influence of events and structure (or in other words, the impact of individual actions versus impersonal factors like traditions, norms, and institutions) scholars have engaged in for decades.

Besides this renewed interest in the role of individuals in shaping politics, researchers have begun more in-depth explorations into the elusive world of emotions as a decisive factor in political matters. Clinical psychologist and political strategist Drew Westen described the political brain as an emotional brain, "not a dispassionate calculating machine, objectively searching for the right facts, figures, and policies to make a reasoned decision."[5] Westen primarily concentrates on electoral politics and voters' feelings toward candidates, or

3 David Bell, "Donald Trump Is Making the Great Man Theory of History Great Again," *Foreign Policy*, January 12, 2017, https://foreignpolicy.com/2017/01/12/donald-trump-is-making-the-great-man-theory-of-history-great-again/.

4 See Douglas J. Hoekstra, "The Politics of *Politics*: Skowronek and Presidential Research," *Presidential Studies Quarterly* 29, no. 3 (1999): 657-671, and Stephen Skowronek, "Theory and History, Structure and Agency," *Presidential Studies Quarterly* 29, no. 3 (1999): 672-681.

5 Drew Westen, *The Political Brain: The Role of Emotions in Deciding the Fate of the Nation* (New York: PublicAffairs, 2008), xv.

what he calls "the marketplace of emotions." Other scholars have investigated the outbreak of major conflicts through the lens of emotions, for instance the U.S. Civil War and the Cold War.[6] Some historians took a more biographical approach to determine how emotions influenced the decisions of prominent foreign policy strategists such as George Kennan and Henry Kissinger.[7] In a study of the transition from Franklin Roosevelt to Harry Truman in 1945, historian Frank Costigliola discovered how personality and emotions even shaped postwar relations between the United States and the Soviet Union. With Roosevelt instead of Truman at the helm after the defeat of the Axis powers, the alliance between the two superpowers might not have disintegrated so quickly, Costigliola argued.[8] In short, contingency, personality, and emotions have become important determinants in political history, complementing more historical institutionalist approaches that foreground structure and impersonal forces over individual agency and the unpredictability of the electorate.

Frank Costigliola's chapter on FDR and Truman appeared in *Recapturing the Oval Office*, a book that seeks to "bring the presidency back into" academic research on U.S. political history. For quite some time, the American Political Development (APD) school dominated this field. APD researchers take a structural approach; they are primarily interested in the historical formation of governmental institutions.[9] In line with *Recapturing the Oval Office*, our book attempts to refocus the attention on the White House, but from a biographical perspective. The contributions to this volume approach the presidency as a personal affair, shaped, in part, by the character, virtues, and flaws of those occupying the Oval Office. As such, it builds on scholars' renewed emphasis on individual agency, by bringing the personal aspect of the presidency back into the narrative of U.S. political history. Our choice for a biographical approach follows from this regenerated interest in the personal. Biography investigates

6 Michael E. Woods, *Emotional and Sectional Conflict in the Antebellum United States* (Cambridge: Cambridge University Press, 2014); Frank Costigliola, *Roosevelt's Lost Alliances: How Personal Politics Helped Start the Cold War* (Princeton: Princeton University Press, 2012).

7 Frank Costigliola, "'I React Intensely to Everything': Russia and the Frustrated Emotions of George F. Kennan, 1933-1958," *Journal of American History* 102, no. 4 (March 2016): 1075-1106. See also Barbara Keys, "Henry Kissinger: The Emotional Statesman," *Diplomatic History* 35, no. 4 (September 2011): 587-609.

8 Frank Costigliola, "Personal Dynamics and Presidential Transition: The Case of Roosevelt and Truman," in *Recapturing the Oval Office: New Historical Approaches to the American Presidency*, eds. Brian Balogh and Bruce Schulman (Ithaca: Cornell University Press, 2015), 50.

9 See for an overview of APD Scott C. James, "Historical Institutionalism, Political Development, and the Presidency," in *The Oxford Handbook of the American Presidency*, eds. George C. Edwards and William G. Howell (Oxford; Oxford University Press, 2009).

whether persons were representative of their time or deviated from it, sometimes at specific moments.[10]

In addition to his work on the role of emotions in politics, Costigliola has also pointed out how individuals can change the course of history at "critical junctures." At these instances, "the otherwise immovable structures ... temporarily become plastic [and] the personality of key leaders can make a decisive and lasting difference."[11] Costigliola's emphasis on individual agency is of particular relevance for this volume. Moreover, a biographical approach does not just illuminate the life of individuals, but also gives insight into specific historical periods. Historian Kenneth Greenberg explained this double function of biography in a review of the life story of James Henry Hammond, an antebellum planter-politician from South Carolina. According to Greenberg, biography, "when done well, can offer the opportunity for synthesis; a world can manifest itself in the life of a person."[12]

The biographical contributions to this volume investigate the relation between personality and presidential politics. Personality here is understood as the myriad ways in which formative factors and events like upbringing, family, hometowns and regional identity, education, career, and life events shape the character of future presidents. Presidents bring this personal background to the White House, and the person they have become up to that point often affects and explains their performance in office, as well as why they sought that office in the first place.[13] This book also analyzes the strategies presidents used to shape how voters (and posterity) viewed their performance by actively assuming a character role or persona.[14] Persona is not synonymous with presidential personality, but refers to the roles individuals (in this case presidents) adopt to further specific goals. All presidents play such roles, from Washington taking on the mantle of statesmanship to George W. Bush's folksy pater-

10 Hans Renders and Binne de Haan, "The Challenges of Biography Studies," in *Theoretical Discussions of Biography: Approaches From History, Microhistory, and Life Writing*, eds. Hans Renders and Binne de Haan (Leiden and Boston: Brill, 2014), 5.

11 Costigliola, "Personal Dynamics and Presidential Transition," 38-39.

12 Kenneth S. Greenberg, "Why Masters Are Slaves," review of *James Henry Hammond and the Old South: A Design for Mastery*, by Drew Gilpin Faust, *Reviews in American History* 11, no. 3 (1983): 386.

13 See for more on this Marcia Lynn Whicker's introduction to a special issue on "The Human Presidency" of the *Presidential Studies Quarterly* 29, no. 1 (March 1999): 7.

14 The word "persona" stems from the term used in ancient Roman theater to denote the masks that actors would don to assume a specific character in the play. See B.L. Ware and Wil A. Linkugel, "The Rhetorical Persona: Marcus Garvey as Black Moses," *Communication Monographs* 49, no. 1 (1982): 50.

nalism.[15] Some of the presidents discussed in this book were fixated on their personal reputation and legacy.

The volume opens with two reflections on the role biography and psychohistory play (or have played) in the study of the presidency. In his opening chapter, veteran presidential biographer Nigel Hamilton notes the importance of the biographical method in assessing the role of individual agency of those occupying the Oval Office. Ideally, Hamilton argues, the biographer and historian work together in symbiosis: "each one acting to inform and challenge the other." Citing his own work on Franklin Delano Roosevelt as commander in chief, Hamilton demonstrates how the biographical method can serve as a "corrective" to existing misunderstandings in historical scholarship. In such cases, the biographer helps breathe new life in the ongoing discussion about the impact of presidential personality on policy and history.

In his contribution to the volume, Arthur Eaton analyzes the connections between psychohistory, a biographical genre that was once very popular, and presidential history. Psychohistory, Eaton explains, is an "interdiscipline" that combines a (Freudian) psychoanalytic mode of examination and history to explain the personality and psychological problems of powerful historical figures like Adolf Hitler and Martin Luther. As Eaton shows, American presidents proved an irresistible object of study for psychohistorians. Following in the footsteps of Freud – whose notorious psychoanalysis of Woodrow Wilson appeared posthumously in 1967 – a growing number of historians published presidential 'psychobiographies' in the 1960s and 1970s that sought to push the boundaries of the discipline. The new 'vision' psychohistorians like Robert Lifton and Nixon-biographer Bruce Mazlish articulated, was met with hostility by traditional historians, who considered it a controversial branch of study. While hardly practiced today, Eaton shows the fascinating place psychobiography once occupied in presidential historiography. Its focus on the person of the president touches on many of the themes pursued in this volume.

David Zarefsky's case study discusses the origins of Abraham Lincoln's evolving position on slavery. Lincoln, of course, has no shortage of biographers, but his personal views on slavery and his sincerity and commitment to abolition remain a puzzle for historians. Zarefsky explains how Lincoln's upbringing and early experiences as a frontier lawyer and Whig-politician helped him formulate seven commitments with regard to slavery that shaped his time

15 See for instance Evan Cornog, *The Power and the Story: How the Crafted Presidential Narrative Has Determined Political Success from George Washington to George W. Bush* (New York: Penguin, 2004).

in office. In the process, Zarefsky shows that Lincoln was neither the "great" nor reluctant emancipator that he is often made out to be, but someone whose views were shaped and influenced by his personal background and experiences.

President Andrew Johnson is the main character in Mark de Vries's chapter. A slave-owning Tennessee Democrat who sided with the Union and became Lincoln's running mate, Johnson is best known for his clash with Radical Republicans over the goals of Reconstruction. Few historians look favorably upon Johnson's presidency, but De Vries demonstrates that the very traits that disqualified Johnson in the eyes of his biographers – including his temper and racist convictions – supplied the passion and determination to effectively obstruct the Radical Republican Reconstruction program. De Vries explains how Johnson adopted a strict constitutionalist Jacksonian persona in his dealings with administrators responsible for the actual implementation of Reconstruction in for example Louisiana to rally support as well as advance the careers of like-minded politicians. As De Vries shows, Johnson's personal style of politics brought him dangerously close to impeachment, but also paved the way for the post-Civil War racist Redeemer governments of the 1870s. Because of this controversial legacy, scholars have consistently judged Johnson as one of the worst presidents in U.S. history.

In contrast with Johnson, Franklin Roosevelt appeared to be much more preoccupied with how his presidency would be remembered. FDR actively employed the past on the campaign trail and as president, often to depoliticize his own position. Yet in doing so, he was very much involved in shaping the memory of himself and of his administration, seemingly without a self-serving political aim. Sara Polak shows how FDR's political acumen, norm-breaking, and astute 'juggling' of political expectations represent his elusive personality. She suggests that his approach to curating his future image offers the most productive inroad into understanding the connections between personality and presidency. Besides being the chief executive, Roosevelt also was a public historian of sorts who consciously constructed apolitical tributes to his presidency, often through forging so-called indexical connections between himself and concrete outcomes of his policies and programs. To a certain extent, the seemingly apolitical nature of FDR memory culture explains his continuing popularity, also among scholars.

In his chapter, Dario Fazzi takes a closer look at Eleanor Roosevelt, whose liberal internationalism was firmly grounded in her upbringing. Born into a patrician East Coast family, Roosevelt's awareness of *noblesse oblige* activated a sense of social duty that became "her most important guiding principle." Eleanor not only elevated the post of First Lady to a politically significant position, but also continued her social activism in fighting poverty and standing up for women's and civil rights during the Depression Era. Fazzi argues how this progressive domestic work translated to a strong internationalist agenda in foreign politics. As such, Eleanor Roosevelt played a pivotal role in attempts to globalize the New Deal.[16]

In his contribution to the volume, Robert Mason analyzes the multifaceted political persona of Dwight Eisenhower. The roots of Eisenhower's position as one of the most popular presidents in recorded history during his time in office, Mason explains, were located in his ability to portray himself as above parties. Eisenhower held no political office before running for president. He framed himself as a war hero, peacemaker, and father-figure (to his soldiers as well as to the nation) instead. This resulted in what Mason calls a "nonpolitical politician," making people identify more with his office than with the Republican Party. Paradoxically, as Mason shows, this nonpolitical persona meant that efforts to transfer Eisenhower's personal popularity to the Republican Party as a whole were largely unsuccessful. During his time in office, the Republican Party operated in Eisenhower's shadow, which was also a cause of the Republicans' rightward shift.

Regional background informs Keith Finley's chapter on Lyndon Baines Johnson. Finley states we need to know about Johnson's Texas roots in order to understand his later politics; his parents and his upbringing in the Hill Country profoundly shaped his personality, a personality that determined the form and scope of LBJ's Great Society program. Johnson's policies at home and abroad were "clearly a product of his Texas-sized dreams and personality," Finley argues. As a young boy, Johnson wanted the adulation of his mother, who in turn expected excellence from her son. In later years, similar quests for recognition determined his political personality, in combination with rather paranoid ideas about East Coast intellectuals looking down on a politician from the countryside.

By the time Eisenhower's VP Richard Nixon became president in 1968, the GOP had become a much more ideologically-driven party. Through a case study of the Office of Telecommunications Policy (OTP), Kathryn Cramer Brownell explores how the interaction between Nixon's personality and institutional factors shaped his presidency. The OTP "provides an opportunity to examine the intersection between the personal and the broader cultural

---

16 Recent scholarship on the Depression era in the United States calls attention to the global aspects of the New Deal. See for example Kiran Patel, *The New Deal: A Global History* (Princeton: Princeton University Press, 2016).

environment and institutional structures in which Richard Nixon operated," Brownell writes. Considering Nixon's tense relationship with the press, a study of his attitudes toward communication policy reveals how presidential personality can have a considerable impact on federal decision-making.

In line with Finley's chapter, Maarten Zwiers also concentrates on regional identity and family background to explain the rise (and fall) of Jimmy Carter. Zwiers analyzes Carter's 1976 presidential campaign as a telling prelude to his presidency. Like Johnson, Carter's parents had a forceful influence on his personality. Masculinity, regional identity, and religion made the Carter campaign a very distinctive phenomenon with a highly personalistic nature. However, the 'good old boy' club that was the basis for Carter's successful bid for the White House eventually undid his presidency. After victory, latent feelings of regional inferiority, in combination with religious zeal and an obsession with control, rose to the surface and handicapped the Carter administration.

Jelte Olthof concludes the volume with an analysis of the politics of persona practiced by the 45th president, Donald Trump. Drawing on rhetorical theory, Olthof shows how Trump crafted a public persona as a successful and ruthless blue-collar billionaire as early as the late 1960s. He consistently fashioned this self in his public performances, his best-selling book *The Art of the Deal*, and on the campaign trail. In the case of Trump, Olthof argues, persona and person have become so intertwined, that it is hard to make out who the 'real' Donald Trump is. This entanglement has important implications for his behavior as president and his accountability to the American electorate. Although the Trump administration is a particularly dramatic example of how the complicated interaction between personality, persona, and individual agency often determines the operation and impact of presidential politics, all contributions to this volume emphasize the importance of individual agency in understanding the presidency and the workings of U.S. political culture.

CHAPTER 1

The Symbiosis between Biography and History

Nigel Hamilton

1 Of Power and Agency

Every four years, via an Electoral College, the voters of the United States elect the man or woman who will be their next president and chief executive. Each election entitles the winning presidential nominee to 'rule' for the following four years, come war or peace. But ever since the Twenty-Second Amendment was passed in 1951, no individual may run for more than two elections. Understandably that Amendment was a reaction to the unique fourth term for which Franklin Delano Roosevelt insisted upon running in 1944 – an election that prompted his Republican opponent, Thomas Dewey, to declare: "four terms, or sixteen years, is the most dangerous threat to our freedom ever proposed."[1]

American politicians, legislators, and commentators worried that, even in the midst of a world war, four terms for the same president was inimical to American-style democracy – and who can blame them? Not only were the powers vested in the president as commander in chief of the U.S. military enormous, but so were the burdens placed upon the president in a nation that had been dragged into global conflict at Pearl Harbor. Could any human being be expected to bear those responsibilities sagely and sanely for more than eight years? After all, President Woodrow Wilson had been felled by a massive stroke in 1919, toward the end of his second term and some months after the ending of World War I. His true condition had been kept secret, even perhaps from himself – for he had then decided to run for a third term in 1920 (He failed, however, to get the Democratic nomination).

Franklin D. Roosevelt's dire medical condition, in mid-1944, was similarly withheld from the public, though it was becoming visibly apparent to all who met him.[2] In terms of his health – hypertensive cardiac disease – he should not have been permitted to run, Dr. Frank Lahey (head of the Lahey Clinic

1 David M. Jordan, *FDR, Dewey, and the Election of 1944* (Bloomington: Indiana University Press, 2011), 290.

2 Robert Ferrell, *The Dying President: Franklin D. Roosevelt, 1944-1945* (Columbia, MI: University of Missouri Press, 1998), 17.

© KONINKLIJKE BRILL NV, LEIDEN, 2020 | DOI:10.1163/9789004422643_003

and medical consultant to the president) warned White House doctor Vice-Admiral McIntire. McIntire, in turn, told the president.[3] But the advice became only one factor in Roosevelt's decision to run – though it did force him to take the matter seriously when recommending a new vice-presidential nominee at the Democratic Party convention.[4] Roosevelt went on to win a fourth term – but within three months of his fourth inauguration was dead.

My point here is this: the power, authority and potential influence of the individual who is elected to the presidency is not merely theoretical. However much as historians we may question individual agency – the ability of a single individual to affect the course of events – we are, when analyzing the American presidency, faced by the reality of real executive power. We may seek to document and interpret the full variety of political, economic, social, and cultural patterns that help us understand the course of U.S. history, but we should be mindful that Congress itself was certainly under no illusions about the paramount agency of that individual, once elected, to affect the fortunes of the nation (and other nations) once installed in the White House. That power may subsequently be contested by Congress and the Supreme Court, exercising their constitutional checks and balances, but in a world in which the U.S. became the dominant world power militarily in 1945, the president's role remains a crucial keystone in the American political system.

In seeking to assess the role and effective agency of the president as they have been exercised in U.S. and world history, then, we need not be coy in paying close attention to the particular individual occupying the Oval Office. Which leads us to the question, who is best equipped to record, understand, and assess a particular chief executive: the historian or biographer? I ask this because, in studying the past, we surely need both: each one acting to inform and challenge the other. Biography and history have always enjoyed a symbiotic relationship, ever since classical times. The earliest great biographers *were* historians, after all – Plutarch, Suetonius, Tacitus – who wanted to capture more deeply the individual personalities of their subjects, but also to examine their effect or agency upon others, and their times.[5]

The symbiotic relationship between biography and history, let us be honest, has varied in quality over the millennia. As I have argued in "Biography as Corrective," however, there has recently been a significant shift or turn in

3 Harry Goldsmith, *A Conspiracy of Silence: The Health and Death of Franklin D. Roosevelt* (New York: iUniverse, 2007), 170-171.

4 Ferrell, 78.

5 Nigel Hamilton, *Biography: A Brief History* (Cambridge, MA: Harvard University Press, 2007), 25-27.

the biographical perspective.[6] What had appeared to some to be an alarming tendency in the 1980s to value the personal over the political, or the private person over worldly achievement, has developed for the most part into a more serious desire by biographers to review and assess critically the public lives and achievements of their chosen subjects and to use 'deep scholarship' to challenge, where necessary, complacent or facile judgments of historians in painting the past. Nowhere has this shift been more evident than in the study of the U.S. presidency. Biographies such as Robert Caro's multi-volume life of Lyndon Johnson or Edmund Morris's multi-volume life of Theodore Roosevelt or Lou Cannon's multi-volume biography of Ronald Reagan have set new standards in the forensic re-examination of past presidents: their characters, certainly, but also their interactions with those around them, and their effect on their times, both for good or ill, in the judgment of the author.[7]

The number of biographies of U.S. presidents being undertaken today seems also to be increasing. While to some extent this reflects the commercial book market in a celebrity age, it should be noted that the trend is not confined to commercial publishing; it is evident in university press publications also. The phrase 'definitive biography' may have passed out of favor – reviewers accepting that no such thing is possible, or even desirable – but there appears to be a widespread recognition that historians have failed to fully explain the American past, especially the presidential past. In this respect modern biographers, collectively, may be said to have set new standards of scholarship that made the work of American historians, in relation to the agency of the presidency, often seem shallow and disappointing. Let me illustrate this through a case study of President Franklin Delano Roosevelt in his role as U.S. commander in chief, directing the most destructive war in human history: World War II.

2 Historians on FDR as Commander

Article II, Section 2, of the U.S. Constitution states that the "President shall be Commander in Chief of the Army and Navy of the United States, and of

6 Nigel Hamilton, "Biography as Corrective," in Hans Renders, Binne de Haan, Jonne Harmsma, eds, *The Biographical Turn: Lives in History* (London: Routledge), 15-30.

7 Robert Caro, *The Path to Power* (New York: Vintage, 1982), *Means of Ascent* (New York: Vintage, 1990), *Master of the Senate* (New York: Vintage, 2002), and *The Passage of Power* (New York: Vintage, 2012); Edmund Morris, *The Rise of Theodore Roosevelt* (New York: Coward McCann, 1979), *Theodore Rex* (New York: Random House, 2001), and *Colonel Roosevelt* (New York: Random House, 2010); Lou Cannon, *Governor Reagan: His Rise to Power* (New York: PublicAffairs, 2003), and *President Reagan: The Role of a Lifetime* (New York: PublicAffairs, 1991).

the Militia of the several States, when called into the actual Service of the United States." This responsibility, for good or ill, is of great importance in peacetime: the president is empowered to appoint and discharge officers, is expected to work with Congress to finance the U.S. military, even its allies, to further American interests, and has to meet potential threats from abroad. In war, however, that presidential responsibility becomes of even greater significance. Many of America's forty-five presidents have been war presidents, including Madison, Jefferson, Polk, Lincoln, McKinley, Wilson, Franklin Roosevelt, Truman, Eisenhower, Lyndon Johnson, Nixon, George H.W. Bush, George W. Bush and Obama. The greatest responsibility of all, without question, was the one shouldered by President Roosevelt in the case of World War II: the most destructive, global war in human history.

Why, then, did historians for the most part decline to record, analyze, and assess FDR's tenure as U.S. commander in chief in World War II after the war was won? Despite multitudes of 'official,' government-sponsored and published military ('Greenback') histories of the U.S. military's role in World War II, no single history or historical account of President Roosevelt's role as *summo imperio*, or American commander in chief during the war, was ever published. A full volume, *The Supreme Command*, was devoted to General Eisenhower's command of the D-Day invasion and subsequent campaign in Northwest Europe, for example; yet how exactly the actual U.S. commander in chief, Franklin Delano Roosevelt, exercised his ultimate military authority, in a global war in which an estimated 60 million people died, simply went unexamined in any detail by historians.[8]

In part, of course, this was because historians of the presidency were not military historians. For their part military historians were very willing to tackle American military operations and strategy, yet found themselves both tentative and ignorant of the president's role, which lacked the same military paper trail they were used to. Wherever documentation was thin, they turned to the postwar autobiographical accounts of those officers who had held important roles in the fight: from the secretary of war, Henry Stimson, to the Joint Chiefs of Staff, Marshall, King and Arnold, and to regional and field commanders, from MacArthur to Nimitz, Bradley to Patton. And, unusually, to a British historian's work: that of Winston Spencer Churchill.

Churchill was, of course, half-American. He also possessed unique credentials for chronicling the military direction of World War II on the part of the Allies, namely that he himself had been quasi-commander in chief of all British

8 Forrest Pogue, *The Supreme Command* (Washington: U.S. Department of the Army, 1954).

and British Empire forces in the conflict, having made himself also minister of defense once appointed British prime minister on May 10, 1940. As one wit would put it, Churchill had, when losing the elections in 1945, proceeded to "win the war a second time – first in winning it, then in writing how he'd won it." His magisterial six volumes, *The Second World War*, made abundantly clear the central, defining role he himself had played.[9] He had, after all, directed not only the forces of Great Britain and its colonies, but those of its dominions, Canada, Australia, New Zealand, and South Africa, too, where their respective prime ministers had granted him that authority. He had, he narrated, masterminded the overall strategy pursued by the Allies and even – since he considered himself a trained soldier and liked to wear military uniform – had a guiding hand in directing military operations in the field.

Published between 1949 and 1953, the six-volume account helped Churchill win the Nobel Prize for Literature in 1953. In the United States, *The Second World War* came to take pride of place upon the shelves of every public and personal library of the nation. Indeed, Churchill became as venerated as any American politician in U.S. history – the more so for his warnings of Soviet communist Cold War intentions. The sway of the *Second World War* over World War II historical and military studies (on both sides of the Atlantic) was thus unparalleled, not least because Churchill had managed to purloin all 10 Downing Street government papers on leaving office in 1945, and had used a small army of historians to help him construct his masterpiece, one that would come to rival the great works of Xenophon and Julius Caesar. Its influence on historians – official, academic and independent – even to this day cannot be overstated.

Since President Roosevelt died in 1945, Churchill moreover had *carte blanche* to describe his dealings with the U.S. president, his fellow commander in chief during the war. Anxious to win back the prime ministership of Great Britain he had lost in the British General Election of July 1945, Churchill had a personal and political agenda in painting a self-portrait as the primary author of Allied victory in World War II. President Roosevelt, by contrast, was pictured as a kindly, avuncular, and essentially compliant colleague in his wheelchair, while warrior Churchill himself determined the military course of the war.

After an excellent half-century run, however, Churchill's self-aggrandizing account eventually had its day. In 2005 the British historian David Reynolds published a careful, extended analysis of each volume of *The Second World*

9 Winston Churchill, *The Second World War*, 6 vols. (Boston, MA: Houghton Mifflin, 1949-1953).

War in a book he titled *In Command of History: Churchill Fighting and Writing About The Second World War*.[10] Reynolds dissected Churchill's masterpiece from beginning to end, exposing what he called the work's "willfully inaccurate account" of the war, with innumerable examples of "sleight of hand," and "blatant pieces of distortion."[11] Subsequent twenty-first century histories of Churchill's wartime military leadership have also begun to reflect this more critical assessment of Churchill's account.[12] In the United States, however, the damage that Churchill's narrative did to the perception of President Roosevelt's military role in directing the war was severe and lasting. Given the lack of comparable records or an autobiographical account by the president himself, it proved difficult for historians to contest Churchill's version of war at the very top.

It is in this context that I would like to offer my own experience to illustrate how a revisionist presidential biographer operates today, not only in illuminating the actual agency of the president in question, but in challenging historical platitudes and received opinion. For the stakes involved in World War II were profound, affecting hundreds of millions of people. The role and agency of President Roosevelt in ensuring the military defeat of Nazi Germany was, I believe, crucial, and has been seriously misrepresented by historians. Had Prime Minister Churchill prevailed at the war's highest direction, it is entirely possible that the war against Hitler would not have been won by the Allies.

3 The Role of Biography

I confess that when in 2009 I began my study of FDR as commander in chief of the U.S. Armed Forces I had no particular agenda, beyond filling in what I thought to be a major historiographical lacuna. There had been a book, titled *Commander in Chief*, published by Eric Larrabee twenty years before.[13] Of the ten chapters in the work, however, only one had addressed the role and performance of President Roosevelt, the rest being devoted to his subordinates: Marshall, King, Arnold, Vandegrift, MacArthur, Nimitz, Eisenhower, Stilwell,

---

10 David Reynolds, *In Command of History* (New York: Random House, 2005).

11 Reynolds, 379, 378, and 382.

12 See Carlo D'Este, *Warlord: A Life of Winston Churchill at War, 1874-1945* (New York: HarperCollins, 2008), Max Hastings, *Winston's War: Churchill 1940-1945* (New York: Knopf, 2010), inter alia.

13 Eric Larrabee, *Commander in Chief: Franklin Delano Roosevelt, His Lieutenants & Their War* (New York: Harper & Row, 1987).

and LeMay. This was very much representative of U.S. military history up to that time, and I had no reason to contest the wide-angled focus save that, as a seasoned biographer rather than as an historian, I was skeptical.

The great American historian of the U.S. Navy in World War II, Eliot Morison, had claimed FDR "never imagined himself to be a strategist," and "in general followed the advice of the Joint Chiefs of Staff," while Secretary of War Stimson had claimed that General Marshall's "views guided Mr. Roosevelt throughout."[14] U.S. commanders, for their part, were on record having claimed they only rarely saw the president. General Marshall, Chief of Staff of the U.S. Army, said he often had not seen the president "for a month or six weeks." General Stillwell was more damning; he considered the president a "rank amateur in military matters," and – even more pejorative – a man "completely hypnotized by the British," who had "his ear, while we have the hind tit."[15]

Such claims intrigued me, since they could not all be true. If FDR was guided by Marshall and the Joint Chiefs of Staff "throughout," and they disagreed with British Mediterranean strategy for defeating Hitler in World War II, how could FDR have also been hypnotized by Churchill? Moreover, regarding Churchill I had my own biographical reservations. For a period of ten years I had been the authorized biographer of Field Marshal Montgomery, Churchill's primary commander in the D-Day invasion and thereafter.[16] It was quite clear from Montgomery's papers, and from talks I had with Montgomery himself before his death, that the field marshal revered Churchill as prime minister but considered him a "hopeless" quasi-commander in chief of British Empire forces. In his view Churchill was Victorian in his understanding of modern war, wildly opportunistic, devious, a poor picker of men, and "all over the place" in terms of military strategy.[17] In short, I began researching *FDR at War* with an open mind, yet skeptical whether historians had really gotten to grips with FDR's own role and agency as commander in chief. As far as possible, therefore, I set out to try and reconstruct the war for the first time strictly from the president's point of view. We had heard out the others – the secretary of war, the Joint Chiefs, the commanders, and Churchill. It was time to describe and examine, as far as possible, how FDR himself had seen the war, wearing his mantle as U.S. commander in chief.

---

14 Samuel E. Morison, *The Two Ocean War: A Short History of the United States Navy in the Second World War* (Boston, MA: Little Brown, 1963), 583.

15 Quoted in Nigel Hamilton, *The Mantle of Command: FDR at War, 1941-1942* (Boston, MA: Houghton Mifflin Harcourt, 2014), xiii.

16 Nigel Hamilton, *Monty*, 3 vols. (New York: McGraw Hill, 1981, 1984 and 1987).

17 Field Marshal Montgomery to author.

The research process of determining the actual agency of a particular individual in history is, in the end, a biographical as well as a historical challenge. What does this challenge boil down to? In my case, it involved interviewing the last surviving officer from the wartime Map Room, which FDR had set up at the White House in 1942. It necessitated trawling the archives of the FDR Library in Hyde Park, from Roosevelt's Map Room papers to the President's Secretary's Files. And it necessitated piecing together all records of meetings between the president and his advisers, as well as other trusted colleagues (such as the Canadian prime minister Mackenzie King, who would often stay in the White House with the president). Taking these preliminary research steps, I was struck by how much more in control of ultimate decision-making FDR was than I had realized or been led by historians to believe. Moreover, I was impressed by how much more strategically President Roosevelt thought than had been chronicled. Which raised the interesting question: what, exactly, is the role of a nation's commander in chief during wartime?

Churchill, in his great self-portrait, had pictured this role as a Roman Caesar in action. Indeed, Churchill was famous for the "Action This Day!" tags he would append to documents he sent out. He had a bedroom in his underground headquarters (now a museum) in London and was a whirlwind when inspecting and visiting troops, squadrons, and naval units, both at home in Britain and in the field.[18] It was, in other words, very much a role he played – active, inspirational, decisive, courageous. So colorful and effective did it seem in retrospect, moreover, that American historians assumed it to be a model of how to direct the armed forces of a great nation as commander in chief. What they did not take into account was the negative side of such 'hands-on' agency: that Churchill's very activity, as British prime minister and minister of defense, was certainly inspirational, but also a model of willful, often blind interference that would have lost Britain the war had it not been for his American counterpart who proved the rock on which the war was actually directed and won by the Allies: the U.S. president.

In the tradition of Abraham Lincoln in the Civil War, Franklin Roosevelt was emphatic in presenting himself to the public as its civilian commander in chief. Unlike the British prime minister, Roosevelt had never worn a uniform, despite having wanted to attend the Naval Academy when young. However, he had been an avid reader of naval history, had been appointed assistant secretary of the navy in the Woodrow Wilson administration, and had visited the

18 The Churchill War Rooms (Formerly Cabinet War Rooms), a division of the Imperial War Museum, London.

European battlefields during World War I. He was also interested in aviation, not only as transport but as a growing offensive (and defensive) weapon in modern war. He had been the first presidential nominee to fly to his party's national convention in 1932, and once elected had come to see air power as the critical factor in modern strategy. His efforts to harness U.S. manufacturing to mass production (first to reinforce European democracies, then to build up America's own offensive arsenal) were not the actions of a spectator, but of a leader wanting to face an ultimate enemy armed with its best weaponry, combined with an overwhelming scale of U.S. mass-production.[19]

Such was the well-known background of FDR's ideas about the role of commander in chief during peacetime. But how did he operate in wartime? What was his relationship with his military Chiefs of Staff? How did he see his own role? How effective (or not) was he in exercising ultimate command of American forces? And how did he influence, or how was he influenced, by his allies, in particular his fellow commander in chief, Winston Churchill? In this regard I believe the serious modern biographer resembles a cryptologist, for they are both seeking to crack a code. How did Roosevelt operate as commander in chief, and how effective or ineffective was he? Those were the unexplained mysteries that historians had not resolved, at least not to my satisfaction as a biographer and military historian. And to see if I could crack it, I decided to piece together what I had discovered about a secret meeting FDR held even before the war had begun for the U.S., namely his secret trip aboard a heavy naval cruiser, the USS Augusta, to meet with Churchill in mid-August of 1941, together with his Joint Chiefs of Staff.

It was the trip's detailed reconstruction that first demonstrated to me just how little FDR relied on the advice of his Chiefs of Staff, let alone that he was almost exclusively "guided" by them, as Morison claimed. As the president's air chief Lieutenant-General "Hap" Arnold noted in his diary of the trip: "where are we going? And why?"[20] General Marshall was equally in the dark, admitting later he "had no knowledge" of the impending discussions with the British military team Churchill was bringing to Newfoundland, "until we were well up the coast on the cruiser Augusta."[21] Using the diaries, letters, notes, and later accounts of participants on both American and British sides, that first meeting between potential allies gave me, as a biographer, a fascinating fresh perspective on FDR: how exactly he exercised his presidential and military authority, how he handled his military advisers, and how he handled Churchill. The

19 Hamilton, *The Mantle of Command*, 388.
20 Ibid., 11.
21 Ibid., 15.

British prime minister had hoped the meetings, held aboard their respective battleships off the coast of Newfoundland, was to announce the president's decision to enter the war on the British side. Instead, the president demanded that Churchill sign an Atlantic Charter in which the signatories agreed to "respect the rights of all peoples to choose the form of government under which they will live," a knife that struck at the heart of Churchill's refusal to grant India self-government and his postwar colonial aspirations.

What thus impressed me as a biographer was that, in assembling such a huge amount of documented detail, it proved possible to get a new biographical handle on a president whose intentions and modus operandi had largely eluded historians for seven decades and to clear up myriad misunderstandings, misreadings, and misinformation in the case of Churchill's own romanticized account (I had access to a very detailed diary kept by Churchill's deputy military assistant, Ian Jacob, whom I had gotten to know very well while working on my Montgomery trilogy in the 1980s). As a biographer, I felt I had broken the code and that the decrypts would enable me to go on 'reading' Roosevelt's mind and behavior in subsequent episodes and landmark events of the war and its military direction.

If cryptology is a feature of modern forensic biography, so too can modern biography be considered a form of detective non-fiction in its process. For once I understood how FDR had come up with the idea of a first meeting with Churchill; how he had gone about it, who he took with him (including the assistant secretary of state, Sumner Welles, whom he had instructed to begin preparing a charter-like document and then fly to Newfoundland to join him), how he had negotiated with Churchill, and how he had trained his own chiefs of staff merely to listen to their British opposite numbers but offer no strategic opinions themselves, let alone plans. I thus felt well-equipped to critically follow the actual footprints of the U.S. commander in chief, from the moment the war began for America on December 7, 1941, when the Japanese attacked Pearl Harbor and Hitler declared war on the United States, to the bitter end – and to do so in a wholly fresh way. This might well involve a rewriting of presidential history, I recognized as I proceeded, but such an approach was, I had come to recognize, a response to the great challenges of modern biography: namely using the detailed biographical lens to review and question long-established versions of history and where necessary correct them.[22]

I should emphasize that this biographical task, involving 'deep scholarship,' is not cosmetic. We are not talking here of merely adding a better understanding of the president's character or personality, though this may be a benefit.

---

22 Ibid., 3-40.

We are talking about using the biographer's investigative focus to re-construct, where appropriate, history, if history is the way we see the past. It is also about reconsidering an individual's impact or agency on others, and upon the course of events. Following the metaphor of forensic reconstruction or detective non-fiction, I therefore divided *The Mantle of Command* into a series of fourteen episodes I could re-examine and re-record biographically, just as I had done with the Atlantic Charter meeting.

Let me give one more example of how this approach altered the conventional historical understanding of Roosevelt, both as president and U.S. commander in chief. This was FDR's decision to overrule General MacArthur, his military commander in the field in the Philippines, and to resist any suggestion of surrender at Bataan in February 1942. Once again, this was a decision only the commander in chief could make; General Marshall only had an ancillary, rather than 'guiding' role. MacArthur had himself been Chief of Staff of the U.S. Army in the 1930s, when Marshall was but a colonel. MacArthur's increasingly panicky cables from the Malinta Tunnel on Corregidor Island had not impressed the president, and the story of how, on 9 February 1942, he firmly put MacArthur in his place at a signal moment in history (and in complete contrast to the British in Singapore, where the huge garrison was surrendered to a small Japanese army virtually without a fight) demonstrated just how steely FDR could be, when necessary.[23] As Marshall later confided to his biographer, Forrest Pogue, it was at that point "I decided he was a great man."[24]

FDR's willingness to use his constitutional authority to override his generals in war was an aspect of the Roosevelt presidency that increasingly engaged me, both as biographer and historian. Marshall and his fellow Chiefs of Staff subsequently pressed the president to authorize an invasion of northern France (the so-called Second Front) in 1942. Once again, the president simply overrode them. He was concerned that, apart from hostilities in the Pacific, American forces had never been in battle with the Wehrmacht. But if not a cross-Channel invasion, where could American forces be put into combat to learn the crucial lessons of modern war?

In military history, Roosevelt's decision to override his generals and instead opt for an American invasion of Northwest Africa (Operation Torch) had generally been ascribed to the influence of Churchill, who later claimed parentage of it in *The Second World War*.[25] As a biographer I was again dubious, since I

23 Ibid., 195-206.
24 Ibid., 180.
25 Ibid., 102-103, 105.

saw no evidence of FDR ever being 'hypnotized' by Churchill. Secondly, the unpublished diaries of the British ambassador to Washington, Lord Halifax, that I consulted gave the lie to Churchill's later account. The ambassador visited the White House in the fall of 1941 and heard directly from the president how his strategic mind was working with regard to an invasion of North Africa.[26] Administered by Vichy authorities under only token German control, U.S. troops would be able to strike the Wehrmacht where it was weakest, at the extremity of its lines of communication, where temporary reverses would not affect the outcome of the campaign. Moreover, if the British were able to hold Rommel's Axis forces in Libya and Egypt, a strategy of crushing German and Italian forces in North Africa between them could be pursued. Again, this involved overriding the most vigorous opposition of Roosevelt's own generals and Secretary of War Stimson, who came close to mutiny. Stimson in fact openly bet the president such an invasion of Northwest Africa would fail.[27] Given that the "Torch" invasion proved a signal success and that the president's strategic and operational concerns were validated at Kasserine in February 1943 (i.e. a defeat, but one that allowed the U.S. military to learn crucial lessons in modern combat in a relatively safe theater of war), it was a remarkable example of individual agency in both presidential and military history – one that, remarkably, had never been recognized, let alone assessed by historians.

4 Biography and History

Of course, not all of FDR's strategic and military decisions proved as straightforward as "Torch." Indeed, the problem for a biographer who focuses on one particular aspect of a subject's life can be the overlap between that chosen aspect and others. How to stay close to FDR's military direction of the war, for example, without encompassing the *political* aspects of grand strategy? Certainly, in continuing to follow FDR's wartime trajectory as commander in chief, I have found the political dimensions of Allied wartime policy more and more interwoven with the decisions U.S. and British leaders had to make. Yet even here, a biographical lens is important in getting to the very heart of history. Hitler, for example, believed the D-Day invasion would be the "deciding" battle of World War II. Yet if it was so critical to the ultimate outcome of World War II in Europe, why did Winston Churchill (behind the scenes) endanger

26 Ibid., 110.
27 Ibid., 355-356.

the very transatlantic alliance he had done so much to further, and why did historians for the most part cover this up? Furthermore, in terms of the U.S. presidency, how did FDR handle this opposition by America's most important military ally in the war?

Twice in 1943, Churchill met with President Roosevelt to try and get Britain out of its commitment to participate in a cross-Channel Second Front invasion of northern France, claiming that Britain's disastrous one-day raid on Dieppe in 1942 had proven that such an Allied invasion was bound to fail. Each time Roosevelt had to overrule his primary coalition partner, as I have narrated in *Commander in Chief: FDR's Battle with Churchill, 1943*.[28] Churchill was nothing if not obstinate, however. His third and final confrontation with FDR over Operation Overlord took place in Cairo and Tehran at the end of November 1943, yet to this day no historian has been able to adequately explain why the prime minister was willing to threaten to resign as British prime minister rather than stand by the written agreement he had recently made at Quebec on behalf of the British Empire: a formal commitment to mount D-Day in the spring of 1944, only five months away.

Again, given the defining importance of D-Day in the military history of World War II, as well as the crucial importance of U.S.-British unity in the days before President Roosevelt's first meeting with Joseph Stalin, how is such a puzzle still unresolved by historians? Why *did* Churchill try to dissuade President Roosevelt from going ahead with the D-Day plans? Moreover, while in Tehran, why did he continue arguing to the very edge of ruining the first summit between the three leaders in order to try and get his way? Was it for political reasons? If so, which reasons? To secure the Balkans for the western rather than the eastern Allies? To force Turkey into the war on the Allied side? To atone in some way for his failure in forcing the Dardanelles at Gallipoli in 1915? In the hope of a domino effect that would somehow trigger the collapse of the Third Reich, like that of the Second Reich in 1918? Or to avoid high casualties in a D-Day invasion, that would affect British manpower in the final years of the war and disable British control of its postwar revived colonial empire?

There were clearly many factors involved in Churchill's quasi-meltdown (leading to a physical meltdown, in the form of pneumonia) in November and December 1943. What is clear to historians of the presidency is that the matter of agency (i.e. the motives of both FDR and Churchill and the extent to which these played out in the historic meeting in Iran that decided the biggest

---

28 Nigel Hamilton, *Commander in Chief: FDR's Battle with Churchill, 1943* (Boston, MA: Houghton Mifflin), in extenso.

issue of the war in Europe) is a contested region of history, one where both the historian and the biographer must exercise their respective, overlapping skills.

5 Conclusion

I have now completed the third and final volume of *FDR at War*.[29] The research and writing of the trilogy demonstrated to me (and hopefully to the reader) how crucial a fresh and challenging biographical approach can be to the history of the presidency within the larger canvas of the American past. As in all history, moreover, there are insights to be gained that help us understand *other* eras too and that are applicable to similar or comparative cases. For example, Plutarch's *Parallel Lives* (or paired biographies) sought to identify common moral virtues as well as failings. Certainly, modern biographies of U.S. presidents serve to show us, at close quarters, how different individuals have exercised their ultimate presidential power, for good or ill.[30]

In my own case, looking at the manner how Franklin Roosevelt performed his role as U.S. commander in chief in World War II raises interesting historical parallels with former and succeeding presidents. With Lincoln and his generals in the Civil War, certainly, but also how Eisenhower used his experience of supreme theater command in World War II to guide his actions as later president and commander in chief during the Cold War.[31] Also why President Truman (an artillery officer in World War I) eventually felt compelled to recall General MacArthur during the Korean war. Or more recently, why President Obama dismissed General Stanley McChrystal in Afghanistan.[32] Conversely, in reverse cases senior military commanders have occasionally influenced the U.S. commander in chief in ways that suggest diminished agency on the part of the president, as one might argue was the case with President

---

29 Nigel Hamilton, *War and Peace: FDR's Final Odyssey, 1943-1945* (Boston, MA: Houghton Mifflin, 2019).

30 See for example Nigel Hamilton, *American Caesars: Lives of the Presidents, From Franklin D. Roosevelt to George W. Bush* (New Haven: Yale University Press, 2010).

31 See inter alia James Macpherson, *Tried by War: Abraham Lincoln as Commander-in-Chief* (New York: Penguin Press, 2008) and Stephen Ambrose, *Eisenhower: Soldier, General of the Army, President-Elect President* (New York: Simon & Schuster 1983), and *Eisenhower: The President* (New York: Simon & Schuster 1985).

32 See H.W. Brands, *The General vs. the President: MacArthur and Truman at the Brink of Nuclear War* (New York: Doubleday, 2016) and Jonathan Weisman, "McChrystal Out; Petraeus In," *Wall Street Journal*, June 23, 2010.

Johnson during the Vietnam War. Such relationships between individuals – and their oft-conflicting roles – illuminate the constantly changing power-dynamics between the president as an individual and the armed forces in American democracy. Moreover, they are once again in the public mind, with the contentious Trump administration. No definitive accounts, we know, are ever possible. What is clear though, is that the task of modern biography is central to an appreciation of the agency and performance of each president: a symbiosis between history and biography that would surely satisfy the ghosts of Plutarch and Suetonius.

CHAPTER 2

U.S. Presidents and Psychohistory

Arthur Eaton

In June 1976, the American Psychiatric Association (APA) published a report titled "The Psychiatrist as Psychohistorian." In the document, a committee of psychiatrists investigated the dangers – including the threat to United States national security – of a phenomenon known as psychohistory.[1] In this chapter, I will investigate three psychoanalytic studies of U.S. presidents, attempt to explain their crucial role in the development of the psychohistorical movement, and discuss their wider cultural and intellectual significance. These case studies provide further insight into the formation of psychohistory as an intellectual interdiscipline, as well as into the dominant conception among a number of scholars in the United States that obtaining knowledge about the personality of political leaders would prove essential in evaluating their behavior and conduct. As such, it is an illustration of what has been called the 'psychologization' of U.S. politics in the decades following World War II, as well as the 'Americanization' of psychoanalysis in those decades.

Psychohistory is an academic interdiscipline, born out of the fusion between psychoanalytic thought and academic historiography, conceived in the late 1950s. It experienced the height of its popularity and influence in the 1960s and 70s. Today there are still a number of practitioners of psychohistory, although their influence on the broader fields of historiography and psychoanalysis has diminished considerably. In its prime, the psychohistorical movement consisted of a group of scholars, both psychologists and historians, who shared an interest in the promotion and development of a Freudian historiography. Prominent members of the movement included Robert J. Lifton, Bruce Mazlish, Charles B. Strozier, Peter Loewenberg, Lloyd deMause, and Peter Gay. The movement produced two influential journals: *The Journal of Psychohistory* and *The Psychohistory Review*.[2] The former is still published intermittently; the latter is now defunct. Initially, it was the psychohistorians' aim to establish teaching programs at universities, promote psychohistorical knowledge and

1 Charles K. Hofling, *The Psychiatrist as Psychohistorian: Report of the Task Force on Psychohistory of the American Psychiatric Association* (Washington: APA, 1976).

2 The earliest editions of the Journal of Psychohistory appeared as *The History of Childhood Quarterly – The Journal of Psychohistory*.

© KONINKLIJKE BRILL NV, LEIDEN, 2020 | DOI:10.1163/9789004422643_004

practice in general, and, for a number of them, to create independent psychohistorical institutes. Although it eventually lost its association with psychohistory as a movement, one of the most important platforms for the development of psychohistorical thought was the annual 'Wellfleet meetings' held by psychiatrist Robert J. Lifton in his vacation home in Wellfleet, Massachusetts.[3]

As Petteri Pietikainen and Juhani Ihanus have pointed out, two formative events mark the beginning of the development of psychohistory as an intellectual movement and the idea that the development of a specifically Freudian approach to academic history was possible and desirable.[4] First came William L. Langer's presidential address "The Next Assignment," delivered to members of the American Historical Association (AHA) in December 1957. In that speech, Langer argued explicitly for the development of a Freudian approach to history.[5] His brother, Walter C. Langer, was a psychoanalyst who had worked with Anna Freud. He had coordinated the compilation of a 1000-page psychoanalytic report on Adolf Hitler's personality for the Office of Strategic Services (the OSS) during World War II.[6] On the basis of psychological analyses, Walter and his colleagues had predicted that, faced with defeat, Hitler would commit suicide. Through the work of his brother, William Langer had become convinced of the usefulness of psychoanalytic theory in the analysis of historically significant characters, living or dead.

The second marker was the publication of psychoanalyst Erik H. Erikson's book *Young Man Luther: A Study in Psychoanalysis and History* (1958). Erikson's work was highly esteemed in academic circles and reached a wide readership. The book contained a psychological analysis of the early-modern church reformer Martin Luther. Erikson attempted to show how the young Luther gained his religious following by 'working through' (in the psychoanalytic sense) some of the psychological problems that were common to his generation of men. In the book, Erikson tried to construct a theory of the leader-led

---

3 In their paper "On the Origins of Psychoanalytic Psychohistory," Petteri Pietikainen and Juhani Ihanus have shown the importance of Robert J. Lifton's so-called Wellfleet Gatherings in the development of early psychohistory. In this paper they have laid the groundwork for any studies on the history of psychohistory.

4 Petteri Pietikainen and Juhani Ihanus, "On the Origins of Psychoanalytic Psychohistory," *History of Psychology* 6, no. 2 (2003).

5 William L. Langer, "Presidential Address Delivered at the Annual Dinner of the American Historical Association the Statler Hotel, New York City, December 29, 1957," *American Historical Review* 63, no. 2 (January 1958): 283-304.

6 Published in 1972 as: Walter C. Langer, *The Mind of Adolf Hitler: The Secret Wartime Report* (New York: Basic Books, 1972).

dynamic, using a mix of psychoanalytic theory and historical data. The work indirectly grappled with questions about the rise to power of Adolf Hitler. As many psychohistorians were preoccupied with similar questions about leadership, the 'Luther book' (as Erikson referred to it himself) became a blueprint for the work done by them.[7] Erikson was a friend and mentor to Robert J. Lifton and he attended Lifton's psychohistorical Wellfleet meetings until his health deteriorated in the 1980s.[8] Although Erikson never considered himself part of a psychohistorical movement, he was considered a leading figure by many of the psychohistorians. Both the work of Erikson and the work of the Langer brothers rested firmly on the idea that persons in a position of power could – and should – be subjected to psychological analysis. In 1965, Lifton received a large grant from the American Academy of Arts and Sciences for the first official meeting of what was then called the 'Group for the Study of Psychohistorical Process,' to be held in Wellfleet. This is often seen as the starting point of the psychohistorical movement.[9] However, for a long time after its establishment, the term 'psychohistory' remained what Claude Levi-Strauss called an "empty signifier" – a word with no stable meaning anchored to it.[10]

Loosely united by the shared aim of creating a Freudian approach to history, psychohistorical authors attached a wide variety of meanings, definitions and methods to the term 'psychohistory.' In so far as the psychohistorians were following in the footsteps of Erikson and the Langer brothers, a strand of biographical narratives emerged under the banner of psychohistory that employed psychoanalytic terminology and focused on leaders – spiritual, intellectual, political – and the interaction with their followers.[11] Why did a particular personality appeal to a group of followers in a specific historical context? How did the personalities of leaders shape their decision-making? How, in turn, did leaders proceed to influence the thoughts and feelings of their followers? These were questions, formulated in the wake of World War II, many psychohistorians sought answers to. The so-called 'psychobiographical'

7 For example, some years later, books were published with titles such as: Richard Lebeaux, *Young Man Thoreau* (Amherst: University of Massachusetts Press, 1989) and Burke Wilkinson, *Young Louis Fourteenth: The Early Years of the Sun King* (Basingstoke: Macmillan, 1970).

8 Personal communication with Lifton, May 22, 2015.

9 It is, for example, mentioned as such in: William McKinley Runyan, *Psychology and Historical Interpretation* (New York: Oxford University Press, 1988).

10 Claude Levi-Strauss, *Introduction to the Work of Marcel Mauss* (London: Routledge & Kegan Paul), 63.

11 This is analyzed at length in: Charles B. Strozier and Daniel Offer, *The Leader: Psychohistorical Essays* (New York: Plenum Press, 1985).

narratives that they produced often focused on U.S. presidents.[12] Below I will discuss three of these narratives and show how all three, each in their own way, were significant in the construction of psychohistory as an intellectual movement.

1 The Case of Tommy W.

Although the early psychohistorians all shared the belief that psychoanalytic theory could make a contribution to the study of history, the nature of the interaction was never fully agreed upon. Some psychohistorians believed this was a good thing. Robert Lifton for example wrote: "The Faustian intellectual temptation is to dismiss the paradox and make things simple. We do better, I am certain, to embrace the paradox. For it can be energizing."[13] For him, as for Erikson, psychohistory was best left undefined and open to interpretation. In that way it could remain a malleable field and practice, without running the risk of degenerating into orthodoxy and rigid methodologies. Others, particularly the psychohistorians who believed that Freudian psychoanalysis was a 'hard' science (a prevalent belief in the 1960s), found this difficult to accept. Proponents such as MIT historian Bruce Mazlish believed that if psychohistory was to be of value, it had to somehow adhere to fixed rules and produce verifiable results.[14]

This tension at the heart of psychohistory led to much misunderstanding about the field and discipline. In any case, the psychohistorians' inability to come to a consensus over the exact nature of their endeavor meant that the early psychohistorians spent a lot of time and effort setting up spaces for debate – newsletters, journals, conferences, and informal meetings. It also meant they were concerned with the 'image' of psychohistory. The posthumous publication of Sigmund Freud's analysis of Thomas Woodrow Wilson in 1967 illustrates this preoccupation.

---

12 Later, when psychohistory became a more established discipline in the late 1970s and early 1980s, certain authors – such as William McKinley Runyan – would distinguish between 'psychohistory' and 'psychobiography.' As the term psychohistory became more and more controversial, and psychobiographers started to develop their own set of methodologies, some psychobiographers distanced themselves from psychohistory as a term and movement.

13 Robert J. Lifton, "On Psychohistory," in *Explorations in Psychohistory: The Wellfleet Papers*, eds. Robert Jay Lifton and Erik Olson (New York: Simon and Schuster, 1974), 24.

14 Personal communication with Mazlish, January 15, 2014.

In 1973, Robert Coles, a fellow traveler of the psychohistorical movement, looked back on the achievements of psychohistory thus far and wrote: "In the name of 'applied psychoanalysis' the lives of an assortment of political leaders, generals, artists and writers have been examined, and as one goes through those attempts, one keeps coming back to [Freud's] Leonardo study – and to Freud's superior qualities as a thinker and writer."[15] This opinion was shared by many psychohistorians. Although Erik Erikson had shown that psychoanalysis and historiography had things to teach to each other, many psychohistorians believed that it was ultimately Sigmund Freud who had laid the groundwork for psychohistorical thought.[16] In general, then, they considered his application of psychoanalytic ideas to historical characters exemplary. There was, however, one notable exception to this rule. Freud's work on Woodrow Wilson: *Thomas Woodrow Wilson: Twenty-Eighth President of the United States – A Psychological Study*.

The book was co-authored by William C. Bullitt, a diplomat and a former analysand of Freud. It was published posthumously in the United States in 1967, to rather devastating reviews. William Bullitt had worked as an American diplomat and foreign correspondent in Europe under President Woodrow Wilson. Bullitt was analyzed by Freud in the 1920s. After the analysis, Freud and Bullitt agreed to write a psychoanalytic study of President Wilson – Bullitt provided the data on Wilson's life and Freud and Bullitt would then together write an analysis of his personality. When the book appeared, many years after Freud's death, the response to *Woodrow Wilson* amounted to no less than widespread disavowal, bordering on pandemonium. On the eve of the book's publication in the 1960s, the American Psychoanalytic Association discussed denying Freud's authorship as a possible PR strategy.[17] Erik Erikson suggested in a review for *The New York Review of Books* that Freud could have only agreed to such a "disastrously bad" publication because Bullitt helped him and his family escape from the Nazis.[18] Anna Freud reportedly "disliked the book" as soon as she read it. She "had hopes that it could be changed to a large extent.

15 Robert Coles, "Shrinking History Part 1," *The New York Review of Books*, February 22, 1973, 15-21.

16 See, for one of many examples, the introduction to Charles B. Strozier and Daniel Offer, *The Leader: Psychohistorical Essays* (New York: Plenum Press, 1985).

17 "Annual Meetings – May, 1967," *Bulletin of the American Psychoanalytic Association*, 23 (1975), 887-906. Review of William Bullitt and Sigmund Freud, "Thomas Woodrow Wilson: A Psychological Study" (1967), in *The New Statesman and Nation*, May 12, 1967, 653-654.

18 Erik H. Erikson, "The Strange Case of Freud, Bullitt, and Woodrow Wilson: I," *The New York Review of Books*, February 9, 1967: 3-6.

This proved impossible."[19] In a review, historian A.J.P. Taylor wondered: "How did anyone ever manage to take Freud seriously?"[20] Publishers marketed the book as "Freud's only study of a politician of his own time."[21]

Much like the psychoanalysts, the psychohistorians, aware of the importance of this document for their budding movement, were keen to show that Freud could not have been the author of certain passages. John Voss, the executive officer of the American Association of Arts and Sciences, who had just procured a large grant for the upcoming two Wellfleet psychohistory gatherings, wrote in a letter to Erikson: "I suggested to Bruce [Mazlish] that it might be interesting to do a computer-word analysis of the text to find out how much of it was Freud and how much of it was Bullitt. My guess would be that the actual author of 90% of the volume would be the latter."[22]

But in his introduction to the book, Freud clearly stated: "For the analytic part we are both equally responsible; it has been written by us working together."[23] It is significant that the Bullitt-Freud book appeared in 1967. The first Wellfleet psychohistory gathering was held in 1966, and interest in the application of psychoanalytic thought to history was growing steadily around that time.[24] Psychohistorians were afraid that the publication of the book would endanger their movement. To the psychohistorians, *Woodrow Wilson* became an example of how psychoanalytic theory should not be applied to history, and therefore how psychohistory should not be written. In his review, Erikson was particularly distressed by the authors' denigrating use of the name 'Tommy' when they referred to the young Woodrow Wilson. In content, however, the work does not essentially differ much from Freud's earlier historical works. Much as in Freud's biographical work on Leonardo da Vinci, Bullitt and Freud reconstructed Wilson's childhood, and from those constructions went on to analyze his behavior as president. In fact, it seems likely that Freud did have something to do with the analysis, and that the book was later re-written, or

---

19 Letter from Anna Freud to Paul Roazen, dated March 15, 1967. Quoted in Todd Dufresne, *Freud Under Analysis: History, Theory, Practice: Essays in Honor of Paul Roazen* (London: Jaron Aronson Inc., 1997), 282.

20 Quoted in Peter Gay, *Freud for Historians* (Oxford: Oxford University Press, 1985), 93.

21 *Psyche. Zeitschrift für Psychoanalyse* 62 (2008): 61.

22 Letter from John Voss to Erik Erikson, February 3, 1967. Container 11, Erik H. and Joan M. Erikson papers, 1925-1985, Houghton Library, Harvard College Library, Harvard University.

23 See introduction to Sigmund Freud and William C. Bullitt, *Thomas Woodrow Wilson, Twenty-eighth President of the United States: A Psychological Study* (Boston: Houghton Mifflin, 1967) xiv.

24 Personal communication with Lifton, May 22, 2015.

finished by William Bullitt. The authors focused specifically on Wilson's relationship with his father:

> The outlets employed by Wilson's Ego for his passivity to his father were all outlets approved by his Super-Ego. His chief outlet was through direct submission to the will of his father. He did what his father wanted him to do and did not do what his father did not want him to do. He accepted his father's thoughts without question and his father's leadership with adoration.[25]

As Erikson remarked in his review, it is unlike Freud to speak about the ego in hydraulic terms such as "outlets," and yet the theory applied is solidly Freudian. Erikson grudgingly agreed with Freud and Bullitt's interpretation. "For one does find in the lives of a number of men and women of messianic bent and historic performance a comparable relation of parent and child, which makes it incumbent on the child to fulfill the parent's ideal image and to redeem his own shortcomings."[26] Some of these more primitive dynamics, Erikson held, were correctly suggested in the book. "Yet the decisive factors in any historical study are not only how the parent could coerce the child, and the child convince the parent," he thought, "but how the child became a man who could make his contemporaries believe that he was filling a place in history, that he was a principle force in history."[27]

Why was Erikson, the informal mentor of the psychohistorians, so enraged by the book? In part, he missed the sociological and historical context to Wilson's life in Freud and Bullitt's work. In other words: it was not enough like his own work. It was only through his own approach, in which he did not only try to understand the personality dynamics of a particular individual, but also their historical context and significance – as he had done in *Young Man Luther*, that he felt the fields of history and psychoanalysis merged successfully into a psychoanalytic viewpoint. What Erikson missed in the Woodrow Wilson book were the questions on the dynamics between leaders and followers. Why had he been a failure in the eyes of his followers? Why was his legacy tainted? In his own work, Erikson tried to embed the psychoanalytic actor in their historical context. In this way, he sought to find out why a person became attractive as a leader to their followers. These were not the questions that Freud and Bullit sought to answer. Their analysis of the president resembled earlier

---

25 Freud and Bullitt, *Thomas Woodrow Wilson*, 65.
26 Erikson, "The Strange Case of Freud," 5.
27 Ibid., 5.

attempts to 'psychoanalyze' historical characters by psychoanalysts. The book on Woodrow Wilson did not fit the image that the psychohistorians were trying to fashion of their movement and its heritage – a movement that was increasingly focusing on the leader-led dynamic and the analysis of historically significant persons in the present.

2 Psychological History

To understand properly what the aims of the psychohistorians were, and from which intellectual traditions they emerged, it is crucial to understand their academic context. The decades after World War II saw the flourishing of social sciences in the United States. Anthropologist Clifford Geertz put it as follows: "It was, in any case, social science in full cry; headier and more confident than ever before or since."[28] As a result, traditionally popular subjects such as history were increasingly losing numbers of students to subjects such as sociology, anthropology, and psychology. In addition, historians in the U.S. were encouraged to tread into the limelight of public debates and share their knowledge with a wider public, which led to the popularization of history as a semi-literary genre. In its traditional form, academic history was increasingly perceived as having lost relevance in the modern world.[29] As a result, there emerged a strong tendency toward interdisciplinarity in academic history. Professional historians began increasingly to supplement their methodologies with elements derived from the social sciences. Such developments culminated in the creation of influential journals such as the *Journal of Interdisciplinary History*, published first by MIT Press in 1969. The aforementioned tendencies are reflected in an article published in the *New York Times* in 1971, which reported on a conference on interdisciplinary history, organized by leading historian Arthur M. Schlesinger Jr. A quote from the article served as *The Times*' 'Quotation of the Day':

> Armed with computers, statistics, psychoanalysis, sampling techniques, economic models and other tools of modern social science, younger historians have established a wide beachhead in the discipline that Prof.

28 Clifford Geertz, *After the Fact: Two Countries, Four Decades, One Anthropologist* (Cambridge, MA: Harvard University Press, 1995), 100.

29 For a discussion, see Anna Green and Kathleen Troup, *The Houses of History: A Critical Reader in Twentieth-century History and Theory* (New York: New York University Press, 1999).

> C. Vann Woodward of Yale, former head of the American Historical Association calls a 'living fossil from the pre-scientific age.[30]

Historiographical debates at this time centered around the question whether or not historians should be employing socio-scientific methods. We see what can be best described as a generation gap between a group of traditional historians and a younger generation of historical scholars that sought the help of socio-scientific methodolgy. One of the most influential documents in this debate was a book titled *Clio and the Doctors* (1974), written by well-known historian Jacques Barzun. In the book he took up arms against the generation of young interdisciplinaries.[31]

Barzun's book was a fierce statement. It defended 'traditional' history against the tendency to, in his words, "graft upon history such neighboring knowledge as wears the aspect of science."[32] One such neighboring discipline was psychoanalysis and the main target of Barzun's book – the 'doctors' referred to in the title – were the psychohistorians. In a defense of psychohistory published in the *New York Times*, sociologist Richard Sennett called Barzun's book "sad" because it represented, in his view, an "aristocratic" view of history. He accused Barzun and his fellow-traditionalists of first being "inclined to snoot at both psycho-history and quanto-history as interesting oddities at best" and now, when psychohistory was receiving a lot of favorable responses in academic circles, by labeling them a menacing threat.[33]

3 The Case of Richard N.

Although the book at no point mentioned his name, *Clio and the Doctors* was aimed specifically at the work of one of Barzun's former students: Bruce Mazlish. Instead, Barzun attacked "the author of a psycho-historical study of Richard Nixon."[34] This study would play an important role in determining how psychohistory and psychohistorians were perceived. Mazlish was professor of

30 Robert Reinhold, "Historians Find Fresh Answers with Tools of Social Science," *New York Times*, July 3, 1971. 27.

31 Jacques Barzun, *Clio and the Doctors: Psycho-history, Quanto-history, & History* (Chicago: University of Chicago Press, 1974), x.

32 Ibid., 11.

33 Richard Sennett, "Review: Clio and the Doctors," *The New York Times*, October 20, 1974, 413.

34 Barzun *Clio and the Doctors*, x.

history at MIT and gained notoriety with his psychoanalytic study of the personality of Richard Nixon, titled *In Search of Nixon*. Mazlish considered himself a pioneer of the psychohistorical movement and set up the earliest Wellfleet meetings together with Robert J. Lifton; he was one of the earliest advocates of psychohistory as a semi-independent discipline. In his book on Nixon, he wrote: "Psychohistory is not *merely* the application of psychoanalysis to history but a true fusion of the two, creating a new vision."[35] This new vision was inspired by Mazlish's interactions with William Langerformer, president of the AHA.[36] Bruce Mazlish had been inspired by William Langer's presidential address in 1957, in which he argued for the use of psychoanalysis in history. Mazlish was a great believer in interdisciplinarity and had been in psychoanalysis himself after the break-up of his first marriage.[37] He was convinced of the scientific status of psychoanalysis.

Mazlish went 'in search of Nixon' in 1968. In fact, he did not so much start off in search of Nixon himself, as he did in pursuit of what he thought were the *predictive* qualities of psychohistory. Through his connection with William Langer, Mazlish was aware of the OSS Hitler-study written by Walter Langer during the war.[38] Like many, he had been impressed by the fact that Langer and his team had predicted Hitler's suicide. As a result, Mazlish now intended to prove (or disprove) that psychohistory had limited predictive qualities.[39]

In 1968, Mazlish coordinated a secret group of academics with the aim of analyzing the personality of the presidential candidate for the next election: Richard Nixon or Hubert Humphrey. For the project, Mazlish sounded out "five or six outstanding scholars – other historians, political scientists, and psychoanalysts" on their willingness to participate in a team inquiry into the psychodynamics of the prospective president.[40] Each of the members, using their own set of theories, was asked to write an analysis of the candidate. Afterwards, a group portrait would be assembled. In addition, alternative 'scenarios' of the "major problems and events that might confront the president" would be written up and predictions about his behavior in such stressful situations added.[41] Mazlish started his own research, approached a number of organi-

35 Bruce Mazlish, *In Search of Nixon: A Psychohistorical Inquiry* (Baltimore, MD: Penguin Books, 1974), 152.

36 Personal communication with Mazlish, January 15, 2014.

37 Ibid.

38 Ibid.

39 Mazlish, *In Search of Nixon*, vi.

40 Ibid.

41 Ibid.

zations, but none agreed to participate. For lack of finances the project was finally aborted.[42]

The preliminary studies, however, did not go to waste. On 19 January 1970, Mazlish presented a paper on Nixon at a meeting of psychohistorical scholars, based on the initial research he had done for the canceled Nixon project.[43] The paper was later published in slightly altered form by the *Journal for Interdisciplinary History* at MIT. The published paper in turn formed the basis of the book *In Search of Nixon: A Psychohistorical Inquiry*, which was published in early 1972, before the Watergate scandal was properly uncovered. In a revised edition of the book in 1973, written while many of the facts about Nixon's involvement in the scandal were still unknown or yet to be verified, Mazlish cautiously remarked that "[Nixon's] predilection for denial, as we have described it, has been greatly in evidence throughout the unfolding of Watergate… These and other characteristics that we have tried to analyze reappear compulsively."[44] Several decades later, Mazlish put it more directly: "I was a prophet!"[45] In truth, Mazlish did not predict anything even close to the Watergate scandal and in fact he never claimed to have done so. The book was a portrait of Nixon based upon all available sources, including the ones about his childhood. Without access to any first-hand accounts of the president's personality, Mazlish had to make do with speeches, autobiographical writings, and second-hand accounts of Nixon's life and behavior. He was aware of the limitations of this approach, but stressed that he believed an analysis of the available materials might still be fruitful.

He tried to answer the question what, in his view, makes a psychohistorical approach more (or less) than an application of psychoanalytic theory to a historical figure. "For example," he wrote, "psychohistory allows us, indeed forces us, to take seriously Nixon's role as president. Many of his decisions will emerge from the demands or constraints of his role rather than his personality … Psychohistory tries to take that fact seriously."[46] Psychohistory, he went on to argue, also directs attention to the way in which the subject's personality has been shaped by the values and institutions of the society they grew up in and to the ways in which they reflect, influence, and confirm those values and institutions. It is this last emphasis that aligned Mazlish's approach

---

42 Ibid., vii.

43 Ibid., vii.

44 Ibid., xii.

45 Tomasz Pawelec, "Bruce Mazlish: Pioneer Psychohistorian," *Clio's Psyche* 3, no. 3 (December 1996): 78.

46 Mazlish, *In Search of Nixon*, 11.

with that of Erikson and it was also exactly this part that was missing from the Nixon book. In the preface he wrote: "In fact, what I am offering is primarily a brief psychological sketch of Richard Nixon, informed by an awareness of psychohistorical theory and practice – and a good deal of humility."[47]

Mazlish's portrait of Nixon was of a man haunted by his mother's dislike of warfare and his father's competitiveness: an ambivalent president who dealt with his ambivalence by projection of aggression onto others. "He is a man," Mazlish wrote,

> haunted by his father's failure and driven to avoid that failure for himself and to redeem it for his parent. He compensates for lack of native abilities, where this is the case, by enormous hard work and persistence. ... He has had a serious problem with death wishes and anxiety in relation to his brothers, Eisenhower, and himself.[48]

Up to a certain extent, Mazlish argued, these character traits correspond to those of Americans in general.

> For [Nixon] and for us ... dedication to peace has a corresponding element in powerful aggressive impulses and a tremendous competitive drive to win, and avoid any semblance of 'defeat.' The compassion for the needy finds a companion in the desperate need to always feel strong and to reject feelings of passivity and dependency.[49]

In Search of Nixon revealed an underlying belief that psychoanalysis was a scientific discipline, as well as a strong conviction that a psychohistorian could, given enough data, come to verifiable conclusions about a subject's personality. From *In Search of Nixon* it would seem that Mazlish believed that psychoanalysis – even the psychoanalysis of a historical actor conducted at a distance in space and time – could produce a form of (relatively) certain knowledge. He did not shy away from applying psychoanalytic thought to living subjects, either. In the first chapter, "The Nixon Problem," he wrote that "the American President is so powerful that 'analysis' of his 'personality' is both necessary and justified."[50] Nixon emerged from Mazlish's book as a botched American hero: incapable of dealing with his own weakness and therefore prone to falseness

47 Ibid., vii.
48 Ibid., 142.
49 Ibid., 142.
50 Ibid., 3.

and trickery. It was not exactly a prediction of the Watergate scandal, but it was an evaluation of the president's character that would not be contradicted by the unfolding of events.

Undoubtedly, the book on Nixon dealt with a leader's appeal to their followers and in that sense was more properly psychohistorical than Freud and Bullitt's analysis of Woodrow Wilson. Yet the book about Nixon gained a very problematic status within the psychohistorical movement. It was one of the points of contention between founding scholars Robert J. Lifton and Bruce Mazlish.[51] Was it the task of the psychohistorian to apply psychoanalytic knowledge to living political figures? Bruce Mazlish believed it was. Robert J. Lifton, less convinced of psychoanalysis's scientific status, was not so sure. Their differences can be traced back to their dissimilar intellectual backgrounds.

4 The Case of Barry G.

To understand the context of Mazlish's attempt to psychoanalyze Richard Nixon from a distance, it is crucial to see that while psychohistorians were shaping their movement, psychoanalytic terminology and thought had permeated American culture at large. As such, it also entered into the country's political debate. Shortly before the 1964 presidential election (Lyndon Johnson versus Barry Goldwater), newly founded *Fact Magazine* polled members of the American Psychiatric Association, asking them whether conservative candidate Goldwater was mentally stable enough to become president of the country. The cover of the November-December issue gave the answer: "1,189 psychiatrists say Goldwater is psychologically unfit to be president!"[52] The issue's title in full was: "The Unconscious of a Conservative: A Special Issue on the Mind of Barry Goldwater." The thrust of the two main articles was that Goldwater had "a severely paranoid personality and was psychologically unfit" to become president.'[53]

The publication of the article led to a lawsuit. According to the official jury report, the articles tried to support the thesis that Senator Goldwater was mentally unstable "by citing allegedly factual incidents from his public and private life and by reporting the results of a 'poll' of 12,356 psychiatrists," together with

---

51 Personal communication with Mazlish, January 22, 2014.

52 "The Unconscious of a Conservative: A Special Issue on the Mind of Barry Goldwater," *Fact Magazine*, issue 5 (1964).

53 Ibid.

a sampling of comments "by the 2,417 psychiatrists who responded to the poll questionnaire."[54] It was by no means the first instance of the pathologizing of political preference in the U.S. media. Around the same time, *Harper's* published a piece titled "The Paranoid Style in American Politics," written by Columbia historian Richard Hofstadter.[55] He argued that (Goldwaterite) conservatism could and should be regarded as a mental illness.[56] In the court case that followed the publication of the article in *Fact Magazine*, a federal jury awarded Barry Goldwater $1 in compensatory damages; $25,000 in punitive damages were claimed from Ginzburg, the editor in chief and publisher of the magazine.[57] *Fact Magazine* ceased to exist. The incident moreover led to an amendment of the American Psychiatric Association's ethics principles later. The amendment became known as 'section 7.3,' or the 'Goldwater rule,' and stated that it was forbidden for members of the APA to comment on the mental states of individuals without having examined them personally.[58] No such rule, however, was put in place for historians.

Several years later, in 1976, the American Psychiatric Association published a short document entitled *The Psychiatrist as Psychohistorian*. Spurred by the Goldwater controversy some years earlier, shocked by the publication and success of Bruce Mazlish's book on Nixon, the aim of the document was to assess to what extent psychohistorical studies were impinging upon the privacy of the persons studied if these persons were still alive; to look critically at the discipline's methodological underpinnings; and to determine if the analysis of persons "in a significant and sensitive government position – such as a Secretary of State" (the author here is alluding to the psychohistory of Henry Kissinger that Mazlish was preparing at the time) might "place the subject, and therefore the Nation, at a disadvantage in negotiating with foreign powers."[59]

The authors of the document were convinced that psychoanalytic profiles compiled by intelligence agencies "in the service of national interest" were

---

54 http://www.supremecourtopinions.wustl.edu/files/opinion_pdfs/1969/69-687.pdf (Accessed on September 13, 2016). 4.

55 Richard Hofstadter, "The Paranoid Style in American Politics," *Harper's Magazine* (November 1964): 77-86.

56 Ibid., 77.

57 http://www.supremecourtopinions.wustl.edu/files/opinion_pdfs/1969/69-687.pdf (Accessed on September 13, 2016). 4.

58 Questions surrounding this issue have come under scrutiny again at the time of writing, see Benedict Carey, "The Psychiatric Question: Is It Fair to Analyze Donald Trump From Afar?" *The New York Times*, 15 August, 2016.

59 Hofling, *The Psychiatrist as Psychohistorian*, 10.

of value.[60] By implication, they were now determining if psychohistory could also be deemed a national security threat. According to the authors, psychiatrists made for especially dangerous psychohistorians, for two reasons, worth quoting in full:

> (1) By reason of his special perceptive and deductive skills and his special knowledge of depth-psychology, the psychiatrist as psychohistorian is often in a position to discern certain things about the subject's mind and behavior that are not discernible to the subject himself or to those observers lacking the special training and knowledge. (2) By reason of his special status as a physician, a psychiatrist, and a scientist, the author is, to a considerable extent, accepted by a large segment of society as having special powers, and his report is therefore likely to be taken very seriously, often as having even greater authority than he claims for it… In a case in which the psychiatrist had reasonably ample data – let us say, interviews with the subject, interviews with persons on familiar terms with the subject at various periods of his life, access to some of the subject's speeches, writings and behavior in the public domain – his psychohistorical analysis of the subject would, at least in theory, be analogous to clinically deductive reports of X-ray films of the patient's body.[61]

The document betrays some interesting assumptions about psychiatry and psychoanalysis: first, that "depth-psychology" was based upon, and produced, a "special knowledge" which was only accessible to those who had gone through proper training; second, that it was a science, which, if based on enough data, produced certain knowledge, analogous to the physician's knowledge of a patient's body. Also, that this knowledge was obtainable through the use of documents and interviews with the patient and people surrounding the patient and was therefore not contingent upon the psychoanalytic (or otherwise therapeutic) process itself. Finally, the passage above seems to acknowledge that "physician," "psychiatrist," and "scientist" were terms that, in the public's imagination, were invested with a considerable amount of authority, an authority that was put at risk by the association of psychiatry and psychohistory and the use of the latter by non-specialists, such as journalists and historians. John Mack, who was a member of the task force, explained: "Although some of us felt there could be exceptions, we were trying to avoid

60 Ibid., 13.
61 Ibid., 9.

the irresponsible armchair stuff that pretends to be clinical."[62] The psychiatrists were fighting a losing battle, as "the actual practice of psychoanalysis" increasingly became "less important than its cultural impact."[63]

Finally, the task force concluded that there was nothing improper or unethical (even if written by a psychiatrist) about a study such as the one written by Walter Langer about Hitler for the OSS. If an extreme situation warranted it, psychiatrists and historians were allowed – even expected – to serve their country. In fact, in times of peace, the authors could find no fault in producing "for confidential use of government officials" psycho-profiles and psychobiographies of significant international figures whose personality formation needed to be understood "to carry out national policy more effectively."[64]

The authors held that "this type of activity blends by almost imperceptible degrees into common practices of educational institutions, businesses, charitable organizations, and so on, many of which compile basically harmless files or 'dossiers' on the tastes, likes and dislikes, biases, and eccentricities of key individuals with whom they must deal."[65] Only when a person under scrutiny was currently alive *and* a fellow-citizen or a functioning component of the same nation as the writer, did ethical considerations "assume considerable weight."[66] It would only be ethical for a psychiatrist to write and publish a psychohistory, psychobiography or psycho-profile of a living person if the subject had been informed, and had freely given consent for personal interviews and publication. That meant Mazlish's 'psychohistorical inquiry' of Nixon was suspect.

From the taskforce's perspective, then, psychohistory not only impinged upon the privacy of individuals and possibly formed a threat to national security; in its crudest form, it also jeopardized the authoritative position of psychiatry as a profession. In an interview with the *New York Times* in response to the report's publication, Mazlish dismissed the worries expressed in the document: "It staggers me to imagine that the Syrians could read my book and say, 'Ah, now we know how to deal with Kissinger.' That's a fantasy."[67] To be on the safe side, Mazlish decided to drop the term psychohistory from the title of his psychohistory of Henry Kissinger. The cover of that book simply read:

62 Philip Noble, "A Controversial Discipline," *New York Times*, October 10, 1976.

63 Quoted in Lawrence R. Samuel, *Shrink: A Cultural History of Psychoanalysis in America* (Lincoln: University of Nebraska Press, 2013), xiii.

64 Hofling, *The Psychiatrist as Psychohistorian*, 12.

65 Ibid., 13.

66 Ibid.

67 Quoted in Noble "A Controversial Discipline."

Kissinger: The European Mind in American Politics. A Biographical Inquiry by Bruce Mazlish.[68]

5 Conclusion

Psychoanalytic analyses of U.S. presidents played an important role in the construction of the psychohistorical movement. The psychohistorical movement, in turn, played an important part in bringing the study of the personalities of presidents to the attention of the wider public in the United States. In part, it was the application of psychoanalytic thought to living politicians that discredited the psychohistorical movement in the eyes of professional historians and psychoanalysts.

In the case of Freud's analysis of Woodrow Wilson, published in English in the 1960s, the psychohistorians were quick to distance themselves from this work. They viewed it as an unsophisticated form of applied psychoanalysis that might damage the reputation of their budding movement. The psychohistorians' mentor Erik H. Erikson objected to the work because it did not, in his view, set psychoanalytic theory to work productively within history. His own analysis of Martin Luther tried to go beyond applied psychoanalysis by showing how psychoanalytic theory could shed new light on the leader/led dynamic. In the wake of World War II and the rise of Adolf Hitler to power in Germany, Erikson was grappling with the question how a leader becomes attractive to a large group of followers. This question preoccupied many of the early psychohistorians. Bruce Mazlish was inspired by the work of William Langer, who as president of the American Historical Association had advocated the use of psychoanalysis in history, and by his brother, Walter C. Langer, who had written a report on Adolf Hitler for the OSS during World War II. In the report, Walter Langer predicted that Hitler would, if confronted with certain circumstances, commit suicide. Inspired by this work, Mazlish started to advocate the application of psychoanalytic thought to living politicians in the 1960 and 1970s. To test the predictive capacities of psychohistory, Mazlish attempted to set up a group that would analyze the personality of Richard Nixon. The project was aborted for lack of funding. He did, however, write his own psychohistorical study of Nixon. Concerned by the work being done by Mazlish and others, the American Psychiatric Association banned members

68 Bruce Mazlish, *Kissinger: The European Mind in American Policy* (New York: Basic Books, 1976).

from analyzing living political figures and published a document *The Psychiatrist as Psychohistorian* in 1976, in which they advise not to analyze living political figures, as these analyses might prove detrimental to U.S. national security.

Although psychohistorical studies were still being published, by the late 1980s psychohistory had lost its status as a promising new field of research.[69] Due to inherent strife in the psychohistorical movement and changing interpretations of Freud in the United States (the shift from a biologistic interpretation to a more hermeneutic interpretation through the introduction of works by French theorists such as Jacques Lacan), the application of Freudian theory to historical subjects lost its novelty and prestige inside and outside of academia.[70] Concomitantly, the belief that political leaders could or should be 'analyzed' – in part due to the aforementioned 'Goldwater Rule' – receded into the background. The idea that 'psychohistory' might, one day, become a (semi-)independent discipline was, at this time, abandoned by its earliest proponents. As the psychohistorical movement lost its impetus, many ideas professed by psychohistorians were adopted by scholars of various stripes. Applications of psychological and psychoanalytical ideas to groups and individuals continue in the fields of 'psychosocial studies' and 'psychoanalytic studies' and in the wider field of biography. At the time of writing, interest has rekindled in the early attempts to apply psychological thought to political figures, due to the election of eccentric businessman Donald J. Trump as the 45th president of the United States.[71]

69 See for instance: Michael Rogin, *Fathers and Children: Andrew Jackson and the Subjugation of the American Indian* (New Jersey: Transaction Publishers, 1991). This work, clearly psychohistorical in its theme and execution, makes an effort to distance itself from the term *psychohistory* and the psychohistorical movement in its introduction.

70 An exploration of the many causes for the decline of psychohistory exceeds the scope of this paper. For further discussion of the history of psychohistory from the perspective of an active psychohistorian, I would refer the reader to Elovitz, Paul, *The Making of Psychohistory* (London: Routledge, 2018).

71 Debate about the application of psychological thought to living historical figures continues, for instance surrounding the work: Bandy X. Lee (ed.), *The Dangerous Case of Donald Trump* (New York: Thomas Dunne Books, 2017), to which Robert J. Lifton, once a staunch disputant of applied psychohistory (to living historical figures), made a contribution.

CHAPTER 3

Origins and Development of Lincoln's Antislavery Policies

David Zarefsky

Concluding the second volume of his magisterial political biography of Abraham Lincoln, Sidney Blumenthal observes that Lincoln "forged himself in a world of uncertainty" and that "the arc of his story was uneasy, unpredictable, and often unintended" but "his thoughts and words were the careful result of his intense consciousness."[1] This is a more nuanced view than many judgments of Lincoln. Within a generation of his death, Lincoln was idealized in public memory, associated with a variety of contemporary causes for which public support was sought. Initially, this was part of the drive for inter-sectional reconciliation. Perhaps the zenith of hagiographic treatments was the publication of Carl Sandburg's multi-volume *Abraham Lincoln: The Prairie Years* and *Abraham Lincoln: The War Years* during the 1920s and 1930s, although Lincoln was also a source of national inspiration during the years surrounding World War II and the Cold War.[2]

By the late twentieth century, however, the hagiographic view of Lincoln was in decline. Through the lens of the civil rights movement and changing attitudes toward race, his flaws seemed larger.[3] His persistent support for colonization (returning freed slaves to Africa), very tentative moves toward supporting Blacks' right to vote, rejection of social equality of the races, and even his occasional indulgence in racist jokes, were argued to be truer signs of his character than some of his more forceful and eloquent statements. As for his being the 'Great Emancipator,' recent scholarship has emphasized the

---

1 Sidney Blumenthal, *Wrestling with His Angel, 1849-1856* (vol. 2 of *The Political Life of Abraham Lincoln*) (New York: Simon and Schuster, 2017), 481.

2 See Merrill D. Peterson, *Lincoln in American Memory* (New York: Oxford University Press, 1974) and Barry Schwartz, *Abraham Lincoln and the Forge of National Memory* (Chicago: University of Chicago Press, 2000) on the emergence of public memory of Lincoln. The Sandburg biography is *Abraham Lincoln: The Prairie Years*, 2 vols. and *Abraham Lincoln: The War Years*, 4 vols. (New York: Harcourt, Brace, 1926-1939).

3 This more recent phase in Lincoln's public memory is examined in Barry Schwartz, *Abraham Lincoln in the Post-Heroic Era* (Chicago: University of Chicago Press, 2008).

© KONINKLIJKE BRILL NV, LEIDEN, 2020 | DOI:10.1163/9789004422643_005

roles played by many, including the enslaved, in moving from slavery to freedom.[4]

But Lincoln's story is more complicated than these extreme versions. He was not simply the convenient agent for views about slavery that were 'in the wind' at the time. He was neither the Great Emancipator of popular stereotype nor the racist and reluctant emancipator of the anti-stereotype.[5] Rather, he was a man whose early experiences and involvement in the political struggles of the 1850s shaped his beliefs about slavery, governing the actions he would take on this topic as president. In developing that claim, this chapter will review briefly Lincoln's early encounters with slavery and then will characterize views that emerged from his attention to and involvement in the politics of the 1850s. The final section of the chapter will illustrate how Lincoln drew from this mix of personal experience and political thought to shape the actions he pursued as president.

1 Lincoln and Slavery: The Early Years

American slavery was complicated. Introduced to support agriculture in Virginia in 1619, it spread to other colonies over the next 150 years. By the time of the American Revolution, slavery was lawful in twelve of the thirteen colonies, but it was concentrated in the South. In the quarter-century after independence, it was essentially eliminated in the northern states. There were diverse reasons for its abandonment: a growing moral revulsion toward the institution, but also the fact that slavery became unprofitable on the small farms and rocky soil of New England, in contrast to the plantation agriculture of the South. Moreover, while the means of removing slavery sometimes was manumission, often it was to sell slaves farther south, bringing profit to the owners undertaking the sale. Even after northern states abandoned slavery, they continued to profit from it – especially the emerging class of Northern manufacturers who could obtain raw mate-

---

4 This issue is discussed in James M. McPherson, *Drawn with the Sword: Reflections on the American Civil War* (New York: Oxford University Press, 1996), 192-207; and Leonard L. Richards, *Who Freed the Slaves? The Fight Over the Thirteenth Amendment* (Chicago: University of Chicago Press, 2015).

5 See, for example, Lerone Bennett, Jr., *Forced into Glory: Abraham Lincoln's White Dream* (Chicago: Johnson Publishing, 2000); Fred Kaplan, *Lincoln and the Abolitionists: John Quincy Adams, Slavery, and the Civil War* (New York: HarperCollins, 2017).

rials such as cotton much cheaper because the crop had been picked by slave labor.[6]

Conflicting views about slavery dominated the period of the national founding. The only hope for union lay in the ability to finesse, if not completely to avoid, the issue. Thomas Jefferson's draft of the Declaration of Independence contained, as one of the specific grievances against King George III, the allegation that he was responsible for the introduction of slavery into the American colonies. The passage was removed before the Declaration was approved by the Second Continental Congress. Some critics thought slavery not such a bad thing and did not believe it belonged in a list of grievances; others thought it unfair to blame the king for introducing a system that had been embraced by many of the colonists themselves.

At the time of the drafting of the Constitution, it became clear that the new nation could either address the slavery issue directly or preserve the union, but not both. Delegates to the Constitutional Convention from North and South Carolina and Georgia made clear that they would bolt if the slave trade were not adequately protected.[7] The final version did not mention the word *slave* or *slavery* (a fact that Lincoln would find highly significant) but it did make several concessions to the peculiar institution. Perhaps the most significant was 'the 3/5 compromise'– a provision that, in allocating representation to Congress, as well as direct taxes, among the states, 3/5 of the number of slaves would be added to the total number of free persons (although, of course, slaves were not eligible to cast votes – not even 3/5 of a vote – for those representatives). This was a compromise between southerners who wanted 100 percent of the slaves to be counted and northerners who wanted none. This provision gave slaveholding states a bonus in Congressional representation and also in the electoral vote assigned for choosing the president. This move had a significant effect early on: were it not for the 3/5 bonus, John Adams and not Thomas Jefferson would have been elected in 1800.

A second provision stipulated that the international slave trade could not be restricted for twenty years, until 1808. Here too, motives were mixed. Some wished to restrict the slave trade as a step toward the gradual abolition of slavery itself, but others wanted to drive up the value of their existing investment.

---

6 The history of slavery in the colonies and early republic is examined in Ira Berlin, *Many Thousands Gone: The First Two Centuries of Slavery in North America* (Cambridge, Mass.: Harvard University Press, 1998).

7 The disputes at the Constitutional Convention are described in Berlin, *Many Thousands Gone*, and in James Oliver Horton and Lois E. Horton, *Slavery and the Making of America* (New York: Oxford University Press, 2004).

Some who favored unrestricted trade in slaves wanted a source of cheap labor; others wanted to attract more slaves to the United States where they would be treated better than elsewhere. The twenty-year retention of the slave trade was one side of a bargain. In return, the Constitution provided that navigation acts could be passed by simple majority in Congress, which northern states desired rather than requiring a two-thirds majority that some southern supporters of free trade wished to impose.

The third Constitutional provision governing slavery was the requirement that fugitives be delivered up to their owners when caught. But the Constitution did not specify whose requirement it was to do this deed. To implement owners' rights to reclaim their escaped slaves, Congress passed a fugitive slave act in 1793 and would pass a stronger one in 1850.

During the country's early years, there was no consistent policy about slavery. Congress prohibited it in the Northwest Territory but allowed it in the Southwest Territory. Parts of the Northwest Territory tried unsuccessfully to introduce it later. If there was any consensus, it was that slavery was a domestic institution under the control of the states and was not within the enumerated or implied powers of the Federal Government. The question of Congress's role to regulate slavery in the *territories* was raised in the controversy over Missouri's application for admission as a state. Unlike states, territories were under the control of the Federal Government. The resulting controversy threatened to destroy the Union. In his old age, Thomas Jefferson called the question "a fire bell in the night."[8] It was settled by compromises, balancing the admission of Missouri as a slave state with that of Maine as a free state, and then dividing the rest of the territory in the Louisiana Purchase. North of latitude 36°30,' slavery was outlawed; south of that line, it was permitted if desired by settlers who went there.

At least until the late 1820s and early 1830s, many southerners were as ambivalent about slavery as were their northern counterparts. They regarded it as necessary for their agricultural economy, yet many also believed that the institution rested on a shaky moral foundation. Only when abolitionists began in the early 1830s to challenge slavery directly did most Southerners abandon their ambivalent views and mount a full-throated defense. That was when John C. Calhoun began to refer to slavery not as a necessary evil but as a positive good, and other southern spokesmen took up the same theme.

It was into this milieu of ambivalent attitudes about slavery that Abraham Lincoln was born on February 12, 1809 in Kentucky, a slave state. When he was

8 Thomas Jefferson to John Holmes, April 22, 1820.

seven years old, his family moved to the new state of Indiana, carved out from the Northwest Territory and therefore free (although numbering supporters of slavery among its settlers). There were several reasons for the family's move, including contested land claims in Kentucky and the possibility of richer soil in Indiana. But among the reasons was that Abe's father, Thomas Lincoln, was uncomfortable living among slave-owners and thought their presence harmful to free labor. This was a common amoral objection to slavery on the part of many Northern farmers. Although Lincoln would differ from his father in many respects, he shared this hostility to slavery.

In 1818, Lincoln's mother died, and the following year Thomas Lincoln remarried. Abe's stepmother, Sarah Bush Johnston, took a strong interest in the boy, recognized his native intelligence, and encouraged him to read. As he carried a book everywhere and sometimes neglected his chores in order to read, his alienation from his father grew. As soon as he could do so after reaching the legal age of 21, Lincoln left the family home (by this time his parents had moved near Decatur, Illinois) and established residence in the small Illinois town of New Salem. He lived there for seven years before moving to Springfield, where he would live until he went to Washington in 1861 as president elect. While in New Salem, Lincoln tried a variety of occupations, including postmaster, surveyor, and tavern-keeper. He was unsuccessful at most of them but meanwhile had become a skilled raconteur and enjoyed the friendship of other men. He served in the militia during the 1832 Black Hawk War, having been elected captain by his men themselves.

Lincoln had several distinctive personality characteristics. Throughout his life he was an adroit storyteller, widely recognized for his humor and wit. He was sociable and enjoyed the company of others. His ambition for fame and desire for upward mobility were also widely known; his law partner William Herndon famously described his ambition as "a little engine that knows no rest." More recently, scholarly attention has been given to Lincoln's persistent melancholy, sometimes bordering on depression.[9] None of these personality factors, however, explains Lincoln's overriding concern for the slavery issue, because that concern originated only with the passage of the Kansas-Nebraska Act in 1854. By that time, Lincoln had been politically active for twenty years. He entered politics as a Whig, supporting Henry Clay and opposing Andrew Jackson. After an initial defeat, in 1834 he was elected to the Illinois House of Representatives. He was re-elected for a total of four terms, after which he returned to Springfield and to the law practice he had established with a

9 For example, see Joshua Wolf Shenk, *Lincoln's Melancholy* (Boston: Houghton Mifflin, 2005).

succession of partners.[10] In 1846 he was elected to a single term in the U.S. House Representatives, the only Whig Representative from Illinois.

During those years, slavery was not an especially salient issue for Lincoln, but he was clearly opposed to the institution. On two occasions he traveled to New Orleans, taking a barge down the Mississippi River to bring goods to market. While there, he observed a slave auction, and on the way he saw a group of slaves shackled together, marched in a coffle to a market, but presumably happy and carefree. After the second of these episodes, he reportedly said to a friend, "If I ever get a chance to hit that thing, I'll hit it hard."[11]

Later in his life, Lincoln would reflect unfavorably on his teenage years. As had been customary, his father had hired him out to work on neighboring farms but kept Abe's earnings for himself. Referring to this experience, Lincoln said that he understood the feelings of the slave because he once had been a slave himself.[12] We may look askance at his equation of his youthful labor with chattel slavery, but the comment is particularly revealing. For Lincoln, the essence of slavery was deprivation of the ability to control the fruits of one's own work. This was not only the loss of economic freedom but also the loss of any ability to rise above the slave's current condition. Without the chance for upward mobility, the slave was consigned to a life of permanent degradation. Even as Lincoln, for most of his life, would disclaim social and political equality between the races, he consistently maintained a commitment to economic equality. As he stated in one of his 1858 debates with Stephen A. Douglas, when it came to "the right to eat the bread, without leave of anybody else, which his own hand earns, [the Negro] is my equal, and the equal of Judge Douglas, and the equal of every living man."[13]

Lincoln entered the Illinois legislature during the mid-1830s, just when abolitionists began to flood the mails with literature and to submit petitions to

---

10 On Lincoln's Illinois legislative career, see Douglas L. Wilson, *Lincoln Before Washington: New Perspectives on the Illinois Years* (Urbana and Chicago: University of Illinois Press, 1997).

11 Lincoln's cousin, John Hanks, related this story. See Benjamin P. Thomas, *Abraham Lincoln: A Biography* (1952; rpt. Carbondale, Ill.: Southern Illinois University Press, 2008), 24. Historians doubt the accuracy of this story, since Hanks left the party in St. Louis and was not with Lincoln in New Orleans. Whether or not the quotation is literally correct, it is an accurate statement of Lincoln's revulsion at the institution of slavery.

12 Cited in Blumenthal, *Wrestling with His Angel*, 147, 376; Michael Burlingame, *The Inner World of Abraham Lincoln* (Urbana and Chicago: University of Illinois Press, 1994), 36.

13 "First Debate with Stephen A. Douglas at Ottawa, Illinois," August 21, 1858, *Collected Works of Abraham Lincoln*, ed. Roy P. Basler (New Brunswick, NJ: Rutgers University Press, 1953), 3: 16.

Congress calling for measures ranging from immediate abolition to dissolution of the Union. These actions aroused an extreme backlash in the South and were hardly more popular in the North. To support the resistance, the Illinois legislature passed a resolution that strongly decried abolitionists. Only Lincoln and another Whig representative demurred. They sponsored an alternate resolution that attracted hardly any support. It stated that the system of slavery was "founded on injustice and bad policy" but went on to acknowledge that abolition aggravated rather than diminished the evils.[14] It was not that abolition was morally wrong but that it was counterproductive. In his law practice, Lincoln was involved in two cases related to fugitive slaves. He won the case representing a fugitive seeking his freedom, and he lost the case representing a master seeking to recapture a fugitive.[15] There is little reason to think he pursued either case less than wholeheartedly, for it was his belief that every client was entitled to the most vigorous defense possible.

During his tenure in Congress, Lincoln was distinguished mostly for his opposition to the Mexican-American War, which was quite popular in the months after it ended successfully for the United States. But as his term was nearing its end, he took one significant action regarding slavery. He introduced a bill calling for abolition in the District of Columbia. Lincoln's bill went nowhere, but his action reveals much about his views on the Constitution. Like almost all Americans, he believed that the Federal Government was powerless to do anything about slavery in the sovereign states where it already existed, but he thought it *could* act with regard to the areas it controlled: the territories and the District of Columbia. Although that would soon change, the status of the territories was settled by the Missouri Compromise. The District of Columbia was the one place where the question was open and Congress could do something to address the embarrassment many northern congressmen felt upon seeing slave pens and auction lots within sight of the U.S. Capitol.

Throughout these early years, Lincoln was a member of the Whig Party, and his political mentor and 'beau ideal' of a statesman was Henry Clay. Clay was a paradoxical figure, a southern slaveholder who opposed slavery. The prototypical Whig, Clay was both antislavery and anti-abolition. He thought slavery was wrong, an evil that must disappear in God's good time. But abolition any time soon would be catastrophic, throwing the races into the impossibility of living together. Clay's preferred solution was colonization, simultaneously

14 "Protest in Illinois Legislature on Slavery, March 3, 1837," *Collected Works*, 1: 75.

15 For a discussion of Lincoln's legal career, see Brian R. Dirck, *Lincoln the Lawyer* (Urbana and Chicago: University of Illinois Press, 2007).

freeing slaves (ideally with the consent of their masters in return for compensation) and deporting them to Africa, their ancestral homeland even though virtually all had been born in America.[16] Colonization was an impractical but elegant solution, appealing to both antislavery and anti-abolition horns of the Whig dilemma. Clay was president of the American Colonization Society from 1817 until his death in 1852. Lincoln was an active supporter until the end of the second year of his presidency.

2 Lincoln and the Politics of the 1850s

After Lincoln left Congress, he returned to his private law practice, increasingly representing corporate clients and rising into the upper-middle class of Springfield society. There is little reason to think he was occupied with the slavery question until his nemesis, Senator Stephen A. Douglas, introduced the Kansas-Nebraska Act in early 1854. By repealing the Missouri Compromise, the Act raised the possibility that slavery, formerly excluded from the Nebraska Territory, might be introduced there, and by extension into other new territories as well.[17] The subsequent story of the politics of slavery between 1854 and 1860 is intricate and complex.[18] Against the backdrop of this ongoing controversy, Lincoln awakened his interest in slavery and gradually worked out his system of beliefs. Here are its major tenets.

First, Lincoln advocated not the abolition of slavery but its containment. He reconciled his strong antislavery moral convictions with his belief that government's power to act against the wishes of the slaveholding states was quite limited. He did so by pledging not to interfere with the institution in the states where it already existed, denying that there was any power to do so in any

16 The American Colonization Society and Clay's role in it are described in Richards, *Who Freed the Slaves?*, 50-51.

17 Lincoln claimed in closing his 1858 Senatorial campaign that, while he was not insensitive to ambition, he would forswear any political office if the Kansas-Nebraska Act could be repealed and the Missouri Compromise restored. "Fragment: Last Speech of the Campaign at Springfield, Illinois," October 30, 1858, *Collected Works*, 3: 334. He had stated that it was the Kansas-Nebraska Act that reawakened his interest in politics because it denied the claim that slavery was in the course of ultimate extinction. See "Speech at Chicago, Illinois," July 10, 1858, *Collected Works*, 2: 484-502.

18 For discussions of the politics of slavery, see Blumenthal, *Wrestling with His Angel;* Michael Burlingame, *Abraham Lincoln: A Life* (Baltimore: Johns Hopkins University Press, 2008), 2 vols.; and Ronald C. White Jr., *A. Lincoln: A Biography* (New York: Random House, 2009).

case, but was unalterably opposed to its spread to any new territory. In his 1854 'Peoria speech' and subsequently, he distinguished between the existing institution and its spread.[19] Containment became the core of the new Republican Party's platform and represented the lowest common denominator on which virtually all Republicans could agree. It accommodated those who opposed slavery on moral grounds and also those who opposed extending slavery to the territories because they wanted Blacks, whether slave or free, excluded from the territories. At various times between 1854 and 1860, including the 1858 debates with Douglas, Lincoln espoused both of these positions. Yet more often he would see containment as a fitting response, despite its moderate nature, to his moral condemnation of slavery. Besides his legalistic argument about limited powers, he explained why during the Douglas debates, using a disease analogy: "You may have a wen or a cancer on your body and not be able to cut it out lest you bleed to death, but surely it is no way to cure it to engraft it all over your body."[20] Implicit here is Lincoln's belief that immediate abolition would be counterproductive.

Second, Lincoln did not profess to know what to do about the immediate problem. "If all earthly power were given to me," he said at Peoria, "I should not know what to do, as to the existing institution."[21] He ticked off a number of possibilities – deportation, a caste system, even freedom with equality. Of this last option, he stated frankly, "My own feelings will not admit of this, and if mine would, we well know that those of the great mass of white people will not."[22] But ignorance about the proper short-term policy would not be disabling, because of the third major belief in Lincoln's schema.

Third, Lincoln believed that containment would alter the dynamics of slavery over the long term, leading eventually to emancipation. He thought that slavery must either expand or die. Confined to where it already existed, it would deplete the soil, reducing crop yields below the point of profitability. Once that happened, slavery would no longer make economic sense. For this reason, Lincoln maintained, the public mind would "rest in the belief that it is in course of ultimate extinction."[23] Presumably, slave states on their own

19 "Speech at Peoria, Illinois," October 16, 1854, *Collected Works*, 2: 248. Lincoln had made substantially the same speech two weeks earlier, at Springfield.

20 Lincoln invoked the analogy to cancer during the final debate with Stephen A. Douglas, in Alton, on October 15, 1858. See *Collected Works*, 3: 313.

21 "Speech at Peoria," *Collected Works*, 2: 255.

22 "Speech at Peoria," *Collected Works*, 2: 256.

23 "'A House Divided': Speech at Springfield, Illinois," June 16, 1858, *Collected Works*, 2: 461. For a discussion of whether containment really would lead to extinction, see Martin B. Duberman, *The Antislavery Vanguard: New Essays on the Abolitionists* (Princeton: Princeton University Press, 1965), 402.

would abolish it voluntarily. This was not unlike the way that slavery had actually disappeared from the North. Lincoln was willing to wait a long time – he would sometimes target the year 1900, sometimes a century or more – so long as the public mind would be confident of the ultimate result. When he became president, he would be willing to speed the process along by offering financial incentives to slave states abandoning slavery or to individual slaveholders who freed their slaves. But it was precisely this public confidence in slavery's ultimate demise that he thought was undermined by the Kansas-Nebraska Act.

Fourth, however, Lincoln did not believe that slavery could be kept out of new territories except by its explicit and enforced prohibition. He differed with his Whig heroes Henry Clay and Daniel Webster, both of whom thought that climate and soil conditions would keep slavery out of the Mexican cession, notwithstanding the Compromise of 1850 that opened New Mexico territory to proslavery settlement. Even more did he differ with his rival Stephen A. Douglas, who thought that Nebraska Territory would be unlikely to attract slaveholders even with the repeal of the Missouri Compromise. To the contrary, Lincoln observed, the facts of the *Dred Scott* case demonstrated that slavery tended to spread to new territory even in the face of a restriction presumed by all to be valid at the time.[24] How much more, then, could it spread when the law was officially neutral. And if slavery ever were allowed into new territory, that would be the game. If slaveholders settled in a new territory, those hostile to slavery would stay out, knowing that free labor could not compete economically with slave labor. Slave territories would beget slave states, thwarting Lincoln's goal of bringing the institution of slavery to an end.

Fifth, Lincoln identified his positions with those of the nation's founders. He maintained that they, like he, were opposed to slavery; that they accepted its existence for the sake of the union; but that they believed that Congress had the power to regulate it and signaled that a future Congress should use that power to bring about slavery's demise. Of course, the founders never were confronted with precisely the same question as were Lincoln and his contemporaries. As a result, there was no direct evidence of their intentions. Rather, inferences could be drawn from bits and pieces of selected evidence. Most thoroughly in his 1860 Cooper Union speech, Lincoln examined votes taken and notes written by the signers of the U.S. Constitution, to reach the conclusion that a majority of them thought Congress had power over slavery in the territories and should exercise it. As for the remaining signers, in most cases they left no record of their views and cannot be assumed to have disagreed

24 "Third Debate with Stephen A. Douglas at Jonesboro, Illinois," September 15, 1858, *Collected Works*, 3: 130.

with the majority.[25] In addition to this historical exegesis, Lincoln cited several other signs of the founders' presumed intentions: the commitment in the Declaration of Independence that all men are created equal, the prohibition of slavery in the Northwest Ordinance passed under the Articles of Confederation and its reaffirmation by the First Congress under the Constitution, the absence of the word 'slavery' in the U.S. Constitution (so that once slavery was eliminated, Lincoln said, the great document would be without blemish), and the action by Congress to abolish the international slave trade at the very first moment that doing so was Constitutionally permissible.

Of course, Lincoln was not the only figure in the slavery controversy who appealed to the memory of the founders. Directly challenging Lincoln's Scriptural formulation that "a house divided against itself cannot stand," Douglas pointed out that the founders *made* the country divided half slave and half free, and chided Lincoln for setting himself up as wiser than they.[26] To this taunt, Lincoln denied that the founders *made* the country divided but insisted that they *found* it that way and, not knowing what to do about it, left it that way for the time being but signaled their disapproval and their hope for its eventual demise.[27] When Douglas and other critics accused Lincoln of charging the founders with hypocrisy, since most of them were slaveholders themselves and did not immediately liberate their slaves after declaring that all men were created equal, Lincoln replied that their statement was aspirational rather than descriptive. It was "a standard maxim for free society," a goal constantly to be pursued and gradually approximated.[28]

One might wonder why Lincoln and others spent so much of their rhetorical energy on the question of what the founders would have done. The answer is that the 1850s were years of filiopiety.[29] The founders had all died but were just out of reach; their lineal descendant, Henry Clay, had died only a few years before. They were the subjects of almost universal veneration. If one could identify one's position with that of the founders, it was as if one could prevail on the complex question of slavery itself.

25 "Address at Cooper Institute, New York City," February 27, 1860, *Collected Works*, 3: 522-550.

26 "First Debate with Stephen A. Douglas at Ottawa, Illinois," August 21, 1858, *Collected Works*, 3: 8.

27 Lincoln expressed this sentiment often. For example, see his statement in the first debate, *Collected Works*, 3: 18-19; and in the third debate, *Collected Works*, 3: 117.

28 "Speech at Springfield, Illinois," June 26, 1857, *Collected Works*, 2: 406.

29 On this topic, see George B. Forgie, *Patricide in the House Divided* (New York: W.W. Norton, 1979).

Sixth, Lincoln did not believe that southern slaveholders were responsible for the 'peculiar institution.' He viewed them, like their northern counterparts, as captives of circumstance. He sometimes expressed the view that if their positions were reversed, northerners would behave like southerners and vice-versa.[30] Lincoln did not avoid blaming southerners just to be nice. He saw the problem of slavery through a wider lens – as a structural problem afflicting the economy and culture of both North and South. He referred not to "Southern slavery" but to "American slavery," and he pointed out how manufacturing, in particular, gained from a slave economy. The benefit of seeing the problem in these terms is that it is possible to presume the good will of all sides and success can be had through changing an impersonal system rather than overpowering evil individuals.

Seventh and finally, Lincoln gave great weight to the power of public opinion and those who mold it. What the public believes is a reality in its own right. The reason that the slavery controversy had been capable of settlement by compromise prior to the Kansas-Nebraska Act, Lincoln maintained, was that "the public mind was confident in the belief that slavery was in the course of ultimate extinction."[31] Confident in that belief, the public could accept deviations as expedient compromises not challenging the principle. This is how Lincoln rationalized both the Missouri Compromise and the Compromise of 1850. But the Kansas-Nebraska Act was different, because its core principle was official indifference with respect to slavery. Now the public mind was aroused as never before, and Lincoln believed that it would stay that way until the restoration of the Missouri Compromise.

Stephen A. Douglas came in for special criticism by Lincoln because of his role in shaping public opinion. Many people waited to form their own opinions, Lincoln suggested, until they knew what viewpoint Douglas had adopted. When Douglas proclaimed that he "[didn't] care" whether new territories accepted or rejected slavery, he was coaching public opinion not to care about it either: the message underlying "I don't care" was that "you needn't care."[32] In thus disabling public resistance to slavery's spread, Douglas was doing the work of a conspirator to make slavery national. Sometimes Lincoln explicitly posited the existence of such a conspiracy; at other times he said he could not be sure whether there was a plot or not but that the unsettled state of current

30 For example, "Speech at Peoria," *Collected Works*, 2: 255.

31 "First Debate with Stephen A. Douglas at Ottawa," *Collected Works*, 3: 18. The same sentiment had been expressed in the "House Divided" speech.

32 "First Debate with Stephen A. Douglas at Ottawa," *Collected Works*, 3: 27.

public opinion closely resembled what a conspiracy would try to achieve.[33] Lincoln consistently held that his real adversary was not the southern slaveholder or proslavery advocate but the northern moderate who trivialized the issue, wearing down the public opprobrium over slavery and its extension, thereby preparing the way for slavery to be legalized everywhere.[34]

Lincoln believed that the Supreme Court was especially sensitive to public opinion, because it relied on public acceptance to give legitimacy to its decisions. He held that the Court waited to issue the *Dred Scott* decision until the presidential election of James Buchanan signaled that the country would acquiesce in it.[35] *Dred Scott* held in part that no territory could outlaw slavery. All that was needed to extend slavery nationwide was another decision, a hypothetical 'Dred Scott II,' holding that no *state* could exclude slavery. The Court was unwilling to issue such a decision just now, Lincoln speculated, because it would lack a supportive public opinion. But that situation could change once Douglas traveled the country proclaiming that slavery was such a trifling matter that he cared not whether it was voted down or voted up. That was the threat Lincoln would dedicate himself to meeting. He would reaffirm the underlying moral claim against slavery, would restore public confidence that it was in course of ultimate extinction, and he would do so by containing slavery where it already existed, preventing its spread.

These seven key commitments, influenced by Lincoln's own experience and his involvement in the politics of the 1850s, would shape his thought and action once he was elected president of the United States.

3 Lincoln and the Presidency

Enough southerners shared Lincoln's belief that slavery must expand or die that they viewed the very fact of his election as an existential threat to the 'peculiar institution.' In a significant radicalization of southern opinion in the weeks following the election, seven states seceded from the Union, beginning with South Carolina on December 20, 1860, and ending with Texas on February 1, 1861. As president-elect, Lincoln made no public statements, both to preserve

33 For example, Lincoln offered both the "strong" and "weak" versions of the conspiracy allegation in the "House Divided" speech. See "'A House Divided': Speech at Springfield, Illinois," June 16, 1858, *Collected Works*, 2: 465, 467.

34 This was the sentiment expressed toward Lincoln's conclusion in the final debate, at Alton. See *Collected Works*, 3: 312-316.

35 "'A House Divided,'" *Collected Works*, 2: 463.

his flexibility later and to avoid deliberate misinterpretation of what he might have said. In consequence, he enjoyed no presidential honeymoon and found it necessary immediately upon taking office to articulate his policy to deal with the secession crisis. The announcements in his First Inaugural Address, and his subsequent statements and actions, were affected by his pre-presidential experience.

With his antislavery convictions checked by legal and political realities, Lincoln devoted his First Inaugural Address to establishing that there was no just cause for attempting to break up the Union. The cause of seven states' attempting to secede was, he said, "unwarranted apprehension" that the advent of a Republican administration would threaten their peculiar institution. He reassured Southerners, whom he referred to as his "disaffected fellow countrymen" (not allowing that secession was even a possibility) that such was not the case. He quoted his earlier speeches in which he had pledged not to interfere with slavery in the states where it existed, and went so far as to indicate he would accept a proposed Constitutional amendment guaranteeing it there in perpetuity. He argued that secession was both physically and legally impossible and held that attempts to break up the Union were therefore "insurrectionary or revolutionary, according to circumstances."[36] He then announced his administration's policy, which conceded as much as possible to the southern states without yielding the basic principle of national sovereignty. Beyond holding the federal forts that had not already been surrendered, there was little that his Administration would do to corral the rebellious southerners.

On the most obvious level, Lincoln's speech was an attempt to conciliate Southerners and urge them to back away from the precipice of disunion. But if that effort were to fail and war were to come, Lincoln structured the situation so that the South would be seen as the aggressor.[37] As he said, "the government will not assail *you*. You can have no conflict, without yourselves being the aggressors."[38]

When a ship attempted to resupply Fort Sumter, a federal outpost in the harbor of Charleston, South Carolina (and one of only two federal forts in the seceding states remaining in Union hands), Confederate forces launched an attack and the war was on. As Lincoln had hoped, there was overwhelming northern support for putting down the southern resistance. But the effort to

36 "First Inaugural Address – Final Text," *Collected Works*, 4: 265. Presumably, the "circumstances" were whether or not the effort was successful.

37 This argument is developed in David Zarefsky, "Philosophy and Rhetoric in Lincoln's First Inaugural Address," *Philosophy and Rhetoric* 45, no. 2 (2012): 165-188.

38 "First Inaugural Address," *Collected Works*, 4: 271.

do so led four additional states to secede. Lincoln called Congress into special session, to meet on July 4, in order to request funds and forces for what everyone mistakenly thought would be a short and simple war. He defined the issue as whether a freely elected government could preserve itself in the face of armed resistance too strong to be checked by the ordinary police power. Slavery was still not what the war was about, although all recognized it as the underlying issue. But if the Union could be restored, Lincoln remained confident that that issue could be resolved through the passage of time and the working of economic incentives.[39]

Accordingly, Lincoln countermanded emancipation orders issued by two of his generals, John C. Fremont and Benjamin Butler, in the districts they controlled. Fremont's action, in 1861, was overruled on the merits, and Butler's, in 1862, on the grounds that any decision about emancipation as a war measure must be made by the commander-in-chief, not a subordinate in the field. But Lincoln moved gingerly in that direction by signing, if not vigorously implementing, the First and Second Confiscation Acts passed by Congress. These acts accepted, for the sake of argument, the southern contention that slaves were property, and provided that they could be seized as contraband if used in aid of the rebellion. The Second Confiscation Act was the broader in its interpretation of what counted as aiding the rebellion. It did not take a great leap of logic to justify emancipation on the same basis as confiscation.

And Lincoln's thought was evolving. As the war dragged on inconclusively, with Union forces suffering repeated military defeats in the East, the president began to imagine emancipation as a war measure. If he could induce more slaves to desert their masters and come behind the Union lines, he would weaken the resources available to support the Confederate military effort and strengthen those supporting the Union, all at one stroke. A secondary consideration was that European governments who were considering extending diplomatic recognition to the Confederacy might be deterred from doing so by the fact that the North now would be fighting for a moral objective, not just a return to the *status quo ante*.

Still, Lincoln was not yet ready to act. First, he would make an effort to encourage voluntary emancipation, beginning with the border states. These were the four slave states that remained in the Union: Maryland, Delaware, Kentucky, and Missouri. If they could be induced to act, other states farther south might follow suit without the federal government coercing them –

39 For a description of Lincoln's proposed economic incentives, see Richards, *Who Freed the Slaves?*, 45-52. Lincoln elaborated these proposals in his 1862 Annual Message.

which Lincoln continued to believe he lacked authority to do. So he offered to compensate states that abolished slavery or masters who individually freed their slaves. The cost would be amortized over a long time, and in any case would be lower than the cost of fighting the war. In addition, Lincoln reaffirmed his support for colonization – the voluntary resettlement of newly freed slaves outside the United States, either in Africa or in Central America. To Lincoln's great regret, not a single border state had taken up his proposal nor were either slaveholders or free Blacks attracted to the prospect of colonization in any significant numbers. Nor were they attracted when the president repeated these proposals in his Annual Message of December 1, 1862, where he proposed them as Constitutional amendments.

But Lincoln continued to mull over emancipation as a war measure. He drafted a proclamation but kept it under lock and key. On July 22, 1862, he read it aloud to his Cabinet, inviting comment on the details but not on the decision itself. At the suggestion of Secretary of State William Henry Seward, he withheld its issuance pending a northern military victory, so it would not seem like a desperate gasp from a nation facing defeat. When the Confederate invasion at Antietam Creek, Maryland was repulsed in September, that was deemed enough of a victory. So on September 22 he proclaimed that if the rebellion had not ceased in a hundred days' time, on January 1, 1863 he would declare the slaves then in rebellion to be "then, thenceforward, and forever free."

After he had resolved to issue the proclamation, but before he had done so, Lincoln met in August with a delegation of influential free Blacks in Washington. He urged them to take the lead in colonization, expressed the view that Blacks and whites could not coexist peacefully in the United States if slavery were to be abolished, and implied that his listeners were being selfish by disregarding his invitation to deport themselves.[40] Read today, this is one of Lincoln's most embarrassing public statements, especially when one remembers that he already had decided on emancipation. One has to wonder if he really thought he could avoid issuing the proclamation, or if, alternatively, he was going through the motions in order to convince northern whites opposed to emancipation that he had exhausted every other alternative.

The week after receiving the delegation of African Americans, Lincoln was the nominal recipient of an editorial in Horace Greeley's *New York Tribune* in the form of an open letter. It claimed to represent northern public opinion in

40 "Address on Colonization to a Deputation of Negroes," August 14, 1862, *Collected Works*, 5: 370-375.

calling to transform the war into a moral crusade against slavery by ordering emancipation. The president replied by letter to one of Greeley's competitor newspapers. Still not willing to tip his hand about what he had prepared, he wrote that his object was "to save the Union, and is not either to save or destroy slavery." He went on to elaborate that if he could save the Union by freeing all the slaves, he would do that; if by freeing none of the slaves, he would do that; and if by freeing some and leaving others in slavery, he would take that course.[41] What is significant, of course, is that while he continued to maintain that the war was about preserving the Union, privately he had decided that emancipation was a necessary means to that end. The country could not be reunited half slave and half free, and the Union could not prevail without the military, diplomatic, and psychological boost provided by making emancipation an aim of the war.

Several curious features of the Emancipation Proclamation are worthy of brief note. First, it applied only to the areas then in rebellion. The specific states, and parts of states, were enumerated in the Proclamation itself. These, of course, were precisely the areas where Lincoln lacked the power to enforce the Proclamation. This curious fact has led some critics to allege that the president's action was insincere, that he did not really support emancipation but was doing the bare minimum that the military situation required.[42] But a more plausible interpretation is that Lincoln's view about the Constitution had not changed. He still believed he lacked power to interfere with slavery in the states where it existed – except as an exercise of the war power. If emancipation was to be justified as a means to put down rebellion, then logically it must be limited to areas in rebellion. This did not mean that it had no effect elsewhere. It was a powerful incentive to slaves to desert their masters and join Union forces, and it was a signal that as the Union armies advanced, emancipation would accompany them.

Second, the Proclamation is virtually devoid of moral force. As the historian Richard Hofstadter famously remarked, it "has all the moral grandeur of a bill of lading."[43] This is also explained by its purpose as a military document. But it also may have been calculated as a way to avoid arousing opposition from northerners hostile to the emancipation project. And a third notable feature is that Lincoln proclaimed the slaves free "then, thenceforward, and forever."

---

41 "To Horace Greeley," August 22, 1862, *Collected Works*, 5: 388-389.

42 On this point, see especially Bennett, *Forced Into Glory*.

43 Richard Hofstadter, *The American Political Tradition and the Men Who Made It* (New York: Knopf, 1948). For a discussion of this allegation, see Allen C. Guelzo, *Lincoln's Emancipation Proclamation: The End of Slavery in America* (New York: Simon and Schuster, 2005).

Of course, the goals of the Proclamation could be achieved only if slaves were promised freedom permanently. One could not expect them to risk their lives for a benefit that could be taken away. Yet it was dubious that the exercise of the war power could outlast the war. Lincoln several times stated that no slave freed by the terms of the Proclamation would ever be returned to slavery, but it was not at all clear that he could enforce that promise.

As noted above, between the issuance of the preliminary and final Proclamations, Lincoln delivered his 1862 Annual Message. While he insisted, "I cannot make it better known than it already is, that I strongly favor colonization," he also began to argue – for the first time – that emancipation without deportation would not be so bad. Some of the objections to it, he suggested, were "largely imaginary, if not sometimes malicious." He refuted the claims that freed Blacks would take jobs from whites, that they would overwhelm the North, and that their very presence would threaten public safety.[44] To be sure, these were not full-throated defenses of emancipation, much less of racial equality. The arguments are cast in the subjunctive – *if* emancipation were to come, its consequences would be tolerable. The presence of these arguments can be seen both as Lincoln's recognition of how northern public opinion was radicalizing under the impact of war, and as his effort to 'coach' public opinion in a more radical direction. These arguments did not quell northern resistance to emancipation, to be sure. It would continue throughout 1863 and 1864, most notably in contributing to the New York City draft riots in July of 1863. But it gradually became less credible and less vocal. The carnage of war seemed to require such a lofty objective to justify it. And Lincoln made reunion and emancipation his twin and inseparable goals at just about the time that much of the northern public was willing to be convinced. Enacting a presidential role that would be enumerated later by Woodrow Wilson, Lincoln gave voice to the inchoate opinion of the North.

Moreover, the movement of African Americans to the Union side did alter the balance of forces, and after the battles of Gettysburg, Vicksburg, and Atlanta it became clear that the South could not win a conventional war. There were frustrating periods of stalemate, but after the election of 1864 Lincoln actually began to worry that the war might end too soon, before the legal status of the freed slaves was permanently resolved. Accordingly, he took charge of an effort that had been initiated in Congress, to adopt a Constitutional amend-

44 "Annual Message to Congress," December 1, 1862, *Collected Works*, 5: 534-536. For a discussion of this message, see David Zarefsky, "Lincoln's 1862 Annual Message: A Paradigm of Rhetorical Leadership," *Rhetoric & Public Affairs* 3, no. 1 (2000): 5-14.

ment prohibiting slavery, an effort chronicled in Steven Spielberg's 2013 film *Lincoln*.[45]

Lincoln's two most celebrated speeches testify to the evolution of his beliefs about slavery. In the Gettysburg Address, he observed that those speaking at the podium could not hallow the battlefield because the soldiers who had won the victory already had done so. After noting that the nation's original birth had been "dedicated to the proposition that all men are created equal," he urged listeners, instead of consecrating the ground, to rededicate themselves to the cause, so that the nation might enjoy "a new birth of freedom" – this time, purged of the sin of slavery. His long-standing conviction that slavery could be extinguished peaceably proved to be false, yet he saw that reuniting the country required the demise of slavery as a product of the war.

The Second Inaugural Address was Lincoln's fullest attempt to give meaning to the war. It had gone on so long and taken such an unexpected course that it could be explained only in theological terms. To Lincoln, "all know that this interest [constituted by slaves] was, somehow, the cause of the war,"[46] unlike his First Inaugural when he attributed rising tensions to "unwarranted apprehension" among the southern states. The president regarded the war as divine punishment visited on both North and South for the sin of American slavery. He was not strictly impartial in apportioning blame – one side would make war, the other would accept it – but he resisted the victor's temptation to gloat or to victimize the defeated adversary. To be sure, he cast his claims in the subjunctive, saying that "if we shall suppose" that American slavery is an offense against God, "which He now wills to remove, and that He gives to both North and South, this terrible war," we would have no reason to doubt the justice of God's judgment.[47] The subjunctive phrasing protected Lincoln against the arrogance of claiming to know God's will. But his meaning was clear. It took an act of God to supersede all the restraints to emancipation that had been created by man: the economic interest, the racial animus, the political reality, the Constitution, and the law. Racial equality had not arrived; it has not yet. But slavery was gone, through the brave acts of the enslaved themselves, aided by supportive political and moral leaders, among them Abraham Lincoln, who acted when he finally had the chance to "hit [that thing] hard."

Ironically, Lincoln believed that the great events of history were the work of impersonal forces. In 1864, he wrote a Kentucky friend, Albert Hodges, "I claim

---

45 Lincoln's role in this effort is described in Richards, *Who Freed the Slaves?*, although Richards argues that Lincoln came late to the struggle.

46 "Second Inaugural Address," March 4, 1865, *Collected Works*, 8: 332.

47 "Second Inaugural Address," *Collected Works*, 8: 333.

not to have controlled events, but confess frankly that events have controlled me."[48] That may be, but if so it was his gift to be available and in the right place when those forces reached the point at which he could be their agent. His actions were influenced by his own experience, his involvement in the politics of his time, his reason, and his moral convictions. He recognized that the problem of slavery was complex and riven with cross-pressures; yet when the time was right, he found the space in which to act.

48 To Albert G. Hodges," April 4, 1864, *Collected Works*, 7: 282.

CHAPTER 4

Jackson's Heir: How Andrew Johnson Shaped the Post-Civil War Political Order

Mark Leon de Vries

1 Introduction

In November 1865 northern War Democrat Louis Schade wrote President Andrew Johnson a letter of encouragement, reminding him that he had the power to "shape the fate of the country for centuries," and that "history is the only grave, just and impartial judge of human affairs."[1] Johnson did indeed shape the postwar order, but history's (or at least professional historians') judgment has hardly turned out as he or Schade hoped; Lincoln's successor consistently ranks toward the very bottom of scholarly surveys of presidential achievements.[2] Early in the twentieth century, on the other hand, most historians had a far more favorable opinion of Johnson, proclaiming him a hero who "dedicated his whole soul to fight […] tyranny and corruption."[3] Such widely differing assessments mirror the radically changed perspective on the Reconstruction era ushered in by the revisionists of the 1950s onward. By 1969, Eric McKitrick pointed out that Johnson's "reputation has […] been inversely related to that of Radical Reconstruction. As the latter declined, the former – after a few years' lag – rose."[4] As historians increasingly identified Radical Reconstruction as America's 'Unfinished Revolution' that tragically ended in a

1 Paul H. Bergeron, ed., *The Papers of Andrew Johnson: Volume 9, September 1865-January 1866* (Knoxville: University of Tennessee Press, 1991), 415.

2 See the aggregate column of 'scholarly survey results' at https://en.wikipedia.org/wiki/Historical_rankings_of_presidents_of_the_United_States. Johnson does a bit better in surveys of the general population, where he comes in just below the median (2007 Rasmussen poll, cited in Ibid., under 'Popular Opinion').

3 Lloyd Paul Stryker, *Andrew Johnson: A Study in Courage* (New York: Macmillan, 1936), viii; other examples include Robert W. Winston, *Andrew Johnson, Plebeian and Patriot* (New York: H. Holt and Company, 1928); Howard K. Beale, *The Critical Year: A Study of Andrew Johnson and Reconstruction* (New York: Harcourt, Brace and Company, 1930); George Fort Milton, *The Age of Hate: Andrew Johnson and the Radicals* (New York: Coward-McCann, 1930).

4 Eric L. Mckitrick, ed., *Andrew Johnson: A Profile* (New York: Hill and Wang, 1969), viii. Early examples of a critical reevaluation of both Andrew Johnsons and Reconstruction generally include Eric L. McKitrick, *Andrew Johnson and Reconstruction* (Chicago: University of

© KONINKLIJKE BRILL NV, LEIDEN, 2020 | DOI:10.1163/9789004422643_006

'Splendid Failure,' Johnson's rabid racism and implacable resistance to even the most limited of civil rights for the recently freed slaves made him an easy and justifiable target for moral approbation.[5] Indeed, the modern scholarly consensus hardly seems surprising for an unelected and unpopular president, who openly supported white supremacy, had over two-thirds of his vetoes overruled by Congress, was impeached by the House and nearly removed by the Senate.

While Johnson's political goals rankle modern sensibilities sympathetic to the Radical Republicans' pursuit of racial equality, we cannot let this blind us to the fact that measured by his own ambitions, Johnson's presidency was hardly a failure. No recent biographers have disputed either Johnson's racist inclination or temperamental unsuitability for the presidency, but at the same time many acknowledge his personal courage in standing up for his convictions in the face of an increasingly fierce and united political opposition.[6] As a result, he largely succeeded in shaping Reconstruction policy along the lines he envisioned. Despite the laws and even constitutional amendments it passed in response to his intransigence, Congress never fully succeeded in implementing its Radical program in the South and in less than a decade capitulated to southern whites' resistance and acquiesced in exactly the kind of 'home rule' Johnson had envisioned. Even those who argue that Johnson was "the only failure" among otherwise undervalued Gilded Age presidents admit

Chicago Press, 1960); Kenneth M. Stampp, *The Era of Reconstruction, 1865-1877* (New York: Random House, 1965); LaWanda Cox and John H. Cox, *Politics, Principle, and Prejudice, 1865-1866: Dilemma of Reconstruction America* (New York: Free Press of Glencoe, 1963).

5 Eric Foner, *Reconstruction: America's Unfinished Revolution, 1863-1877* (New York: Perennial Classics, 2002); Michael W. Fitzgerald, *Splendid Failure: Postwar Reconstruction in the American South* (Chicago: Ivan R. Dee, 2007). Johnson lacked both the personal charm and the political success that have helped buoy the reputations of presidents such as Woodrow Wilson despite their openly racist opinions and policies: Gary Gerstle, "Race and Nation in the Thought and Politics of Woodrow Wilson," in *Reconsidering Woodrow Wilson: Progressivism, Internationalism, War, and Peace*, ed. John Milton Cooper (Washington, D.C.: Johns Hopkins University Press, 2008), 93-123.

6 Michael Les Benedict, *The Impeachment and Trial of Andrew Johnson* (New York: W.W. Norton & Co., 1973); Albert Castel, *The Presidency of Andrew Johnson* (Lawrence: University of Kansas Press, 1979); James E. Sefton, *Andrew Johnson and the Uses of Constitutional Power* (New York: Little, Brown, 1980); Hans L. Trefousse, *Andrew Johnson: A Biography* (New York: W.W. Norton & Co., 1989); David W. Bowen, *Andrew Johnson and the Negro* (Knoxville: University of Tennessee Press, 2005); David O. Stewart, *Impeached: The Trial of President Andrew Johnson and the Fight for Lincoln's Legacy* (New York: Simon & Schuster, 2010); A more positive assessment of Johnson overall is offered by Paul H. Bergeron, *Andrew Johnson's Civil War and Reconstruction* (Knoxville: University of Tennessee Press, 2011).

that he was "more influential than any other [president] in shaping the way Reconstruction turned out."[7]

From the outset of his presidency, Johnson engaged Republicans in a fierce struggle over what, exactly, Reconstruction was to entail. Was it, as Radical Republicans maintained, a program of 'renovation' in which the South was to be remade in the image of northern Republicans, with substantial civil and political rights for the former slaves? Or was it first and foremost a program of 'restoration,' the purpose of which was to restore the southern states to full self-government and normalized constitutional relations – albeit minus slavery – as soon as possible? Johnson, along with a vast majority of his fellow southerners, clearly envisioned the latter course. Johnson's personal unpopularity and impolitic behavior have often obscured that his policies could count on significant support in the North as well, where a war-weary electorate craved stability and reconciliation first and foremost.[8]

So how did Johnson succeed in securing his long-term policy objectives, even as he seemingly lost every key political battle he fought with the Republicans in Congress? A theoretical framework for understanding this seeming paradox is provided by Gregory Downs and Kate Masur's recent characterization of the postwar federal government as a "Stockade State, a collection of outposts – both military and civilian – powerful within narrow geographical boundaries but limited in their reach [...] beset by both competing power centers and individuals who sought to live beyond the reach of most authority."[9] If Johnson's hard-scrabble roots in Tennessee politics made him ill-suited at winning friends and influencing people in Washington, D.C., it did provide him with a profound understanding of the innate limitations of this kind of federal government. His steadfast support for white supremacy and limited federal

7 Max J. Skidmore, "Introduction," in *Maligned Presidents: The Late 19th Century*, ed. Max J. Skidmore (New York, NY: Palgrave Pivot, 2014), 7, 12; On the extent of Johnson's influence, see also: Trefousse, *Andrew Johnson*, 352; Brooks D. Simpson, *The Reconstruction Presidents* (Lawrence: University Press of Kansas, 1998), 67.

8 David W. Blight, *Race and Reunion: The Civil War in American Memory* (Cambridge: Belknap Press, 2002); Mark Wahlgren Summers, *A Dangerous Stir: Fear, Paranoia, and the Making of Reconstruction* (Chapel Hill: University of North Carolina Press, 2009); Gregory P. Downs, "The Mexicanization of American Politics: The United States' Transnational Path from Civil War to Stabilization," *The American Historical Review* 117, no. 2 (2012): 387-409; Richard Franklin Bensel, *Yankee Leviathan: The Origins of Central State Authority in America, 1859-1877* (Cambridge: Cambridge University Press, 1991), chap. 5.

9 Gregory Downs and Kate Masur, eds., *The World the Civil War Made* (Chapel Hill: University of North Carolina Press, 2015), 6-7; Gary Gerstle makes a similar point in *Liberty and Coercion: The Paradox of American Government from the Founding to the Present* (Princeton: Princeton University Press, 2015), chap. 2.

interference allowed southern whites to mobilize the decentralized and localized legal and political culture in the South in support of maintaining their political, economic, and racial dominance.[10]

Providing substantial (rather than merely pro forma) civil and political equality was a revolutionary project entailing an unprecedented expansion of federal power that would have required a decisive and unified effort by all three branches of the federal government.[11] Instead, Johnson pursued a program of concerted obstructionism that made the failure of Radical Reconstruction all but impossible. Even after Congressional Republicans largely sidelined the president, the conservative regimes he empowered in the southern states provided a formidable bulwark against Congressional attempts to impose far-reaching reforms. Johnson's central role in undermining a more Radical approach to Reconstruction, to be clear, does not necessarily imply that such an approach would have been successful absent his influence. Indeed, a wide body of scholarship reminds us that both large swaths of Congress as well as the Supreme Court remained deeply ambivalent toward the expansion of federal power necessitated by Reconstruction and often acted to limit or curb it.[12] A supportive president was thus hardly a sufficient condition for a different outcome of Reconstruction, but it was almost certainly a necessary one. We have no way of knowing how the postwar dust might have settled

---

10 On the significance of local governance in the 19th century US, especially in the South, see Christopher Waldrep, *Roots of Disorder: Race and Criminal Justice in the American South, 1817-80* (Urbana: University of Illinois Press, 1998); Christopher Waldrep and Donald G. Nieman, eds., *Local Matters: Race, Crime, and Justice in the Nineteenth-Century South* (Athens: University of Georgia Press, 2001); Morton Keller, *Affairs of State: Public Life in Late Nineteenth Century America* (Cambridge: Belknap Press, 1977).

11 On the revolutionary nature of Radical Reconstruction see Robert J. Kaczorowski, *The Politics of Judicial Interpretation: The Federal Courts, Department of Justice and Civil Rights, 1866-1876* (New York: Fordham University Press, 2005), xi-xii; as well as Robert J. Kaczorowski, "Revolutionary Constitutionalism in the Era of the Civil War and Reconstruction," *N.Y.U. Law Review* 61, no. 5 (1986): 863-941.

12 William Gillette, *The Right to Vote: Politics and the Passage of the Fifteenth Amendment* (Baltimore: Johns Hopkins University Press, 1965); Michael Les Benedict, "Preserving the Constitution: The Conservative Basis of Radical Reconstruction," *The Journal of American History* 61, no. 1 (1974): 65-90; Michael Les Benedict, *A Compromise of Principle: Congressional Republicans and Reconstruction, 1863-1869* (New York: W.W. Norton & Co., 1974); Robert M. Goldman, *Reconstruction and Black Suffrage: Losing the Vote in Reese and Cruikshank* (Lawrence: University Press of Kansas, 2001); Ronald M. Labbé and Jonathan Lurie, *The Slaughterhouse Cases: Regulation, Reconstruction, and the Fourteenth Amendment* (Lawrence: University Press of Kansas, 2003); Michael A. Ross, *Justice of Shattered Dreams: Samuel Freeman Miller and the Supreme Court during the Civil War Era* (Baton Rouge: Louisiana State University Press, 2003).

had Lincoln lived or someone other than Johnson succeeded him. What we do know, is that Johnson played a key role in ensuring that it settled on the side of restorationism.

In line with the theme of this volume, this chapter will first briefly explore the personal and ideological outlook that shaped Johnson's approach to the presidency, and in particular to the Reconstruction of the southern states. We will then turn in more detail to how he wielded his influence by exploring his role in shaping the outcome of Reconstruction in one state in particular, Louisiana, which often served as both testing ground and bellwether for national Reconstruction policies.[13] It was here, moreover, that Johnson's obstructionism proved particularly effective. The state's Black electoral majority, large antebellum free Black population, and wartime Reconstruction experience made it perhaps the most promising of all the southern states for Reconstruction to succeed. By the time Grant assumed the presidency in 1869, however, the institutional foundations for such success had been severely curtailed. Johnson had not only hamstrung any attempt by the federal government to provide security and economic opportunities for the freedpeople, but had also consistently supported conservative whites in their attempts to restore a civil government that offered the most limited practical interpretation of freedom for the Black population imaginable.

2 A Jacksonian and a Southerner

Johnson rose to prominence during the Civil War, mostly on the basis of being the only southern senator from a secessionist state to support the Union cause. This "characteristic act of dissociation" by the "outsider" Johnson came at a significant political and personal cost, as it meant bucking the opinion of his southern peers in the Senate as well as his party and associates at home. When Andrew Johnson returned to Tennessee in April 1861, in a last-ditch attempt to keep his home state in the Union, he was physically attacked and nearly lynched by mobs in both Lynchburg and Bristol.[14] Ultimately, however,

13 Ted Tunnell, *Crucible of Reconstruction: War, Radicalism and Race in Louisiana, 1862-1877* (Baton Rouge: Louisiana State University Press, 1992), chaps. 1-3; Peyton McCrary, *Abraham Lincoln and Reconstruction: The Louisiana Experiment* (Princeton: Princeton University Press, 1978); C. Peter Ripley, *Slaves and Freedmen in Civil War Louisiana* (Baton Rouge: Louisiana State University Press, 1976), chap. 9; George C. Rable, "Republican Albatross: The Louisiana Question, National Politics, and the Failure of Reconstruction," *Louisiana History* 23, no. 2 (1982): 109-130.

14 McKitrick, *Andrew Johnson and Reconstruction*, 90; Trefousse, *Andrew Johnson*, 140.

Johnson's independence was more than vindicated, not just by the ultimate outcome of the conflict but also by his personal career. In 1864, after serving as military governor for the Unionist areas of Tennessee, he received the nod as Lincoln's vice-presidential candidate despite – or rather because of – his being a life-long Democrat and a former slaveholder, albeit one who later prided himself for having "owned [and] raised" slaves, "but never sold one." Republicans needed a ticket that could unite the border states as well as northern Democrats behind the war effort.[15]

Johnson's decision to remain loyal reflected his headstrong, irascible, and independent character; his vindication by the war's outcome and his meteoric rise reinforced these traits once he became president. When he received a delegation of southerners not long after acceding to the presidency, Johnson did not miss the opportunity to gloat, reminding them of the "taunts and jeers, the scowls with which I was treated. [...] the circle that stood around me, and [...] the threats and intimidations that were freely uttered by the men who opposed me." He had, however, "lived to see the realization of my predictions and the fatal error of those whom I vainly essayed to save from the results I could not but foresee."[16] He similarly rejoiced when, in his estimation, his own Democratic Party admitted that "its old position untenable, and is coming to ours."[17] Having been proven so utterly right in following his own deepest convictions in 1861 undoubtedly strengthened Johnson's resolve to follow his own convictions and political instincts now that he was president.

Johnson idolized his predecessor Andrew Jackson and adopted a Jacksonian persona that both shaped and justified his core ideological and political convictions. Two of these convictions would prove especially influential for his Reconstruction policies: his commitment to a limited national government and his severe racial prejudice. Johnson's papers are littered by references to Jackson by supporters and admirers trying to gain his ear. A southern newspaper, writing to Johnson early in his presidency, expected him to "be as lenient to the South" as possible. "[N]o man or set of men could control you [...] you had as much of the nerve of Andrew Jackson in you Composition, as any man I ever knew." Even Johnson's critics appealed to him in Jacksonian terms. One correspondent urged him to not treat Confederate leaders le-

15 Paul H. Bergeron, ed., *The Papers of Andrew Johnson: Volume 8, May 1865-August 1865* (Knoxville: University of Tennessee Press, 1989), 61-63; Don E. Fehrenbacher, "The Making of a Myth: Lincoln and the Vice-Presidential Nomination in 1864," *Civil War History* 41, no. 4 (January 2012): 273-290.

16 Bergeron, *Johnson Papers, Vol. 9*, 65.

17 Ibid., 179.

niently, because Jackson's greatest regret was "not having had John C. Calhoun hung."[18]

To Johnson, Jacksonianism implied a commitment to both perpetual Union and limited federal government and strong states' rights (though, obviously, not state sovereignty). As he himself put it, "while I dreaded and feared disintegration of the States, I am equally opposed to consolidation or concentration of power here, under whatever guise or name."[19] A concomitant to his Jacksonian ideology was Johnson's unwavering belief in a strict construction of the Constitution, particularly where it related to federal meddling in state affairs. Considering secession to have been unconstitutional, he firmly believed the southern states had never legally left the Union and thus could and must resume their full independence under civil government as soon as was practicable.

These objectives were reflected in his proclamation establishing a civil government in North Carolina. In a model he would follow in most southern states, Johnson appointed a provisional governor with extensive, albeit temporary, powers limited only by the whim of the president and the presence of federal troops. These governors had the authority to temporarily appoint the thousands of local political and judicial officers responsible for the day-to-day governance of nineteenth-century America. They were also tasked with organizing elections for a constitutional convention. Granting such vast powers to unelected and even federally appointed officials might seem to contradict Johnson's Jacksonian principles, but the substance of their task clearly reflected his Jacksonian ideology. The elections for a constitutional convention were to be based on antebellum – and hence exclusively white – voter eligibility. In North Carolina – as elsewhere – Johnson selected a moderate southern Unionist with little interest in racial equality as provisional governor, signaling his desire for a speedy reunion based on full statehood and white supremacy – terms that reflected this ideology and were embraced by the recently defeated former Confederates.[20] The president hoped such a policy would quickly "see the Union restored as it was previously to the war, or [...] as our Democratic

18 Bergeron, *Johnson Papers, Vol. 8*, 185, 313.

19 Simpson, *Reconstruction Presidents*, 69-71; Trefousse, *Andrew Johnson*, 53; Bergeron, *Johnson Papers, Vol. 9*, 66; Paul H. Bergeron, ed., *The Papers of Andrew Johnson: Volume 10, February 1866-July1866* (Knoxville: University of Tennessee Press, 1992), 152.

20 Mark Wahlgren Summers, *The Ordeal of the Reunion: A New History of Reconstruction* (Chapel Hill: University of North Carolina Press, 2014), 67-69. In the case of North Carolina, the governor was William W. Holden.

friends used to say, 'the Constitution as it is, the Union as it was,' always saving and excepting slavery."[21]

Johnson's policy initially garnered widespread support. Southerners and conservative northern Democrats unsurprisingly applauded his strict construction of the Constitution which did not give "to the general government [...] the power to determine who shall exercise the elective franchise within the limits of a state." Former Democratic New Hampshire Congressman Edmund Burke expressed his "unqualified thanks and gratitude, for the patriotic and noble stand which you have taken in favor of the restoration of the Union upon the principles of the Constitution. I knew you had been nurtured in the school of Jefferson and Jackson." But many Republicans also embraced Johnson's proposal, reflecting the widespread and bipartisan adherence to the ideal of limited national government that pervaded Americans political thinking in the nineteenth century. Prominent abolitionist and Republican Henry Ward Beecher applauded Johnson's narrow interpretation of federal powers. "State sovereignty is heresy," he wrote the president in October 1865, "but state-rights is a reality of transcendent value. And the temptation is very great to employ Federal power in such a way as to make a precedent which bad or weak men, by & bye will use with most disastrous effects."[22] Beecher personally supported the extension of suffrage to the freedpeople, but "it would be attained at too great a price if it involved the right of the Federal Government to meddle with State affairs." He praised Johnson's "clear perception that the welfare of the freedmen depends far more upon the good will of their white neighbors that it does upon northern philanthropy or Governmental protection." In most other cases however, support for Johnson's policies not only reflected a shared understanding of constitutional principles, but also a shared support for a Reconstruction program based on "the intelligent votes of white freemen [...] and not the ignorant suffrages of emancipated slaves."[23]

Although Johnson considered himself a friend and supporter of the freedpeople's interests, his racial prejudices as a southerner and a former slaveholder led him to believe that these interests were best served by upholding white supremacy in the political, economic, and social sphere. His racism and his limited conception of federal authority often exacerbated each other. Had he still been governor of Tennessee, he admitted, he might have supported limited Black suffrage "those who had served in the army; those who could read

21 Bergeron, *Johnson Papers, Vol. 8*, 153.
22 Ibid., 152, 201; Bergeron, *Johnson Papers, Vol. 9*, 93, 269.
23 Bergeron, *Johnson Papers, Vol. 8*, 152; Bergeron, *Johnson Papers, Vol. 9*, 269.

and write, and perhaps a property qualification for others." He considered universal suffrage, however, to be a grave error.[24] Conveniently, his limited conception of federal power implied he had no authority to insist on a policy of universal suffrage which he did not support.

Johnson's Jacksonian beliefs were reinforced by his southern identity, as he shared deeply in the region's racial prejudices. His racism and resulting insensitivity to the challenges and aspirations of the freedpeople is most evident in his interactions with African Americans. In an address to a delegation of Black, mostly southern clergymen, some of whom had only recently been enslaved, Johnson began by proudly stating that "I have owned slaves, raised slaves, but I never sold one." He emphasized how during the war he had personally "risked all in the shape of property, life, an limb [...] sustaining and carrying out the great principle that man could not own property in man." With slavery abolished, however, Blacks need expect no further support, but would have to learn that "freedom simply means liberty to work."[25] When he met another delegation of prominent African-Americans, including Frederick Douglass, some eight months later, his views had not much changed. The true victims of slavery, in the presidents estimation, were not the enslaved Africans, but the poor whites of the South, whom "the colored man and his master, combined, kept [...] in slavery, by depriving him of a fair participation in the labor and productions of the rich land of the country." Douglass's polite, but firm rebuke did not sway the president, whose Jacksonian principles easily buttressed his personal unwillingness to offer federal support for any further expansion of Blacks' civil and political rights. Instead, he suggested, they might consider emigration, as "the colored people can live and advance in civilization to better advantage elsewhere than crowded right down there in the South."[26]

3 Acting on His Convictions

Johnson's political ideology and racial prejudices help explain why he opposed a more forceful policy in support of civil and political equality for the freedpeople, but it remains to be explained how he succeeded in achieving his long-term goals, despite losing so many of his short-term political battles. To understand this, we must turn from his ideological convictions to his day-to-day influence on the governance of the southern states. The disintegration of the

24 Bergeron, *Johnson Papers, Vol. 9*, 180.
25 Bergeron, *Johnson Papers, Vol. 8*, 62.
26 Bergeron, *Johnson Papers, Vol. 10*, 44, 47.

secessionist state and local governments in the spring and early summer of 1865 provided a prime opportunity to reinvent the southern political culture from the ground up. With Congress in recess, Johnson was firmly in the driver's seat and had a huge impact on shaping the postwar South, especially as Congressional Republicans chose to support him during his first year in office.

Johnson used this formidable influence in two crucial respects. On the one hand, in line with his Jacksonian belief in a limited federal government, he severely curtailed the role of both the army and the Freedmen's Bureau. Instead, he ensured that local civil government would have broad and effective authority. If his Jacksonianism explains his preference for vesting power in local and state governments, his southern roots and concomitant racist worldview ensured that these state and local governments would be entirely under the control of the white population – preferably conservative white Unionists, but often even some former Confederates. The freedpeople thus had few opportunities to establish either their economic independence or acquire political power that could help protect them from domination by their former masters. By the time Congressional Republicans began to reassert themselves from the spring of 1866 onwards, they faced an uphill battle against the entrenched power of conservative southern whites empowered by Johnson.

The postwar political developments in Louisiana perfectly illustrate these dynamics. Southern Louisiana had been under federal control since Benjamin Butler captured New Orleans in 1862. When the Freedmen's Bureau was established its assistant commissioner for Louisiana, Thomas Conway, did not need to begin from scratch, but could build on his experience in running the wartime Bureau of Free Labor.[27] In the summer of 1865 he showed himself optimistic on the future of free labor in the state, provided the federal government would guarantee the physical safety of the Black population. Over the summer of 1865, Conway arranged for the distribution of abandoned and confiscated lands to the former slaves and loyal refugees as mandated by the original Freedmen's Bureau legislation.[28] President Johnson, however, quickly

27 On the Freedmen's Bureau in Louisiana see: Howard A White, *The Freedmen's Bureau in Louisiana* (Baton Rouge: Louisiana State University Press, 1970); John C. Rodrigue, "The Freedmen's Bureau and Wage Labor in the Louisiana Sugar Region," in *The Freedmen's Bureau and Reconstruction: Reconsiderations*, eds. Paul A. Cimbala and Randall M. Miller (New York: Fordham University Press, 1999), 193-218.

28 Thomas W. Conway, *The Freedmen of Louisiana. Final Report of the Bureau of Free Labor, Department of the Gulf, to Major General E.R.S. Canby, Commanding:* (New Orleans: New Orleans Times Book and Job Office, 1865), 14, 16-17. 'August 10, 1865, Conway and Howard, Circular No. 7,' *House Executive Document 70, 39th Congress, First Session* (Washington, D.C.: GPO 1866), 16-18.

reversed this policy and ordered all abandoned lands to be restored to their former owners, entrenching local white elites at the expense of the recently freed Black population.[29]

Meanwhile, provisional governor James Madison Wells urged Johnson to get rid of Conway. Wells appealed to Johnson's sectional and racial prejudices, painting Conway a "radical negro suffrage man – [who] thinks the black better than the white man." His policies, Wells warned, would "utterly demoralize the negroes […] to say nothing of the dangerous and vengeful spirit that idleness and want may engender in the breasts of the negroes toward the whites."[30] Johnson agreed and by October 1865 removed Conway from his position. He temporarily appointed his trusted associate General Joseph F. Fullerton in his place. Fullerton issued an "Address to the Freedmen of Louisiana" that immediately made clear they need not expect any but the most minimal support from the Federal government. "Slavery has passed away," he admonished,

> and you are now placed on trial. It is for you to prove that you are able to take care of yourselves, and that you deserved to be made free. […] It is not the intention of the officers of the Bureau to nurse and pamper you, to feed and to cloth you, or to give you any privilege that others do not enjoy. […] Do not believe the idle and malicious stories that have been told you by bad men as to what the government intends to do for you. All had been done for you that you can expect. […] No land will be given to you.[31]

Fullerton reversed many of the policies aimed at supporting the economic and political independence of the freedpeople, by curtailing federal power and vesting governance in local white elites. He closed the Bureau courts, suspended the collection of school taxes, restored land to its former owners, apprenticed countless Black children, and strictly enforced vagrancy laws.[32] Johnson admired Fullerton's approach and when Congress sought to extend

29 'September 25, 1865, Howard, approved by Johnson, Circular No. 16,' National Archives and Records Administration, Washington, D.C., Record Group 105, Microfilm series 1905 [Hereinafter: M1905], reel 53, frame 920; William S. McFeely, *Yankee Stepfather: General O.O. Howard and the Freedmen* (New Haven: Yale University Press, 1968), chap. 6.

30 'July 28, 1865, New Orleans, Wells to Johnson,' James Madison Wells Microfilm, Louisiana and Lower Mississippi Valley Collections, LSU Libraries, Baton Rouge, Louisiana, Mss. 1219.

31 'October 20, 1865, New Orleans, Fullerton, Circular 24, Address to the Freedmen of Louisiana,' M1905, reel 53, frame 925.

32 McFeely, *Yankee Stepfather*, 177-179.

and expand the powers of the Bureau in February of 1866, the president turned to him for advice. Fullerton opposed the bill in no uncertain terms, calling it "class legislation [...] injurious to the freedman in preventing him from acquiring a position as an independent citizen." Johnson borrowed liberally from these Jacksonian arguments in framing his subsequent veto message. Although Congress eventually passed a new Freedmen's Bureau bill over Johnson's veto in July, Johnson continued to undermine the Bureau's attempts to provide legal protection for the freedpeople.[33] With land redistribution off the table, its judicial powers severely restricted, and it funding and manpower precarious, the Bureau was reduced to overseeing a contract system that greatly favored the interests of landowners over those of the Black labor force.

Governor Wells did not only seek Johnson's support in undermining the activities of the Freedmen's Bureau, but also in his attempts to have Black troops removed from Louisiana. Following the surrender, the federal army saw a rapid demobilization. Most northern soldiers had little interest in occupation duties now that the war was won, but for the Black soldiers it was a different matter. To them, the army presented a unique career opportunity. They also had a direct interest in enforcing the more radical aspects of Reconstruction and protecting former slaves from renewed economic and political oppression by their ex-masters. It is not surprising that shortly after the war, inspection officers found the Black troops to be far better disciplined and displaying a better morale than their white counterparts.[34] Conservative southern whites, however, despised the presence of these Black troops who had the temerity to "frequently walk four abreast on our sidewalks while off duty and compel all white persons to give way to them and take the streets."[35]

General Edward Canby, in command of the troops in Louisiana, warned Wells that "the prejudice against color is the substantial foundation of the complaints that are made. The complainants are unwilling to accept from a colored soldier what they would not object to if the sentinel conformed to their prejudices." Ignoring Canby, Wells reported to Johnson that the complaints represented "so true a picture of the baneful influence exercised by the presence and insubordinate conduct of colored troops on the surrounding population of the same color. [...] Wherever colored troops have appeared,

---

33 Bergeron, *Johnson Papers, Vol. 10*, 64-69, 120-127, 157-159; Donald G. Nieman, *To Set the Law in Motion: The Freedmen's Bureau and the Legal Rights of Blacks, 1865-1868* (New York: Millwood, 1979), 109-110, 145-147.

34 'January 11, 1866, New Orleans, Crosby to Insyth,' NARA, RG 393, part 1, entry 4495, box 1; 'February 25, 1866, New Orleans, Nelson to Canby,' Ibid., box 2.

35 'August 18, 1865, Shreveport, petition of citizens to Canby,' NARA, RG 393, part 1, entry 1757, box 4.

their very presence demoralizes the negroes for all purposes of useful industry."[36]

Such warnings fell on sympathetic ears of a fellow southerner. A few weeks earlier, the president had dedicated a large part of a speech to ostensibly thank the colored troops for their loyal service, to issuing stern warnings that reflected his limited faith in their abilities. "Will you," he asked them, "give evidence to the world that you are capable and competent to govern yourselves?" The Thirteenth Amendment notwithstanding, he warned them that "it is for you to establish the great fact that you are fit and qualified to be free. [...] I have to say that a great deal depends upon yourselves. You must give evidence that you are competent for the rights that the government has guaranteed to you."[37] In the immediate postwar year, however, Johnson had few other options than to replenish the rapidly demobilizing army with willing Black recruits. As soon as the situation had stabilized however, he sought to replace them with white volunteers. By the fall of 1867, the last Black soldiers had been withdrawn from the South.[38]

At the same time that Johnson used his influence to curtail the scope and reach of federal enforcement of civil and political equality for the Black population of the South he supported Wells, who rapidly reestablished a civil government in Louisiana dominated by traditional conservative white elites. Wells had been elected lieutenant governor in 1864, under a constitution written by a convention of moderate white Unionists under the protection of military authorities. When Governor Michael Hahn resigned a year later to claim a seat in the U.S. Senate, Wells became governor. The 1864 constitution was never popular. Radical Republicans and freedpeople resented the exclusion of Blacks for the elective franchise, while the vast majority of white conservatives refused to acknowledge the legitimacy of a constitution in which they had had no say.[39]

Wells thus desperately needed to create a broader base of political support to legitimize his own position. He set about using his vast opportunities for patronage in a state where every single office had effectively been vacated to cement support not just among his natural base of conservative Unionists, but

---

36 'August 26, 1865, New Orleans, Canby to Wells,' NARA, RG 393, part1, entry 1738, vol. 79; 'October 20, 1865, New Orleans, Wells to Johnson,' Wells Microfilm.

37 Bergeron, *Johnson Papers, Vol. 9*, 221.

38 Ira Berlin, Joseph P. Reidy, and Leslie S. Rowland, eds., *Freedom: A Documentary History of Emancipation, 1861-1867 – Series II: The Black Military Experience* (Cambridge: Cambridge University Press, 1982), 736.

39 Joe Gray Taylor, *Louisiana Reconstructed, 1863-1877* (Baton Rouge: Louisiana State University Press, 1974), 53-62; McCrary, *Lincoln and Reconstruction*, chap. 8; Tunnell, *Crucible of Reconstruction*, chaps. 3-4.

also many of the more moderate supporters of the Confederacy. As early as May 1865, the New Orleans Unionist Thomas J. Durant warned Johnson that most state and local offices "are now being distributed to men who held commissions in the rebel army, who signed the ordinance of secession in January 1861, who took a leading part in the rebel movement; you can see them now as Judges, sheriffs, and important officers of the new state." Once the areas that had remained under Confederate control were allowed to participate in elections, he warned, unrepentant southerners would overwhelm "the real friends of liberty and Union." James Ready, a physician from Tennessee who had moved to New Orleans decades before, agreed that Wells had turned a complete somerset [sic] and allied himself with a notorious Copperhead, wire-pulling pro-slavery party." His appointments were nothing but the "scum of the Copperhead party down to the meanest rebels in the State."[40]

The president, however, threw his support behind Wells, who promised to line up the vast majority of whites in Louisiana behind the president's conservative plan of Reconstruction. After returning to New Orleans from Washington, D.C., where he had received verbal instructions from Johnson, Wells wrote the president that he had begun the reorganization of the state "bearing in mind steadily [...] your views and injunctions as to the proper mode of proceeding." He felt no qualms about being "less exacting in regards to the antecedents" of parochial officers and "appointed some fine men of resolution and intelligence, who had some military service in the rebel ranks. I will however guarantee their fidelity to the nation and to you its executive."[41]

During the following months, Wells and his most loyal allies, New Orleans Mayor Hugh Kennedy and Thomas Cottman, regularly sought Johnson's support as they clashed with both the military authorities and civilian federal officials, whom they considered "insolent, over-bearing and rapacious." Kennedy warned Johnson that the clerk of the federal poor charged a few dollars to administer the amnesty oath, thus excluding the poor from Johnson's generous provisions. He therefore had taken it upon himself to do so for free to hundreds of people each day. Wells and his allies, meanwhile, regularly pleaded with Johnson to have him appointed as provisional governor, as the president had done in most other southern states, to thus strengthen his authority until new statewide elections could be held. Although Johnson held back on this latter request, he promised Wells every possible support and urged him to

---

40 Bergeron, *Johnson Papers, Vol. 8*, 7, 269; On Durant's background, see Joseph G. Tregle, "Thomas J. Durant, Utopian Socialism, and the Failure of Presidential Reconstruction in Louisiana," *The Journal of Southern History* 45, no. 4 (1979): 485-512.

41 'July 3, 1865, New Orleans, Wells to Johnson,' Wells Microfilm.

get in touch in case any further disagreements arose with General Canby or other federal officials.[42] Although the titular head of the federal government, Johnson's Jacksonian inclination and southern roots made it easy for him to side with local white elites on almost every occasion.

Wells and Kennedy saw the appointment of returning Confederate veterans as a politically expedient, but temporary measure. Mayor Kennedy was sure that "when order reigns again [...] the objectionable can be pruned off." This would prove a critical miscalculation, as by early 1866 Wells began to discover, in Justin Nystrom words, "what a Faustian bargain he had made."[43] In the fall of 1865 he had organized elections for a state legislature in which he ran unopposed except for a quixotic campaign on behalf of the self-exiled former Confederate Governor Henry Watkins Allen. The most significant result of the elections, however, was to usher in a legislature composed mostly of hardline conservatives. Initially Wells and his allies were jubilant about the results, but egged on by the rabidly conservative press from rural parishes, many of these legislators set out to enact a legislative agenda that would drive a wedge in the coalition of conservative Unionists and former Confederates that Wells had hoped to forge.[44] This included an attempt (vetoed by Wells) to suspend the collection of taxes owed over the Civil War years as well as the infamous Black Codes regulating vagrancy, labor tampering, fire arms, and labor contracts which were clearly intended to apply exclusively to the Black plantation laborers. Although Louisiana laws were technically race neutral, the legislators openly envisioned a racial discriminatory application by local officials. Their purpose was to reduce the freedpeople of Louisiana to a condition of political and economic dependence only marginally better than chattel slavery.[45]

President Johnson had regularly backed Wells and New Orleans Mayor Kennedy in their conflicts with military and other federal authorities of which the president was the titular head.[46] But as soon as Wells began to distance

42 Bergeron, *Johnson Papers, Vol. 8*, 114, 236-237, 356, 436; Bergeron, *Johnson Papers, Vol. 9*, 125-126.

43 Bergeron, *Johnson Papers, Vol. 8*, 447; Justin A. Nystrom, *New Orleans after the Civil War* (Baltimore: John Hopkins University Press, 2010), 66.

44 Bergeron, *Johnson Papers, Vol. 9*, 352-353. *Louisiana Democrat*, 10-25-1865, 12-06-1865; *Bienville Messenger*, 01-13-1866.

45 Taylor, *Louisiana Reconstructed*, 100-101. *Senate Executive Document 6, 39th Congress, 2nd Session* (GPO 1867), 181 -187; *Acts Passed by the General Assembly of the State of Louisiana at the Extra Session, Held and Begun in the City of New Orleans on the 23d of November, 1865* (New Orleans: State Printer, 1866) [See Acts 10, 11, 12, 16, 19, and 20 in particular]; *House Report 92, 42nd Congress, 2nd Session* (GPO 1872), 31.

46 See for example Bergeron, *Johnson Papers, Vol. 9*, 98.

himself from the hardline conservatives who now dominated the state legislature, Johnson, in true Jacksonian fashion, threw his weight behind the democratically elected local officials. At its first regular session in 1866, the new legislature immediately set out to organize municipal elections in New Orleans as well as for local officials throughout the state, in the hope of ousting Kennedy and other incumbents who depended on Wells's patronage. Fearful for his position, the governor sought support from Johnson to postpone these elections. President Johnson, however, remained steadfast in his commitment to state autonomy and threatened to have General Phillip Sheridan organize the elections if Wells refused to do so after the legislature overrode his veto of an election bill.[47]

As far as the president was concerned, local elections would bolster the legitimacy of Louisiana's state government and thus accelerate his program of returning the former Confederate States to their regular position in the Union as soon as possible. Coming at the same time as his veto of the Freedmen's Bureau bill, Johnson's support for municipal elections cemented his reputation as an unwavering friend and supporter of conservative southern whites. As one rural newspaper put it, Johnson had shown he "has no objection to the people governing themselves in their own way, as long as they are obedient to the government; and his action has nerved the legislature to throw off the yoke which the present State government had thrown upon it." A planter praised the president as "a friend who will save them from the dreadful fate, which seemed inevitable from northern fanaticism."[48]

The municipal elections held in New Orleans in March resulted in the election of former Confederate Mayor John T. Monroe. Thomas Cottman, who served as Wells's representative in Washington, considered the results an "abuse of confidence, you have so generously reposed in our people, evinced in the recent Municipal election in New Orleans." Although it was Johnson who had personally forbade Wells to postpone the elections, Cottman placed the blame squarely on local military authorities.[49] Louisiana conservatives wasted no time in seeking the president's support in their increasingly fierce struggle against a Unionist governor whom many had not forgiven his wartime loyalty. Monroe immediately wrote the president to emphasize that he had been freely and fairly elected and although Johnson initially upheld General Canby's suspension of the new mayor on a technicality, he quickly issued the necessary

47 Bergeron, 425-426, 652, 654; Bergeron, *Johnson Papers, Vol. 10*, 210-211.

48 *Louisiana Democrat*, 02-21-1866; *Bienville Messenger*, 02-17-1866, 03-03-1866; Bergeron, *Johnson Papers, Vol. 10*, 195.

49 Bergeron, 256-257.

pardon to allow the new mayor to take up his office.[50] By the time parochial elections rolled around a few months later, Wells had lost all semblance of support among Louisiana's white population and conservative editors warned it would be voters' "own fault if the imbecility which now characterizes the office holders throughout the state, shall continue for any length of time."[51]

Finding himself increasingly isolated, Wells now turned to an unlikely source of support in a final attempt to reassert control over affairs in Louisiana. He reluctantly joined in an attempt by more radical Free Staters to reconvene the 1864 constitutional convention in order to extend the vote to the Black population and thus undercut the conservatives who now controlled state politics.[52] This was hardly what Johnson desired, as this would undermine the state's civil authorities, as well as improve the position of the Black population vis-à-vis their former masters – neither of which were results that would please a southern president steeped in the Jacksonian tradition.

Johnson, who had made a career out of following his own instincts, did not make much effort to mend fences with his erstwhile ally in New Orleans. Except for a curt note inquiring by whose authority Wells had convened the convention, the president now largely bypassed the Governor. He communicated instead with the far more conservative Lieutenant Governor Albert Voorhies and State Attorney General Andrew S. Herron. They warned that the convention was leading to mounting tensions in the city, which they blamed on "Violent and incendiary speeches," in which "negroes called to arm themselves" and the president was "bitterly denounced." As the convention approached, Johnson ordered Herron, not Wells, to call on the military authorities for "sufficient force to sustain the civil authority in suppressing all illegal or unlawful assemblies who usurp or assume to exercise any power or authority [...] If there is to be a Convention, let it be chosen fresh from the people of the whole state."[53] Such measures, at the same time, illustrate the limits of Johnson's commitment to local and state sovereignty. When it served his immediate or long-term political goals, he remained willing to use federal forces to protect his interests.[54]

---

50 Bergeron, 266, 290-291; Joseph G. Dawson, *Army Generals and Reconstruction: Louisiana, 1862-1877* (Baton Rouge: Louisiana State University Press, 1982), 32.

51 LD, 66-03-28; Tunnell, *Crucible of Reconstruction*, 102-103.

52 Bergeron, *Johnson Papers, Vol. 10*, 343-344; Walter M. Lowrey, "The Political Career of James Madison Wells," *Louisiana Historical Quarterly* 31 (1948): 1080-1083.

53 Bergeron, *Johnson Papers, Vol. 10*, 750, 752, 760; Nystrom, *New Orleans after the Civil War*, 67.

54 David Brian Robertson argues that throughout American history, arguments about federalism have always served a pragmatic purpose in order to further a substantial policy preference: *Federalism and the Making of America* (New York: Routledge 2017).

The conservative forces in Louisiana, it turned out, could manage quite well without federal support. The city police, under authority of newly installed Mayor Monroe and assisted by a mass of white 'volunteers' had no difficulty breaking up the convention with brutal force, resulting in at least three dozen dead supporters of the convention (most of whom were Black) and countless more injured.[55] General Sheridan warned Johnson in no uncertain terms that "no steps have as yet been taken by the civil authorities to arrest citizens who were engaged in this massacre, or policemen who perpetrated such cruelties." Johnson, however, preferred to listen to reports from his conservative allies Monroe, Voorhies, and Herron, who adroitly painted a picture that reflected his states' rights and racist worldview. They reassured him that "the civil authorities have done their duty" in suppressing a "colored mob, in unison with a few white leaders" that was "well organized" and "well armed."[56]

4 Conclusion

The events in New Orleans severely eroded support for Johnson in the North and led to an increase in the calls for a more radical course of Reconstruction. However, by the time Radical Republicans in Congress assumed control of the Reconstruction process in early 1867, they faced staunch opposition from conservative southern whites entrenched in positions of local power, not just in Louisiana, but across the South. There is of course no guarantee that the struggle for civil and political rights for the freedpeople would have proven any more successful in the absence of Johnson. Ultimately it was an uphill struggle which would inevitably have clashed with widely shared racial prejudices and a political culture committed to decentralized local government. Johnson's opposition, however, doomed Reconstruction to failure even before it had begun.

---

55 For an estimate of casualties, see *House Report 16, 39th Congress, 2nd Session* (GPO 1867), 176-177. For more on the New Orleans "riot" see Donald E. Reynolds, "The New Orleans Riot of 1866, Reconsidered," *Louisiana History: The Journal of the Louisiana Historical Association* 5, no. 1 (1964): 5-27; Melinda Meek Hennessey, "Race and Violence in Reconstruction New Orleans: The 1868 Riot," *Louisiana History: The Journal of the Louisiana Historical Association* 20, no. 1 (1979): 77-91; Gilles Vandal, "The Origins of the New Orleans Riot of 1866, Revisited," *Louisiana History: The Journal of the Louisiana Historical Association* 22, no. 2 (1981): 135-165; James K. Hogue, *Uncivil War: Five New Orleans Street Battles And the Rise And Fall of Radical Reconstruction* (Baton Rouge: Louisiana State University Press, 2006), chap. 2.

56 Paul H. Bergeron, ed., *The Papers of Andrew Johnson: Volume 11, August 1866-Janauary 1867* (Knoxville: University of Tennessee Press, 1994), 18, 25, 37, 44-45; Trefousse, *Andrew Johnson*, 258-259.

During the crucial first year after Appomattox, he neutered the Freedmen's Bureau, limited the authority of military officials, and nurtured state and local governments dominated by unrepentant Confederates. Congress eventually mounted a formidable political opposition that came just one vote short of impeaching him. But by then it was too late. Johnsons steadfast pursuit of his own Jacksonian vison had laid the groundwork for a South that would be dominated by states' rights and white supremacy for another century.

Indeed, when Johnson returned to the Senate in 1875 (the only ex-president ever to do so), he was neither repentant nor cowed. Instead, the only speech he gave there shortly before his unexpected death offered a full-throated vindication of the policies he had pursued as president and a fierce rebuke of his successor Grant for using military force to prop up the Republican state government of Louisiana following the contested 1874 elections.[57] Johnson self-assuredly cited his own policies in 1866 and 1867 as precedent for censuring what he considered a naked power grab by Republicans. To complete his vindication, the Senate's public galleries roared approval at his fierce rebuke of Grant, whom he claimed sought to "inaugurate a system on terrorism, and in the midst of the excitement, in the midst of the war-cry, triumphantly ride into the presidency for a third presidential term; and when that is done, farewell to the liberties of the country."[58]

57 On this so called "Trobriand Coup" see: Taylor, *Louisiana Reconstructed*, 305-307; Dawson, *Army Generals and Reconstruction*, chap. 10; Hogue, *Uncivil War*, chap. 6.

58 Paul H. Bergeron, ed., *The Papers of Andrew Johnson: Volume 16, May 1869-July 1875* (Knoxville: University of Tennessee Press, 2000), 723; Trefousse, *Andrew Johnson*, 372-374.

CHAPTER 5

Franklin D. Roosevelt as an Architect of Public History

Sara Polak

"Man's desire to be remembered is colossal," Franklin D. Roosevelt allegedly said when he observed the Egyptian Pyramids in 1943.[1] This anecdote is often recounted in discussions about Roosevelt's complex attitude toward his own future remembrance. Possibly because of his physical disability – he was paralyzed from the waist down as a result of adult-onset poliomyelitis – he was averse to being portrayed in a figurative fashion, but it would be a mistake to understand his attitude toward his own public image as modest or reticent.[2] The question how he would be represented in the present and remembered in the future occupied him far more intensely than it did for his immediate predecessors and his astuteness in managing that process constitutes a considerable break with tradition. Roosevelt expanded his press and media staff far beyond previous levels, held informal press conferences twice a week (also far more than any previous president), and personally designed and dedicated the Franklin D. Roosevelt Presidential Library, which was the first presidential library in the United States. He favored presenting his work to posing in the flesh. According to chief justice and personal friend Felix Frankfurter, Franklin Roosevelt wanted a small and simple monument, about which he said:

> [It should be] placed in the center of that green plot [in front of the National Archives in Washington, D.C. and should be] a block of about the size of this (putting his hand on his desk). I don't care what it's made of, whether limestone or granite or what not, but I want it to be plain, without any ornamentation, with the simple carving 'In memory of…'[3]

1 Doris Kearns Goodwin, *No Ordinary Time: Franklin and Eleanor Roosevelt: The Home Front in World War II* (New York: Simon and Schuster, 1994), 437.

2 Davis Houck and Amos Kiewe, *FDR's Body Politics: The Rhetoric of Disability* (Texas A&M University Press, 2003), 4.

3 Diary note, cited by Frankfurter himself in "The Memorial to F.D.R.: What the President Wanted," *Atlantic Monthly*, March 1961, 39-40.

© KONINKLIJKE BRILL NV, LEIDEN, 2020 | DOI:10.1163/9789004422643_007

As a result of his own and others' complicated body politics, actual sculptures of FDR (as well as other realistic representations of his body) remain problematic in the United States to this day.[4]

Benjamin Hufbauer and other scholars have argued that Roosevelt created the Franklin D. Roosevelt Presidential Library for various reasons, but at least partly in lieu of more classical iconic self-representational monuments.[5] Franklin Roosevelt did indeed come up with the very concept of the presidential library; he went on to personally design and build his own library on his estate. One consequence of this decision is that his papers are kept and exhibited just a stone's throw from his family home. Upon arrival at the site's visitor center, the majority of visitors purchase a joint ticket that gives access to both sites. As such, the Franklin Roosevelt Presidential Library, deeded by FDR to the National Archives and Records Administration (NARA) and the Springwood Home, which remembers his personal life, administered by the National Park Service (NPS) are deeply connected. Moreover, part of the site, particularly the special exhibition space and portions of the visitor center, were built with funding from the private nonprofit Roosevelt Institute. While NARA and NPS are federal bodies (and therefore non-partisan), the Roosevelt Institute is dedicated explicitly to preserving and presenting the legacy of Franklin and Eleanor Roosevelt. Thus, there are close links between Franklin Roosevelt's private life and persona *and* his political paper trail (and on a meta-level the equally political tradition to build presidential libraries which he engendered) created and reinforced by Roosevelt's own design and by later agents.

While Roosevelt clearly organized his own remembrance in this and other ways, he favored other depictions rather than actual portrayals that resembled him physically. To understand somewhat more systematically what kinds of representation he preferred, the classification of American philosopher and semiotician Charles Sanders Peirce is helpful. He distinguishes between representations that are *iconic* – that is, signs that bear resemblance to their object (for instance a photograph or sculpture), and signs that are *indexical*, meaning that they point toward their object based on a real connection. For instance, much of the clearly visible and omnipresent New Deal architecture in the American landscape continues to index FDR, without representing him through a direct likeness (which would be iconic). Finally, Peirce distinguishes

4 Sally Stein, "The President's Two Bodies: Staging and Restagings of FDR and the New Deal Body Politic," *American Art* 18, no. 1 (Spring 2004): 32-57.

5 Benjamin Hufbauer, *Presidential Temples: How Memorials and Libraries Shape Public Memory* (Lawrence: University Press of Kansas, 2005), 32.

symbolic representations, representations which we do understand, but not because they resemble or point out their object.[6]

Although all three classes of representations of Franklin D. Roosevelt occur, he personally preferred indexical representations of himself to iconic ones. I want to suggest that such indexical representations, while seemingly less focused on his person and more on his work, played an essential role in a broader sense of ensuring FDR's firm position in American memory. Even if he did not yet use the term or the specific jargon, he significantly contributed to shaping the field that has now come to be known as public history. Denise Meringolo shows in her book *Museums, Monuments, and National Parks: Toward a New Genealogy of Public History* that what she terms 'the culture of public history' tends to be historicized as a phenomenon that originated in the 1970s with the Marxist History workshop and other emancipatory movements of those decades, but actually originated some forty years earlier.[7]

In this chapter I will show how Franklin D. Roosevelt was part of that genealogy of public history, in the way that he presented himself and the legacies of his presidency for posterity's sake. At the same time, he actively employed the past to depoliticize himself and his presidential policies to his contemporaries. Both dynamics are similar in their reliance on representing the past to depoliticize issues in the present or future. FDR's political acumen, his norm-breaking behavior, and the ways he presented himself as a candidate and president confounded expectations and may have seemed radical and disrespectful of tradition. He was very mindful of his actions, however; indeed, they were perhaps effective because FDR was cognizant of breaking habits. The same is true for how he acted as a public historian of his own legacy. Both these aspects of his political life are comparable reflections of his personality. A common key factor in FDR's negotiation of the past with regard to his candidacy and presidency and his presentation for the sake of posterity is the fact that he did not seem to do so to blow his trumpet, at least on the face of it. FDR's preference for indexical rather than more obviously self-aggrandizing iconic references to his person and presidency in the American landscape and the nation's consciousness led to a presence that is both subtly political and depoliticized. While it is impossible (and perhaps unnecessary) to decide to what extent this was motivated by a wish to be remembered heroically as a

6 Charles Sanders Peirce, *Collected Papers of Charles Sanders Peirce* (Cambridge: Belknap Press, 1958), 4: 359.

7 Denise Meringolo, *Museums, Monuments, and National Parks: Toward a New Genealogy of Public History* (Amherst: University of Massachusetts Press, 2012), xv-xvii.

statesman, Roosevelt's positioning did contribute crucially to the federal treatment and presentation of natural and cultural heritage and the involvement of historians with tourism. In American memory, the New Deal continues to be indexically connected to Franklin Roosevelt. This connection is strengthened by the fact that the programs' oft-consensual style and extremely wide-ranging and improvisatory nature all resemble Roosevelt's personality too.

1 Franklin Roosevelt as Object and Agent of Public History

In 1936 FDR unveiled the second sculpture at Mount Rushmore, the bust of Thomas Jefferson. In his speech, he reflected on the role of Americans like himself and Jefferson as elements of the future past:

> … we can perhaps meditate a little on those Americans ten thousand years from now when the weathering on the face of Washington and Jefferson and Lincoln shall have proceeded to perhaps a depth of a tenth of an inch – meditate and wonder what our descendants, and I think they will still be here, will think about us. Let us hope that at least they will give us the benefit of the doubt – that they will believe we have honestly striven every day and generation to preserve for our descendants a decent land to live in and a decent form of government to operate under.[8]

By shifting the perspective ten thousand years into the future, Roosevelt suggested that he and his audience in 1936 were part of the same historical moment as Jefferson, whose gigantic bust he had just unveiled. While 'the weathering on the face of Washington and Jefferson and Lincoln' marked their transcendence of eras, those present at the ceremony were part of the era the sculpted presidents are the icons of. Thus FDR, as an American president like the sculpted men once were, implicitly placed himself in their league – a move that appears to have turned out successfully: practically any lay or expert ranking of 'Best U.S. Presidents' since 1945 had Washington, Jefferson, Lincoln, or Franklin Roosevelt in its top three.[9]

8 Franklin D. Roosevelt, August 30, 1936, in Ken Burns, *The Roosevelts, An Intimate History*, PBS, 2014, 1:27-2:30.

9 An insightful overview of various presidential rankings over time (including Gallup, C-SPAN, ABC, Rasmussen) can be found on the Wikipedia page "Historical Rankings of Presidents of the United States" (https://en.wikipedia.org/wiki/Historical_rankings_of_Presidents_of_the_United_States, accessed June 9, 2017).

That task – preservation – is a job that is also a core activity of public historians, although the objects to be preserved are only indirectly related to the "decent land to live in and a decent form of government to operate under" FDR referred to in his Mount Rushmore speech. The use of the word 'preservation' implicitly signals Franklin Roosevelt's (at the time uncommon) interest in historical and natural preservation, which I argue helped shape the context of American public history *avant la lettre*. Franklin Roosevelt was a central player in making the preservation of American landscapes, national parks, and historic sites the business of the federal government, and through the New Deal a key actor in the massive increase of producing new historic sites, monuments, and public art and architecture.[10]

As president, Franklin Roosevelt was driven by a strong personal and political stake in preserving and representing the past to help shape the present and future. To consider him as such opens up an important perspective on how Roosevelt solidified the structural federal position in interpreting American history and shaping historical preservation. Roosevelt was a defining player in enabling and publicly funding the large-scale federally organized preservation and interpretation of the American past. He inherited many of his political positions (and arguably also his keen interest in presenting himself as a break with tradition) from his 'uncle' Theodore Roosevelt, who was elected as a Republican but later ran for president as a Progressive.[11] While Franklin Roosevelt was a Democrat, it is clear that both presidents shared broad political ideals and pragmatism that allowed them to pose as bipartisan. Both also were committed to a stance that Dario Fazzi has termed Rooseveltian in this volume; they personally embodied a transatlantic projection of American exceptionalism.

As a politician and public figure, FDR was highly cognizant of the possible (often self-serving) uses of history, which he regularly employed to allow very broad audiences to feel included or to identify with him. Roosevelt actively used that keen understanding for his own political gain, both on the campaign trail and at other times. He did not personally design, organize, or carry out research, teaching or specific projects to bring history to a larger audience. However, he did fundamentally change the relationship between historians and heritage in a broad sense on the one hand, and federal, state, and local governments on the other. Partly as a result of (or at least coincidental with)

10 Meringolo, *Museums, Monuments, and National Parks*, 110.

11 Theodore Roosevelt was technically only a direct uncle to FDR's wife Eleanor Roosevelt. TR and FDR had blood ties too, though indirect ones: they were fifth cousins.

his own partisan efforts to position himself for future memory, and in relation to history, Roosevelt became a kind of architect on a political and administrative level of current-day public history.

Both Michael Kammen in his paradigmatic history of American uses of the past, *Mystic Chords of Memory*, and Denise Meringolo in *Museums, Monuments, and National Parks* implicitly consider but do not explicitly discuss Franklin Roosevelt as a key player within the genealogy of public history.[12] Instead, they focus on the larger arc of how U.S. Americans and American organizations and the government have treated the past, although both indicate the importance of the New Deal and FDR's administrations. However, intervening in how the past and the then-present might be preserved, interpreted, and engaged with were central on Franklin Roosevelt's agenda, and his personal attitude and approach to these issues shaped his agenda and influenced the relationship between American heritage and government in the decades after his presidency.

2 FDR's Use of History

Although he no doubt realized that it would shape his reputation and future remembrance, Roosevelt engaged with American natural and cultural heritage and historians primarily because he believed this would benefit Americans at the time as well as future American audiences. He was sensitive to the unifying and consensus-building effects of historical analogies and to the potential uses of history and cultural memory. In contrast with Winston Churchill, Roosevelt did not write a history of his own time that claimed narrative authority over the era he had shaped.[13] But he was aware of the many potential uses of the past: to frame a particular perspective on the current political state of affairs, to politically position himself in relation to (and as a successor of) icons from the past, and also to create and propel his own public image into the future, as a political force shaping the future of American preservation. One example Michael Kammen provides of Roosevelt's "shrewd and self-serving" use of the past is his acting on the advice of Assistant Secretary of State R. Walton Moore, who argued in 1936 that "'while the campaign is under way, a stop at Jefferson's

12 Michael Kammen, *Mystic Chords of Memory: The Transformation of Tradition in American Culture* (New York: Random House, 1991), 467; Meringolo, *Museums, Monuments, and National Parks*, 110-113.

13 David Reynolds, *In Command of History: Winston Churchill, Fighting and Writing the Second World War* (London: Allen Lane, 2004).

home might be highly productive in terms of public relations."[14] This campaign stop at a site of memory linked with a great president of the past was similar to the speech at the unveiling of the Jefferson sculpture at Mount Rushmore: Roosevelt stressed his connection with heroic statesmen such as Lincoln and Jefferson, partly in order to associate himself with the entire electorate rather than with Democratic voters only.[15] Thus he created the impression that he was the logical candidate to carry forward the legacy of America's greatest presidents – Kammen even suggests many voters did not realize Roosevelt and Lincoln represented different parties.[16]

Through the use of such strategies, Roosevelt suggested he was a bipartisan president, rising above petty political differences and party politics. He also intuitively avoided to explicitly associate himself with ideological labels such as socialism or liberalism. Roosevelt's lack of ideological profiling has often been regarded a political advantage. In his 2004 book *Franklin D. Roosevelt*, Patrick Renshaw for instance wrote:

> [W]here Hoover's greatest handicap in dealing with the Depression had been his philosophy, FDR's greatest asset was his lack of one. 'Philosophy?' he once quizzically told a questioner 'Philosophy? I'm a Christian and a democrat – that's all.'[17]

In using these extremely broad, mainstream categories, FDR associated himself only with those labels that the overwhelming majority of Americans at the time agreed with, however much they might oppose Roosevelt's actual politics. Roosevelt was successful in presenting a kind of elusiveness or enigma in other contexts too. He used it as a politician to seem less partisan and thus in a sense to depoliticize himself, albeit to his political advantage. There are many instances when Eleanor Roosevelt's far more sharply outlined ideological positions tend to stand in for his seeming vacuity, without firmly committing him to her views.[18] FDR did, both at the time and in later cultural memory, profit from this sense that he was (deep down) more sharply profiled ideologically

14 Kammen, *Mystic Chords*, 452.

15 Ibid., 452.

16 Ibid., 452.

17 Patrick Renshaw, *Franklin D. Roosevelt: Profiles in Power* (Harlow: Pearson, 2004), 100.

18 Thus, although the Roosevelts certainly often disagreed about political matters, Eleanor Roosevelt does offer an inroad into the connections that may be made between FDR's presidential and personal convictions. This is one of the reasons why it makes sense in this particular case to include a chapter dedicated specifically to the First Lady.

than he cared to admit. This worked effectively to keep later Roosevelt narratives intriguing; many popular Roosevelt biographies, but also films like *Warm Springs* or *Hyde Park on Hudson*, claim to finally get to the heart of the 'real' Roosevelt.[19]

His words at the unveiling of the Jefferson memorial at Mount Rushmore illustrate how FDR 'connect[ed] innovation with tradition' in practice: shifting the focus into the future assertively centralized the issue of preservation. As such, preservation not only links up with honoring the past, but also the future. Many of the traditions – material and otherwise – Roosevelt explicitly preserved, rejected, or re-appropriated, therefore became indexes of him. He regularly showed he was prepared to treat the past, customs, and traditions with an irreverence that shocked many contemporaries, but that in effect modernized and therefore strengthened them. The most famous example of this irreverence occurred in 1932 when FDR flew to Chicago to personally accept his nomination for the presidency by the Democratic National Convention.[20] The tradition was that the nominee would await the telegram announcing his nomination at home and accept it there. Part of the force of Roosevelt's response in flying to Chicago lay in the fact that he was indeed awaiting the results at his home estate, but took an airplane – then of course still a relatively novel mode of transport. He could have secretly been staying in Chicago already. But his appearance – literally 'out of the blue' – did not so much cheat the convention, as radically modernize it, while using and paying tribute to the tradition.

In a similar vein, the term New Deal itself provides an example of Roosevelt's negotiation of tradition and innovation. Many elements of its purportedly new programs had already been espoused by Herbert Hoover, who was loudly despised by the Democratic campaign that promised the New Deal. Many other programs were older plans and ideals of the Progressive Era, indeed from the era when uncle Theodore Roosevelt led the country as a progressive Republican.[21] The New Deal was novel in the sense that many of its programs were carried out on a federal level, supported by unprecedentedly large government appropriations and made into law by Congress or mandated through executive order by the President, but the nature and ideas underly-

19 E.g. Jean Edward Smith, *FDR* (New York: Random House, 2007); Geoffrey Ward and Ken Burns, *The Roosevelts: An Intimate History* (New York: Alfred A. Knopf, 2014).

20 Kammen, *Mystic Chords*, 451.

21 Marc Allen Eisner, *From Warfare State to Welfare State: World War I, Compensatory State Building, and the Limits of the Modern Order* (University Park: Pennsylvania University Press, 2000), 349-350.

ing most programs were hardly new. Here too, Roosevelt astutely and rhetorically combined the potential to leverage pre-existing support for domestic programs and policies with the idiom and flair of innovation and radical adjustment to the requirements of a changed world. Although the New Deal was much too large and wide-ranging to have been conceived, planned, managed, and carried out by FDR alone, his name is strongly linked to them in an indexical fashion. In American memory, the New Deal continues to be indexically connected to Franklin Roosevelt. The programs' often-consensual style and extremely wide-ranging and improvisatory nature also all resemble Roosevelt's personality, and were frequently connected to representing him personally.

One of the initiatives that had been around for quite some time but was eventually implemented by FDR was the 1935 Historic Sites Act, which charged the National Park Service with the responsibility of preserving and managing national Historic Sites. NPS director Horace Albright had proposed this measure to FDR. The law explicitly confirmed the central role of the NPS in historic preservation and thus explicitly turned historical preservation into a federal responsibility.[22] A poster designed for the Park Service in 1934 by Dorothy Waugh carried a maxim that, as Kammen wrote, "managed to encapsulate both the customary and the newly expanded roles of the Park Service: 'The Adventures of Today Are the Memories of Tomorrow.'"[23] Both the original role of the NPS in enabling visitors to enjoy the parks and its expanded role in preserving them, in combination with helping park visitors to interpret the sites' history are represented in that slogan, as well as the awareness that 'Today' and 'Tomorrow' are inextricably bound up with 'Memories' of the past. As such, federalizing the management of 'the Memories of Tomorrow' was an important political step. Roosevelt did not request or try to directly assert any influence on the content over 'the memories of tomorrow,' but creating a federal responsibility to manage the representation of the past did imply that public history was both politicized and depoliticized. It was politicized in the sense that the preservation and interpretation of cultural heritage was brought under the eventual auspices of politicians (no longer private tour guides, art collectors, or travel guide publishers) and simultaneously depoliticized, in the sense that the responsible federal agencies, particularly the NPS, in its interpretation and presentation of the past were obliged to steer clear of partisan politics.

---

22 Meringolo, *Museums, Monuments, and National Parks*, 110-112.

23 Kammen, *Mystic Chords*, 468.

3 Depoliticizing the Political

As noted above, Meringolo has shown there is a great deal of continuity in the genealogy of public history, rather than the collapse of an old paradigm and the birth of a new one (located around 1970) that tends to be remembered in historicizing public history as a discipline.[24] On the one hand Roosevelt was a precursor; he would probably not have recognized his work within the terms of the post-modern jargon that characterizes a significant part of public history. On the other, in the 1930s he did already contribute to and reshape the heritage industry by letting public sector or federal agencies manage sites of history, making them more accessible and inclusive. Although in terms of strategies, methods, and discourse Roosevelt was distinctly old-fashioned compared to public historians of more recent decades, in terms of an implicit ideological framework his practice was often similar to later ones.

Franklin Roosevelt, particularly through the New Deal, but also through some of his own personal projects (most importantly the aforementioned design and dedication of the FDR Presidential Library in Hyde Park) involved himself in historical preservation and interpretation of historical heritage to an unusual extent, especially when compared to other American presidents. A key underlying reason to employ the past and to think of projects in the present as future history seems to have been Roosevelt's perception of history and memory as having a potentially depoliticizing force. This went beyond the bipartisanism he tried to project by highlighting his debts to Republican presidents from the past. Through creating federally managed, consensus-based public history sites and practices, he seems to have thought that relatively non-controversial ground could be found for Americans to experience a sense of togetherness.[25]

Kammen argues that using cultural memory to depoliticize the past is a peculiarly American strategy for dealing with national history. Many of Franklin Roosevelt's interactions with history and historical sites can be read as exemplary proponents of that tendency. However, Kammen uses the term depoliticization without making clear what he precisely means by it. When he writes "Americans have been inclined to depoliticize their past," he suggests that American memory tends to become apolitical, in the sense that it loses its political charge, and particularly its link with political party affiliations,

24 E.g. Faye Sayer, *Public History: A Practical Guide* (New York: Bloomsbury, 2015), 11.

25 Karal Ann Marling, *Wall-to-Wall America, A Cultural History of Post Office Murals in the Great Depression* (Minneapolis: University of Minnesota Press, 1982), 210.

which ties in with his idea that voters did not realize Roosevelt and Lincoln led different parties. But by the same token, the fact that Roosevelt could use the depoliticization of the past, or could depoliticize himself through forging a link with national historical figures to his electoral advantage, implies that depoliticization is after all a political phenomenon. Indeed, in FDR's case, it seems to have been a political strategy, though perhaps not so much a strategy driven by ideological convictions as by practical opportunism.

For example, while the New Deal did relatively little for African American citizens, who were extremely hard-hit by the Depression, Roosevelt still became popular among them, primarily because of Eleanor Roosevelt's largely symbolic yet widely appreciated support.[26] Eleanor Roosevelt's role in itself is an interesting example of depoliticization – she was of course not elected, had no formal power, and yet could help to expand the coalition of Roosevelt supporters. This is not to deny Eleanor Roosevelt's good intentions or her important work (both within the formal administration and in the public arena) to promote the emancipation of African Americans, but at the same time, it provided Franklin Roosevelt with the political leeway not to speak out against lynching or to sign the Costner-Wagner bill prohibiting it.[27] This was important in electoral terms, because southern Democrats would probably not have accepted such explicit condemnation of what they considered to be an issue for individual states.

4 Depoliticizing the Past through the New Deal

The 'memory boom' of the last decades – the increased interest in history centered around more or less official historical memory sites on the one hand, and the intense fragmentation of historical narratives through the emancipation of 'lived memory' on the other – has seen a precursor of sorts during the 1920s and 1930s, focused mainly on the importance of preservation and interpretation of cultural heritage sites. Kammen discusses in *The Mystic Chords of Memory* how in the 1920s 'Americana' – objects of American cultural heritage – increasingly became highly sought-after by privately owned museums, individual collectors, and even investors who noted the steady rise in their cultural significance (and therefore monetary value). In the course of the 1930s

26 Clarence Lusane, *The Black History of the White House* (San Francisco: City Light Books, 2011), 222.

27 Lusane, *The Black History of the White House*, 215.

a wide range of efforts to take care of national historic sites emerged. Preservation and cultural memory were incorporated and extended during the New Deal, a move that massively expanded the heritage industry and often turned it into a publicly owned and federally managed enterprise.

The cultural legacy of the New Deal is enormous; it spans a huge range of infrastructural, cultural, and historical sites and artifacts, in large part created by the Works Progress Administration (WPA). The WPA included a wide array of cultural, artistic, and historical projects, producing thousands of post office murals, theater performances, photo series, artworks, books, and films. The WPA and several other New Deal programs (e.g. the Farm Security Administration) also employed professional photographers and film makers to document events such as the Dust Bowl in Oklahoma and elsewhere in the Mid-West, the Great Depression throughout the country, and New Deal laborers at work. Among other things, the Federal Writers Project (part of the WPA) set up the American Guidebook Series, canonizing the historical and natural highlights of each state, and a massive oral history project to record life narratives from the American South, particularly from people born in slavery. Many of these projects employed historians, and many set out to record for the benefit of future historians. Franklin Roosevelt did not personally devise these individual projects, but he did create the social and legal momentum that made them possible on an administrative and political level. Moreover, he strongly supported the individual projects and therefore was a key instigator of the sets of cultural practices and customs that they established. Moreover, first by executive order (June 1933) and later through the aforementioned Historical Sites Act (1935), Roosevelt enabled a radical expansion of the National Park Service and its preservation activities. Like the hundreds of parks, post offices, bridges, and other infrastructural landmarks, many of these projects remain indexically connected with FDR in the collective consciousness. Even if such an indexical link is relatively tenuous, the continued omnipresence of material and textual legacies of the New Deal ensures that Roosevelt remains present in the American landscape.

However, the New Deal's cultural impact was not only at the direct level of cultural and material landscapes, but it also changed the American mindset with regard to its cultural heritage, as Kammen argues:

> There is a very real sense in which Americans broke with an ingrained habit of mind (let the private sector do it) in order to rescue and restore to prominence a range of particular traditions. Needless to say, impoverished yet creative people were also salvaged in the process. That was the

> principal objective, in fact. The circumstances were such that assisting Americans helped to save Americana.[28]

Although at the time the fact that 'impoverished yet creative people' were employed was probably the most visible effect (Kammen focuses on the saving of 'Americana' as a secondary result), the long-term consequence that seems most important was the change in the 'ingrained habit of mind' the WPA and other cultural New Deal programs sparked. This shift from private to public sector in perceived responsibility for 'rescu[ing] and restor[ing] to prominence a range of particular traditions' has had important long-range political implications, which FDR initiated. No longer simply letting 'the private sector do it' was an initial step toward putting the 'public' (sector) in public history, and the projects of many public historians continue to be based on the conviction that historical preservation and interpretation are public affairs. This is on the one hand a relatively radical change in attitude – one that many on the right wing of the political spectrum continue to deplore – and on the other it is a way to ensure that sites of cultural heritage are represented in a 'neutral,' often bland and consensual fashion.

Some, like artist Edward Laning, have argued that the Roosevelts' personal loyalty to their artist friends played a role in the Roosevelt administration's patronage of the arts.[29] Whether or not this loyalty or other aspects were at the heart of Roosevelt's enthusiasm for enabling, preserving, and making accessible public art and heritage, the products of the New Deal in the American landscape have come to function as a reminder of the sense of public responsibility for American heritage forged under his leadership. Through these cultural, artistic, historical, and preservation projects, FDR shaped the landscape, literally and metaphorically, where public history as a discipline could evolve.

History and Americana were also good topics for New Deal art projects, because they tended to seem uncontroversial and because they could be presented as useful to the entire nation. Karal Ann Marling has argued that the 2500 post office murals were historical tableaux "because the past was comparatively non-controversial."[30] Although in the 1930s intense local political conflicts existed about historical representations in post office murals, Marling suggests that historical themes were less controversial than themes from the

28 Kammen, *Mystic Chords*, 444.

29 Cited in Francis O'Connor, "Federal Support for the Visual Arts: The New Deal Then and Now," *The New Deal Art Projects, An Anthology of Memoirs* (Washington, D.C.: Smithsonian Institution, 1972), 90.

30 Marling, *Wall to Wall America*, 211.

present, because a certain taboo rested on representing the Depression and the present of the 1930s.[31] This paradox illustrates the inevitably political nature of using the past as a source of consensus. Shifting the perspective from the present to the past as an artistic theme depoliticized on some level, but any representation of a supposedly consensual past sooner or later runs into political trouble. This dynamic obviously mirrors Franklin Roosevelt's inclination to use historical narratives, settings, and parallels to contextualize himself. Both historical murals and historical contextualization of FDR moved away from the concrete and often painful realities of the present in politics.

However, the past was not only a politically convenient source for artwork; the sense that historical sites and national heritage must be created, interpreted, and made accessible was also fashionable, and had been on the rise since the early twentieth century. Alfred Kazin has called the American Guide Series symbolic of the "reawakened American sense of its own history,"[32] a sense that Roosevelt clearly understood very well and stimulated.[33] This same 'reawakened American sense of its own history' can also be seen in the revival of the interest in slave narratives in the 1920s and 1930s. Originally a genre linked primarily to the antebellum abolitionist movement, recounting the life narratives of freed or escaped slaves, it had waned in the years after the Civil War. The revival, which was more sociological than the original (often highly moralistic) slave narratives, may in part be attributed to the age of the last generation of people who had been enslaved. Several smaller projects to record the stories of former slaves evolved in the 1920s and 1930s, of which the FWP's Slave Narrative Collection project was by far the largest, producing over 2300 interviews. Historian David Brion Davis has argued that this collection of testimonies "is indisputably unique among former slaveholding nations."[34]

So, to conclude, how did FDR's famously glib style, darting attention, and capacity to apparently please all interlocutors manifest itself as actual New Deal policy? First of all, as noted, he managed to put considerable distance between himself and the New Deal while simultaneously becoming indexically connected to it. For instance, the Slave Narrative Collection was not Roosevelt's personal idea (just like many other New Deal programs), but an initiative that sprang from several smaller local projects. Nonetheless, the New Deal massively expanded and federalized the project, synchronizing

---

31 Marling, *Wall to Wall America*, 211.

32 Qtd. In Jerre Mangione, *The Dream and the Deal: The Federal Writers' Project, 1935-1943* (New York: Avon, 1972), 371.

33 Kammen, *Mystic Chords*, 450.

34 David Brion Davis, "Slavery and the Post-World War II Historians," *Daedalus* 103 (1974): 7.

it with Roosevelt's political view that societal issues were best approached through grand projects. As such, it has rightly been connected to his persona. Roosevelt's key political and cultural legacies concern the treatment of the past, be it through preservation, presentation, re-interpretation, or revision. He is a precursor and an architect of modern public history in administrative and infrastructural terms. In his approach to history, FDR looked for ways to arrive at a kind of broad consensus, ideally while still being inclusive of a range of diverging stories. That consensus wants to be depoliticized, which often leads to a degree of blandness. The bland consensus regarding FDR's own role in American history is in part produced by the fact that many of the concerned objects indexically rather than iconically represent his persona, body, or politics. His physical disability may have played a role in establishing this inclination toward indexical referencing, both on his own part and by others who felt uncomfortable representing his body too directly. In any case, that mode of referencing allows for a great deal of interpretative openness. This is by no means ideologically unproblematic, but it does seem to have worked well in creating a largely positive and still evolving space for him in American memory.

CHAPTER 6

"A Different and Better Future": Eleanor Roosevelt and the Global Atlantic

Dario Fazzi

In his second inaugural address, President Franklin D. Roosevelt explained the intimate connection between freedom and equality. In FDR's views, the main task of the U.S. government was to "promote general welfare and secure the blessing of liberty," both at home and abroad. Spreading wealth was the most challenging part of this job, as FDR knew that his administration's duty was not "to add more to the abundance of those who have much," but rather to "provide enough for those who have too little."[1] The rationale behind these words, which in a way summed up the fundamental tenets of the New Deal, testified to the affinity, though intermittent, between the president and his wife Eleanor.[2]

Born in 1884, Anna Eleanor Roosevelt got married to Franklin Delano Roosevelt in 1905. She was a distant cousin of his, but her lineage descended from the Republican – and much wealthier – branch of the knickerbockered Roosevelt family, the Oyster Bay one. Her uncle Teddy was a national hero: colonel of his own regiment in the Cuban War, a talented politician and terrific campaigner, intransigent on financial matters, and a progressive reformist on environmental and social issues. During his time in the White House he substantially modernized the American presidency.[3] In his young niece's eyes, Theodore Roosevelt embodied authority, commitment, and devotion to public duty. He instilled in her the idea that public service and responsibilities were particularly appropriate for people of their class.

Soon, however, Eleanor Roosevelt started being exposed to less aristocratic and much more liberal visions. She spent part of her formative years in

1 Franklin D. Roosevelt, "Second Inaugural Address, January 20, 1937," in *Documentary History of the Franklin D. Roosevelt Presidency*, vol. 50, FDR Selected Speeches, Document 18 (Bethesda: UPA, 2011), 166.

2 Doris K. Goodwin, *No Ordinary Time. Franklin and Eleanor Roosevelt: The Home Front in World War II* (New York: Simon & Schuster, 1994).

3 Serge Ricard, ed., *A Companion to Theodore Roosevelt* (Chichester: Blackwell Publishing, 2011).

© KONINKLIJKE BRILL NV, LEIDEN, 2020 | DOI:10.1163/9789004422643_008

England, where she attended a French-speaking finishing school led by the intriguing mademoiselle Marie Souvestre. Her schoolmistress taught her the love for history, arts, theater, and music; more importantly, Souvestre provided her with a different and complementary worldview. Souvestre was indeed a modern and independent woman who rejected old Victorian social norms and invited her students to do likewise. In her classes, she taught that social and political reforms were the key to overcome exploitation and disenfranchisement.[4]

Back in the U.S. during the early 1900s, Eleanor Roosevelt found a rapidly changing society. New modern technologies and infrastructures were facilitating people's contacts and exchanges, and shortening distances as well. Massive immigration from Europe was reshaping American demographics and posing new challenges to U.S. society at the same time. The Progressive Era was rewriting the contours of American urban life and the governing elites were trying to invent new political recipes for a quickly changing country. It was this fluid context that ignited Eleanor Roosevelt's early social activism.

The idea that the most privileged citizens had to do something for the less fortunate ones was her most important guiding principle. And the reality of New York City at the turn of the century was providing her with plenty of opportunities to put this into practice. Settlement houses and immigrants' shelters became familiar places to her. She visited numerous sweatshops, warehouses, and garment factories in order to gain firsthand experience of workers' difficult conditions. She found solace and personal satisfaction in volunteering for children, unemployed, newcomers, and poor women. She even took her fiancée Franklin on a tour of some of the worst tenement houses of the city. But after her marriage to FDR such a hectic routine had to be (temporarily) interrupted. Social activism had to make room for family duties, and taking care of her children became Eleanor Roosevelt's main task for the rest of the decade.[5]

In 1910, the Roosevelts moved to Albany, where FDR took office as Democratic state senator, thus launching his political career from the same platform that Theodore had used to start his own. Eleanor Roosevelt took advantage of these years of relative isolation from the city and filled with formal receptions to sharpen her political skills and expand her personal network. She attended debates and social gatherings, started being involved in the rising suffrage movement, came into contact with new political allies, and established

4 Blanche Wiesen Cook, *Eleanor Roosevelt: The Early Years, 1884-1933* (New York: Penguin, 1992), 102-124.

5 Brigid O'Farrell, *She Was One of Us: Eleanor Roosevelt and the American Worker* (Ithaca: Cornell University Press, 2010), 6-10.

some of her longest-lasting friendships. Continuing to follow Theodore's footsteps, FDR accepted president Woodrow Wilson's appointment as Assistant Secretary of the Navy and in 1913 he joined the Democratic administration. Once in Washington, D.C., Eleanor Roosevelt made sure that her family was introduced to the most appropriate and influential social circles in town, evaluated FDR's administrative and political experiences, and further increased her political independence.[6]

The outbreak of the war pushed her back to her early social activism. As her biographer and friend, Joseph Lash, later recognized, "the War gave her a reason acceptable to her conscience to free herself of the social duties that she hated, to concentrate less on her household, and to plunge into work that fitted her aptitude."[7] She worked as a volunteer for the American Red Cross, the Navy Relief Association, and in various hospitals and canteens of the capital. Eventually, the Great War transformed her into "an accomplished, widely known, and admired public figure in her own right," one who was able to set her own agenda and fight for her own social and political priorities.[8]

The early 1920s put Eleanor Roosevelt's resilience to the test. She first discovered that her husband had an affair with his secretary and then FDR contracted polio, which condemned him to a wheelchair for the rest of his life. She decided to stay with him and help him to revamp his political career. Along with Louis Howe, she was the mastermind behind FDR's campaign for New York governor, which opened to him another office that had been previously held by his distant cousin Theodore.[9] In these years, Eleanor Roosevelt became "one of New York's leading politicians," a skilled campaigner, and a talented organizer. Upon request from Nancy Cook, who at that time was the secretary of the New York women's division of the Democratic Party, she officially joined the Party and went on a tour of the state to promote and foster women's political participation. This commitment to women's rights led her to edit the Women's Democratic News, a political publication specifically meant to increase women's awareness nationwide, and to join the National

---

6 Allida M. Black, *Casting Her Own Shadow. Eleanor Roosevelt and the Shaping of Postwar Liberalism* (New York: Columbia University Press, 1996), 8.

7 See William H. Chafe, "Biographical Sketch," in *Without Precedent: The Life and Career of Eleanor Roosevelt*, eds. Joan Hoff-Wilson and Marjorie Lightman (Bloomington: Indiana University Press, 1984), 6.

8 Elisabeth Israels Perry, "Training for Public Life: ER and Women's Political Networks in the 1920s," in *Without Precedent*, eds. Hoff-Wilson and Lightman, 44.

9 Julie M. Fenster, *FDR's Shadow: Louis Howe, The Force that Shaped Franklin and Eleanor Roosevelt* (New York: St. Martin's Griffin, 2009).

League Board of Women Voters.[10] In 1924, she was also invited by the Democratic Party's national committee chairman, Cordell Hull, to take charge of an internal women's rights convention.[11]

A few years later, Eleanor Roosevelt began working at the Todhunter School for Girls. This new experience made her believe that she had eventually found her call: education and teaching.[12] She taught courses in American history, literature, and current events. She patterned her teaching techniques on Marie Souvestre, and helped her students to get acquainted with the linchpins of progressive reformism. In the meantime, she was still very active in the New York League of Women Voters, which played an important role in her political education and further improved her social skills. While campaigning for the League, Eleanor Roosevelt learned how to give public presentations, coordinate a wide range of political activities, and lobby for progressive legislation.[13]

This broad social activism not only gave Eleanor Roosevelt public prominence and visibility, but it also enabled her to gain firsthand experience in grassroots campaigning. She learned how to reach out to different audiences. She started mastering a huge variety of communication techniques and media strategies, "which included the use of radio broadcasts, newsletters, and magazines, in addition to such well-tested methods as public debates, speeches, fundraisers, and community events."[14] At the same time, she had the opportunity to cultivate a few pivotal and long-lasting personal contacts, then developed in trusted friendships, as the ones with Nancy Cook, Marion Dickerman, Clarence Pickett, Clark Eichelberger, and Caroline O'Day, all of whom infused into her a constant drive for social reform.

Eleanor Roosevelt soon found her political home in the liberal wing of the Democratic Party, whose socio-political agenda was far more consistent with

---

10 James MacGregor Burns and Susan Dunn, *The Three Roosevelts: Patrician Leaders Who Transformed America* (New York: Groove Press, 2001), 172.

11 Burns and Dunn, *The Three Roosevelts*, 186.

12 Ibid., 192.

13 Maurine Hoffman Beasley, Holly Cowan Shulman, and Henry R. Beasley, eds., *The Eleanor Roosevelt Encyclopedia* (Westport: Greenwood Press, 2001), 313. See also Dario Fazzi, "Eleanor Roosevelt's Peculiar Pacifism: Activism, Pragmatism, and Political Efficacy in Interwar America," *European Journal of American Studies*, 12, No. 1 (Spring 2017), https://ejas.revues.org/11893; Michelle Mart, "Eleanor Roosevelt, Liberalism and Israel," *Shofar: An Interdisciplinary Journal of Jewish Studies* 24, no. 3 (2006): 66.

14 Maurine Hoffman Beasley, *Eleanor Roosevelt. Transformative First Lady*, (Lawrence: University Press of Kansas, 2010), 77; Julieanne Phillips, "League of Women Voters," in eds. Maurine Hoffman Beasley, Holly Cowan Shulman, and Henry R. Beasley, *The Eleanor Roosevelt Encyclopedia* (Westport: Greenwood Press, 2001), 314-316.

her distinctive progressivism than the Republican one. As she wrote in 1923, she considered (liberal) Democrats to be "more concerned with welfare and interests of the people at large, and less with the growth of big business interests," and she shared with them a genuine interest in listening to common people, paying careful attention to their individual and collective needs, and working to improve their actual standards of living.[15]

This inclination to advocate for the most oppressed and the poorest also characterized her years in the White House. She made out of the first ladyship, a constitutionally powerless and theoretically marginal position, an effective office from which to push for a comprehensive progressive agenda. In doing so, she played a pivotal role in moderating FDR's stances, supporting American liberalism's cause within the administration, and counterbalancing the many conservative voices surrounding the president. She was such a constant presence in 1930s American politics, so well connected to Washington's policymakers, that historians have talked about her own New Deal.[16]

In the early 1930s, for instance, Eleanor Roosevelt personally supervised, coordinated, and funded homestead and child-feeding programs in the coal mining areas of Pennsylvania and West Virginia.[17] As Maurine Beasley has acknowledged, the Arthurdale Resettlement Administration Project, which was one of these programs, not only represented "the first effort by a president's wife to become intimately involved in a tax-supported effort for social betterment," but it also "placed her in the forefront of liberals."[18] Along with a few Quaker friends of hers, she also developed *Norvelt*, a self-sufficient community in Pennsylvania that was supposed to provide housing and services and an alternative to unemployment and misery to the coal miners and poor people in the area.[19] Even though critics ridiculed these attempts and dismissed

---

15 Beasley, *Eleanor Roosevelt*, 35; Dan Eshet, *Fundamental Freedoms. Eleanor Roosevelt and the Universal Declaration of Human Rights* (Brookline: Facing History and Ourselves National Foundation, 2010).

16 Frances M. Seeber, "Eleanor Roosevelt and Women in the New Deal: A Network of Friends," *Presidential Studies Quarterly*, 20, no. 4 (Fall 1990): 707-717; Blanche Wiesen Cook, *Eleanor Roosevelt: The Defining Years, 1933-1938* (New York: Penguin Books, 1999); Joseph P. Lash, *Eleanor and Franklin* (New York: Norton & Company, 1971).

17 For a detailed account of the Arthurdale project and Eleanor Roosevelt's role in it, see Nancy Hoffman, *Eleanor Roosevelt and the Arthurdale Experiment* (North Haven: Linnet Books, 2001). See Allan W. Austin, *Quaker Brotherhood: Interracial Activism and the American Friends Service Committee, 1917-1950* (Champaign: University of Illinois Press, 2012).

18 Beasley, *Eleanor Roosevelt*, 138.

19 Norvelt was named as such after EleaNOR RooseVELT. See Timothy Kelly, Margaret Power, and Michael Cary, *Hope in Hard Times: Norvelt and the Struggle for Community During the Great Depression* (University Park: Penn State University Press, 2016).

their poor results, Eleanor Roosevelt remained fully committed to the idea of participatory and communitarian democracy that these experiments were representing, up to the point of busying her agenda with community meetings, devolving part of her lecture fees to these projects, and constantly reporting to the press about their developments.[20]

In so doing, Eleanor Roosevelt distinguished herself from her husband but at the same time complemented neatly his political image. While, as Sara Polak suggests in this volume, FDR strove to earn a reputation as a bipartisan, almost post-ideological president, Eleanor Roosevelt took advantage of her public prominence and communication skills to establish a meaningful connection with several constituencies that the president's necessarily pragmatic agenda would have otherwise alienated. She may have not exerted any direct influence over FDR's decision making or congressional bargaining, as Susan Quinn argues, but she wove his vision into the broader Popular Front culture of the 1930s, thus contributing to historicizing the New Deal efforts.[21] She acted, in other words as her husband's Peter Pan's shadow: free to move, express herself and voice her opinions, but inescapably tied to the projection and contours of his (political) persona.

This mutually advantageous linkage led Eleanor Roosevelt, as first lady, to travel incessantly across the country and closely observe the consequences of the Great Depression. She was constantly confronted with unemployment, starvation, and poverty.[22] In many occasions she faced racial segregation and condemned it not only as immoral but also as inconsistent with the most cherished American values. According to her, there was "no reason why all of the races in this country should not live together, each of them giving from their particular gift something to the other, and contributing an example to the

---

20 On Arthurdale, see Eleanor Roosevelt to W.W. Alexander, January 22, 1938, in Roosevelt Institute for American Studies (RIAS), *The Papers of Eleanor Roosevelt, 1933-1945*, Reel 1, 00002. In another letter to Alexander, who was Arthurdale's administrator at the Department of Agriculture, she presented the story of a boy living in the homestead community whose family could not afford his training, and she admitted: "I have placed several other children from there [Arthurdale] in various capacities in Washington and they all seem to make good. If you think there is any chance, I will pay his transportation and give him enough money to live on until he gets his first pay check." Eleanor Roosevelt to W.W. Alexander, January 11, 1940, RIAS, *The Papers of Eleanor Roosevelt, 1933-1945*, Reel 1, 00008. On her financial involvement, see Bernard Baruch to Eleanor Roosevelt, December 18, 1934, RIAS, *The Papers of Eleanor Roosevelt, 1933-1945*, Reel 1, 00220.

21 Susan Quinn, *Eleanor and Hick: The Love Affair That Shaped a First Lady* (New York: Penguin, 2016).

22 Black, *Casting Her Own Shadow*, 23-28.

world of peace on earth, good will toward men."[23] In promoting civil rights, she oftentimes found herself in opposition to her husband's necessarily pragmatic policy agenda; nevertheless, she kept showing an unremitting courage in defending human dignity and fighting for minority opportunities.[24]

Eleanor Roosevelt's participation in the New York League, her social activism, and her peculiar attention to women's and civil rights did not exhaust the breadth of her political interests. She was indeed very vocal in advocating arbitration, internationalism, and world peace too. In other words, Eleanor Roosevelt's emphasis on social justice and progressive reformism at home translated into liberal interventionism abroad. In line with the internationalist impulse of the 1920s, she made continuous appeals for world cooperation as the only solution to war and the only way to establish long-lasting international stability and peace. For this reason, in the interwar years she favored U.S. participation in the League of Nations and deplored any isolationist tendency within the American political landscape. In 1935, when a pro-isolationist Senate had to vote for the ratification of the World Court treaty, she delivered a rousing radio address in which she called for the benefits of international arbitration. A few years later, she contributed a chapter to Carrie Chapman Catt's book *Why Wars Must Cease*, and wrote *This Troubled World*, dedicating both of these analyses to the necessity for the U.S. to strongly intervene in world affairs to promote democracy, foster world cooperation, and possibly ban war.[25]

Maurine Beasley reads this attitude toward internationalism more as "a repudiation of isolationism" than an "endorsement of American intervention."[26] Considering her conflicting stances on disarmament and on the necessity for military preparedness and conscription, something that led Eleanor Roosevelt to define herself as a "realistic pacifist," Joan Hoff argues that her thinking on foreign policy was often inconsistent. Subscribing to this, Blanche Wiesen Cook prefers to adopt the paradoxical definition of "practical idealist."[27] What

---

23 Eleanor Roosevelt, "The Negro and Social Change," in *Courage in a Dangerous World: The Political Writings of Eleanor Roosevelt*, ed. Allida M. Black (New York: Columbia University Press, 1999), 34-37. See also Mildred W. Abramowitz, *Eleanor Roosevelt and Federal Responsibility and Responsiveness to Youth, the Negro, and Others in Time of Depression*, Ph.D. Dissertation, New York University, 1971, 141-183.

24 Joanna Schneider Zangrando and Robert Zangrando, "ER and Black Civil Rights," in *Without Precedent*, eds. Hoff-Wilson and Lightman, 88.

25 See William H. Chafe, "Biographical Sketch," in *Without Precedent*, eds. Hoff-Wilson and Lightman, 7.

26 Beasley, *Eleanor Roosevelt*, 171 and 179.

27 See Joan Hoff, "Foreign Policy," in *The Eleanor Roosevelt Encyclopedia*, 195.

these definitions tend to underestimate, however, is that Eleanor Roosevelt was quintessentially an *exceptionalist*. To her, the U.S. had a daunting but inescapable task to fulfill, which was nothing less than defending democracy and fostering equality on a world scale. In her own words, "[b]eing a strong nation and having the greatest physical, mental and spiritual strength," gave the U.S. the "tremendous responsibility" to provide the whole world with a vision for the future and lead mankind to a fully democratic development.[28]

However, what made Eleanor Roosevelt's exceptionalism a rather peculiar one, and at the same time fully *Rooseveltian*, was her transatlantic projection of it.[29] To her, the alliance with European democracies was crucial to the success of the U.S. global mission, since transatlantic cooperation was in Eleanor Roosevelt's opinion the only way through which the U.S. could hope to secure democracy and freedom worldwide. While praising transatlantic cooperation, she stressed that the very idea of American isolationism was misleading: "Of course this country still feels very much detached from the rest of the world because of its size and distance, but that will not last forever."[30] Eleanor Roosevelt constantly backed the idea that mutual cooperation across the Atlantic was paramount to the creation of a new, stable, and fair world order.

She also realized very soon that the emergence of authoritarian regimes in Europe was hindering this whole process. In 1936, she confessed to a German friend to consider "perfectly ridiculous that intelligent human beings cannot sit around a table and satisfy their needs [...] It would cost far less to pay for what is wanted than it does for ammunition or to have one generation practically wiped out, to say nothing of the cost that deprivations at home leave us in the way of depleted populations." But in 1939 she was fully persuaded that her

28 Eleanor Roosevelt to Harry Truman, November 20, 1945, cited in Jason Berger, *A New Deal for the World: Eleanor Roosevelt and American Foreign Policy* (New York: Columbia University Press, 1981), 48, and in ed. Steve Neal, *Eleanor and Harry: The Correspondence of Eleanor Roosevelt and Harry S. Truman* (New York: Lisa Drew Book, 2002), 45. See William H. Chafe, "Biographical Sketch," in *Without Precedent*, eds. Hoff-Wilson and Lightman, 23. See also Eleanor Roosevelt, "Keepers of Democracy," in *The Virginia Quarterly Review* 15, no. 1 (1939), in Black, ed., *Courage in a Dangerous World*, 117-120. Eleanor Roosevelt's tireless commitment to democracy made 67 percent of Americans, according to a Gallup poll taken in spring 1940, well disposed toward First Lady's activities, see Goodwin, *No Ordinary Time*, 19. On the concept of exceptionalism, see Ian Tyrrel, "What is American exceptionalism?" online at https://iantyrrell.wordpress.com/papers-and-comments/ accessed on October 13, 2017.

29 Hans Krabbendam and John M. Thompson, *America's Transatlantic Turn: Theodore Roosevelt and the "Discovery" of Europe* (New York: Palgrave, 2012).

30 Eleanor Roosevelt to Mrs. Carola Schaffer Bernstein, January 28, 1936, RIAS, *The Papers of Eleanor Roosevelt, 1933-1945*, Reel 1, 00797.

country had to fight, "because fascism threatened the future of civilization." To her, Americans had the moral duty to restore "democracy and the right of a people to choose their own government without having it imposed upon them by Hitler and Mussolini."[31] Amidst the pivotal political struggle over the Lend-Lease proposal to Britain, she eventually spoke in favor of American action, saying that it was time the U.S. started "thinking about giving something" back to Europe, thus abandoning any reluctance to intervene.[32] As she wrote to U.S. novelist Theodore Dreiser in the spring of 1941, "I do feel that for the future of the world it is vastly important that Great Britain win this war and that the many Democracies that have come under Hitler's rule be restored to independence."[33]

After Pearl Harbor, the focus of the American public debate switched from intervention to war and postwar planning, and Eleanor Roosevelt became part and parcel of that vibrant debate too. In particular, she joined the chorus of liberals who were advocating for the supremacy of the people over the cogency of the nation state, even in the field of foreign affairs. In doing so, she was substantially endorsing FDR's Vice President Henry Wallace's idea of launching, after the war, the so-called "century of the common man."[34] Since she saw "the people's revolution" to be on the move, she believed that the actual geographic boundaries dividing the nations of the world were progressively destined to lose their influence and relevance. It was therefore of the utmost importance to overcome nationalism and particularism and give the whole world the shape of humanity.

Eleanor Roosevelt conveyed her messages on world cooperation and transnationalism unceasingly to the American people, thus paving the way for liberal internationalism to be not only politically viable but also publicly acceptable. Through a number of radio and TV addressees, public lectures, and widely syndicated columns, she kept reminding, especially young people both in Europe and in the U.S., that the ultimate goal of their fight against Nazism and Fascism was not only to restore freedom, but also to build "a different

---

31 Berger, *A New Deal for the World*, 15.

32 Blanche Wiesen Cook, "Turn Toward Peace: ER and Foreign Affairs," in *Without Precedent*, eds. Hoff-Wilson and Lightman 114. Mildred W. Abramowitz, *Eleanor Roosevelt and Federal Responsibility*, 190.

33 Eleanor Roosevelt to Theodore Dreiser, May 3, 1941, RIAS, *The Paper of Eleanor Roosevelt, 1933-1945*, Reel 8, 00468.

34 Henry A. Wallace, "The Century of the Common Man," https://shafr.org/sites/default/files/Wallace%2CCommonMan.pdf, accessed on October 13, 2017. See also, James T. Patterson, *Grand Expectations: The United States, 1945-1974* (New York: Oxford University Press, 1996).

and better future" based on mutual respect among the people of the world.[35] In transatlantic terms, she was trying to *deepen* both the meaning and purpose of the exchange between Europe and the United States. While qualifying the Atlantic space in moral terms, she was in fact assigning it the mission to defend democracy and foster social justice worldwide.[36]

After the invasion of Poland, she started raising private funds for the relief of war refugees. She wrote an open letter asking American and European women's organizations to "join together in a relief organization which shall cover all civilians as they need it, the money to be distributed through the International YMCA, YMCA, Friends Service Committee and Red Cross."[37] Then, she served as honorary vice president of the Non-Sectarian Foundation for Refugee Children, a humanitarian group coordinated by the American Friends Service Committee and organized by Clarence Pickett, whose aim was to shelter young European refugees in the United States.[38] She financially supported the U.S. Committee for the Care of European Children and asked the State Department to take care of a few personal friends she had in Europe.[39]

On April 16, 1943, Eleanor Roosevelt reiterated her liberal vision for a postwar order by foreseeing a process of complete reconfiguration of interclass relations, one that could lead to a renewed "partnership between those who work with their hands and those who work with their heads." These people, in Eleanor Roosevelt's own words, had to "insist on their common interest because they are workers of the world. They are the mass of people who must control their governments in order to have a chance to build a better life throughout the world."[40] In substance, against the false promises of tyranny and totalitarianism, against the impressive growth state apparatuses, against the mechanization and bureaucratization of societies, Eleanor Roosevelt was supporting the benefits of transnationalism.[41]

---

35 Eleanor Roosevelt, *My Day*, January 28, 1942. All the 'My Day' columns are available online through the pages of the Eleanor Roosevelt Papers Project, led by the George Washington University, at https://www.gwu.edu/~erpapers/myday/ accessed on October 13, 2017.

36 Goodwin, *No Ordinary Time*, 30.

37 Eleanor Roosevelt to Bernard Baruch, November 2, 1939, RIAS, *The Papers of Eleanor Roosevelt, 1933-1945*, Reel 00423.

38 Eleanor Roosevelt to Clarence Pickett, April 11, 1940, RIAS, *The Papers of Eleanor Roosevelt, 1933-1945*, Reel 1, 00467.

39 Telegram to Eleanor Roosevelt, October 21, 1942, RIAS, *The Papers of Eleanor Roosevelt, 1933-1945*, Reel 8, 00714; Eleanor Roosevelt to Adolph Berle, June 25, 1940, RIAS, *The Papers of Eleanor Roosevelt, 1933-1945*, Reel 1, 00758.

40 Berger, *A New Deal for the World*, 35.

41 Eleanor Roosevelt, *My Day*, April 18, 1941.

Further explaining her own ideas on postwar reconstruction, Eleanor Roosevelt said that the main objective of the western alliance was a humanitarian one. It had to "alleviate the pangs of hunger for many people throughout the world" and to "give children everywhere the most adequate diet that we possibly can." This meant, in her own words, that after the war the alliance had to foster "a basic change in the old type of economy where power was maintained in the hands of a comparatively small number of people who were influential in world finance and world business." The new global economy Eleanor Roosevelt was envisioning was inspired by liberal values and was based on "freedom for the people of the world as a whole."[42]

In order to substantiate this view on postwar reconstruction, in June 1944 she sponsored a national conference on "How Women May Share in Post-War Policy-Making," which was held at the White House. The participants unanimously acknowledged "her long-time, unflagging interest in the advancement of women," and asked her to encourage "the recent appointments of women as United States delegates to the Food Conference, the United Nations Relief and Rehabilitation Conference, the Conference of Allied Ministers of Education in London, and the International Labor Office Conference." Then, they compiled a roster of qualified women, whose main duty was to draft a plan for postwar cooperation and transnational exchanges, which included more than 200 names and which was presented by Eleanor Roosevelt herself to the president.[43]

The American first lady was calling for a new world order centered on people, on citizens' happiness, on their inalienable right to hope.[44] She deplored the rise of arrogance and egotism and proposed instead an "enlightened self-interest" through which people of the world could understand that wars were detrimental to the whole of civilization.[45] In her view, there would be no victory over Nazism and Fascism without removing the "armed camps" in people's minds – those cultural barriers that kept individuals from mutual understanding.[46] She believed that the establishment of a universal understanding would be a preliminary step and a "prelude to world peace."[47] Thus, drawing

42 Berger, *A New Deal for the World*, 37.

43 A Summary Statement of the Conference on "How Women May Share in Post-War Policy-Making," June 14, 1944, RIAS, *The Papers of Eleanor Roosevelt, 1933-1945*, Reel 20, 00339.

44 Leonard C. Schlup and Donald W. Whisenhunt, eds., *It Seems to Me: Selected Letters of Eleanor Roosevelt* (Lexington: The University Press of Kentucky, 2001), 2.

45 Eleanor Roosevelt, *My Day*, December 13, 1943.

46 Eleanor Roosevelt, "Must We Hate to Fight?" in *The Saturday Review*, July 4, 1942, quoted in Black, ed., *Courage in a Dangerous World*, 136.

47 Eleanor Roosevelt, *My Day*, November 18, 1940.

on the comments of a boy who was looking forward "to the time when the conflict will cease and the real problems of the world can be met by thought and brains," she remarked her confidence in American citizens, writing that her utmost hope was that they would keep themselves from hate, "and act with cool heads but warm hearts, both with our allies and with our enemies at the close of the war."[48] She was, in substance, fostering a broader concept of human welfare that she interpreted as the main springboard for the postwar world order. For this reason, she endorsed several practical proposals and the establishment of a number of international institutions that were meant to help common people, especially in Europe, to recover from the war, such as the idea to create a U.N. sub-commission on the status of women or an agency to defend war refugees' rights.[49]

Consequently, nothing worried her more than the apparently inescapable rise of international tensions that the world was witnessing in the immediate aftermath of the war. In her opinion, these tensions were reawakening some of the old fears that had hindered the progress of democracy in Europe: "In the Balkans, where races are mixed, it has been constantly possible for big powers to incite warfare to keep the people of those countries from developing economic and social security… The Greeks have looked with fear upon their neighbors… The Germans have feared the Russians. The Scandinavians have feared both the Germans and the Russians…"[50] The emergence of the Cold War confrontation was reproducing such schemes of intra-continental division, which she saw as detrimental to the development of a genuine and fruitful transatlantic exchange. And after Winston Churchill notoriously lectured in Missouri, she once again remarked the importance of multilateral cooperation to overcome these divisions and build a stable world order, by arguing that, "instead of running an armament race against each other, […] we the nations of the world should […] use the forum of the United Nations to discuss our difficulties and our grievances." At the same time, she also deprecated the increasing militarization of postwar U.S. foreign policy and disagreed with the building of an intrusive state that, in the name of national security, could eventually undermine American democracy.[51] She agreed with Woodrow Wilson's words

48 Eleanor Roosevelt, *My Day*, June 4, 1943.

49 See, for instance, Eleanor Roosevelt, *My Day*, June 1, 1946, November 11 and 25, 1946. On the Palestinian refugees, see Eleanor Roosevelt, *My Day*, June 14 and 22, 1946 and September 5, 1946.

50 Eleanor Roosevelt, *My Day*, August 10, 1946.

51 With regard to Eleanor Roosevelt's utterances against the building of a national security state and in defense of democracy, see Black, *Casting Her Own Shadow*, 131-170 and Black, ed., *Courage in a Dangerous World*, 221-309.

and ideas that the ultimate target for the U.S. had to be to make the world safe for democracy, but by democracy she primarily meant mutual understanding and safeguarding people's rights.[52]

From the mid-1940s onward, Eleanor Roosevelt progressively projected her own liberal ideas and humanitarianism abroad. Her views were deeply influenced by the many experiences she had gained throughout her public life. Her progressive and reformist drive had induced her to advance the cause of those who were in need of protection, not only at home but on a global scale. Her long-lasting activism, her continuous and simultaneous engagement in social and foreign policy, and her personal quest for rising civic awareness to strengthen democracy transformed her into one of the most prominent representatives and strenuous defenders of American liberalism in the postwar era.

Eleanor Roosevelt's liberalism, however, was fully embedded in her vision of a *global* Atlantic. She believed that the U.S. was destined to play a leading role in the international arena and, following in her uncle Theodore's footsteps, she saw this major involvement as a function of the civilizing mission that the U.S. had to carry out on a worldwide scale. Rather than putting it in racial terms, she preferred to read this mission as part of a global trend leaning toward the affirmation of democracy: a trend whose success went side by side with the strengthening of the transatlantic alliance. In doing so, she was contributing to the launch of the campaign for the defense of western democracy – or the western idea of democracy – that would characterize most of the second half of the twentieth century. She was fully aware that the affirmation of the U.S. as a world power depended on a renewed interaction with Europe. This entailed not only an absolute rejection of any possible isolationist stance, but also the reconfiguration of the transatlantic exchange, which according to Eleanor Roosevelt had to be based on mutual understanding, cooperation, and multilateral diplomacy. In sum, she was revamping a long-standing American impulse to reform the world by bringing common people's perspectives in and by presenting it in transatlantic terms.

The milestone in Eleanor Roosevelt's attempt to shape the world order according to these transatlantic canons was the drafting of the Universal Declaration of Human Rights in 1946-1948.[53] Chairing the committee which drafted

---

52 Elizabeth Borgwardt, *A New Deal for the World: America's Vision for Human Rights* (Cambridge: Harvard University Press, 2005).

53 Ian Tyrrel, *Transnational Nation: United States History in Global Perspective Since 1789* (New York: Palgrave Macmillan 2007) and Ian Tyrrel, *Reforming the World: The Creation of America's Moral Empire* (Princeton: Princeton University Press, 2010).

that document gave Eleanor Roosevelt the opportunity to supervise all of the debates over the philosophical definition of human rights and the duty to negotiate a common frame of reference as well. She was able to puzzle out the ideological wrangles over the legal status of the Declaration. She managed to persuade American and western delegates to include socioeconomic principles in the final document and, at the same time, she boldly rejected Soviet allegations of warmongering.[54] Then, she introduced to the world the results of these long negotiations through an inspiring speech that she delivered in French at the Sorbonne University. She addressed her audience at the peak of the Berlin blockade on September 28, 1948. In that speech, she summed up her visions of peace and transnational cooperation.[55]

According to Eleanor Roosevelt, preserving human freedom was the quintessential element of the San Francisco Charter. Such an emphasis was of utmost importance to France, where the ideal of human freedom had its roots, and in Europe, where that ideal had recently and grievously vanquished tyranny. She explained both the rationale behind the establishment of the UN – the need for world peace – and the general scope of that organization, which was designed to foster multilateral cooperation. But none of these goals could be fully satisfied or achieved, she said, without upholding the "universal respect for, and observance of, human rights and fundamental freedoms for all without distinction as to race, sex, language, or religion." To the "fundamental difference in the conception of human rights" existing between western powers and eastern countries, she countered with the univocal meaning of human freedom, as her husband had already defined it in 1941. On social rights issues, she stressed the importance of supporting free trade unions as well as the right to collective bargaining. Saying that the struggle for democracy and freedom was part of America's duty to preserve international peace and security, she once again reaffirmed her *exceptionalist* posture. But, at the same time, she defended the role of the UN, which had become the primary forum for states to "discuss the issue of human rights." She concluded her speech with an impressive definition of human rights, which were seen as "a fundamental object

54 A complex and detailed account of the Declaration and its enormous impact is given by Mary Ann Glendon, *A World Made New. Eleanor Roosevelt and the Universal Declaration of Human Rights* (New York: Random House, 2001).

55 Berger, *A New Deal for the World*, 67-72 and Tamara K. Hareven, *Eleanor Roosevelt. An American Conscience* (New York: Quadrangle Books, 1968), 235-242. See also Allida M. Black, ed., *The Eleanor Roosevelt Papers: The Human Rights Years, 1945-1948* (New York: Thomson Gale, 2007), 298.

of law and government in a just society," thus confirming a principle that is compelling to this day.[56]

Her insistence on framing the transatlantic alliance as part of a broader institutional framework set up through the UN was instrumental to reinforce – or justify – the existence of a western hemisphere, which in her opinion was both geo-politically and culturally homogenous. Her *atlanticism*, thus, went well beyond the mere support of the Marshall Plan and NATO. With regard to the former, she supported it principally because of its practical consequences and also because it did not contradict the principle of international cooperation.[57] With regard to the latter, her opinions were deeply affected by two events that occurred in 1949, the triumph of the socialist revolution in China and the first successful atomic test in the Soviet Union. She looked at the launch of NATO simply as a move that could protect the U.S.-European allies from Soviet threats. Since Russia had, "while professing a desire for peace, actually shown by its action that it intended to control as many nations as possible by imposing on them Communist ideas," Western European countries needed to be defended in certain ways. But it was clear to her that the scope of the Atlantic Pact was merely to "prevent aggression and to give democracies [...] a sense of security." She repeatedly stressed the defensive nature of the Atlantic alliance and she warned against the risk of instilling a sense of fear in both the Soviet elites and the Russian people.[58]

While rejecting the rise of international tensions between the two blocs, Eleanor Roosevelt remained deeply critical of containment, the domino theory, and atomic deterrence, and she defended on multiple occasions multilateral diplomacy, negotiations and the supremacy of human rights over national security and power politics. From this point of view, she was a pragmatic critic

56 See Mrs. Franklin D. Roosevelt, *The Struggle for Human Rights* (also known as, *The Struggle for the Rights of Man*), Paris, Sorbonne, 28 September 1948 (publication released February 1949), in Black, ed., *The Eleanor Roosevelt Papers: The Human Rights Years, 1945-1948*, 900.

57 Black, ed., *The Eleanor Roosevelt Papers: The Human Rights Years, 1945-1948*, 590.

58 My Day, April 9, 1949. As regards the Atlantic pact, Dean Acheson wanted Eleanor Roosevelt to know that he was working hard so that "its proposed terms [would] be known in time for public discussion before signature." Then, the under- secretary wrote the former first lady and said, "I am sure that when you see the actual terms you will feel much better about it. I will send you a copy as soon as it is released and would be delighted to discuss it with you at any time." See Dean Acheson's letter to Eleanor Roosevelt, March 15, 1949, and the rest of the correspondence in RIAS, *The Papers of Eleanor Roosevelt, 1945-1952, Part 2, General Correspondence 1948-1949*, Reel 12, 00223, 00493; Reel 14, 00965; Reel 18, 00433; Reel 20, 00669; and Reel 25, 00257.

of the Cold War standoff and consistently remained an internationalist, assigning the Atlantic world the global mission to lead the world morally and politically, and in cooperation and not necessarily in conflict with other nations and regions, including the Soviet Union. In her own way, Eleanor Roosevelt bridged interwar progressivism with post-war liberalism, thus paving the way for American policymakers, and above all U.S. presidents, to capitalize on FDR's transformative legacy. The ultimate result of this effort was the (re)invention of the Atlantic not only as a space of competition, hegemony, and dominance, but also – and primarily – as a space of freedom and equality.

CHAPTER 7

War Hero in the White House: Dwight Eisenhower and the Politics of Peace, Prosperity, and Party

Robert Mason

Dwight Eisenhower's career in politics burnished and deployed creatively the enormous popularity that he had gained during his pre-political career – most of all because of his role in leading Allied forces during World War II – and that has few parallels in American history.[1] Popularity was, according to biographer Geoffrey Perret, "Eisenhower's most important political advantage."[2] In some respects, Eisenhower's custody and exploitation of his popularity were a strikingly successful project. Not only did Eisenhower secure two strong victories in winning the White House, but also his approval ratings remained high through much of his time as president (subdued only a little during periods of economic downturn, notably connected with the recession of 1958) – at 65 percent, on average, during his eight years in office. Every year from 1951 to 1960 the Gallup polling organization reported that he was America's most admired man.[3]

To an impressive extent, this popularity, grounded in a pre-presidential career that was nonpartisan and, at first sight, apolitical, survived the challenging transition to a political context that involved bitter contestation not only between the parties but also between Republican factions. More than that, even, studies suggested that positive personal evaluations were yet more extensive among Americans in 1956, at the time of Eisenhower's quest for reelection, than in 1952 – enough to suggest to analysts of public opinion that his reelection success relied more heavily on his personal qualities than on

1 Herbert H. Hyman and Paul B. Sheatsley, "The Political Appeal of President Eisenhower," *Public Opinion Quarterly* 17, no. 4 (1953-1954): 443-460.

2 Geoffrey Perret, *Eisenhower* (New York: Random House, 1999), 491.

3 William I. Hitchcock, *The Age of Eisenhower: America and the World in the 1950s* (New York: Simon & Schuster, 2018), 244. It was as a result of the 1958 recession that Eisenhower's Gallup approval rating dipped below 50 percent for the first time. Jim Newton, *Eisenhower: The White House Years* (New York: Doubleday, 2011), 1. The numbers also reached a record high of 79 percent in the aftermath of the Geneva summit of 1955. Jean Edward Smith, *Eisenhower in War and Peace* (New York: Random House, 2012), 670.

© KONINKLIJKE BRILL NV, LEIDEN, 2020 | DOI:10.1163/9789004422643_009

his presidential achievements.[4] Labeling his success in maintaining popularity the "Eisenhower phenomenon," political scientist John Mueller observes that should a president wish to leave office with buoyant public support, "he should either (1) be Dwight Eisenhower, or (2) resign the day after inauguration."[5] Despite this success, a more ambitious project that Eisenhower pursued experienced failure instead; endeavoring to use his popularity to refashion the GOP (Grand Old Party) in a more moderate form, thus boosting support for the party that had languished in minority status since the time of the New Deal, the project merely boosted the fortunes and prospects of his more conservative rivals.

Until he agreed to enter the race for the 1952 Republican presidential nomination, Dwight Eisenhower's career was entirely outside party politics, and mostly in the army. His family background was poor and in small-town America; born in Denison, Texas, Eisenhower grew up in Abilene, Kansas. Graduating from the U.S. Military Academy of West Point, in 1915, he nevertheless missed frontline duty in World War I. In the army Eisenhower served under a series of successful generals, though his career moved slowly and he remained a major for sixteen years. It would be during World War II that he achieved rapid advancement, and soon fame and eminence, as supreme allied commander in Europe – the significance of which was confirmed by the crowds that greeted him in New York on his return to the United States in 1945, estimated at 4 million to 5 million, the largest in the city's history.[6] At the end of the war in Europe, he served first as military governor of the U.S. Occupation Zone in Germany, before returning to Washington as Chief of Staff of the Army. In 1948, he became president of Columbia University, but in 1951 he went to the North Atlantic Treaty Organization (NATO) as its first Supreme Allied Commander Europe. "Even in a nation which has brought to the surface candidates from such disparate backgrounds as Jackson, Lincoln, Wilson and Willkie," the *New York Times* noted after his presidential nomination, "the rise of General Eisenhower was amazing."[7] With roots in middle America, Eisenhower was everyman escalated to heroic status.

---

4 Angus Campbell, Philip E. Converse, Warren E. Miller, and Donald E. Stokes, *The American Voter* (New York: Wiley, 1960), 56.

5 John Mueller, *War, Presidents, and Public Opinion* (New York: Wiley, 1978), 233.

6 Smith, *Eisenhower*, 446-447. Herbert Parmet writes that when Eisenhower went to Washington at the start of 1953, the crowds there were "the largest for any Inaugural in history." Herbert S. Parmet, *Eisenhower and the American Crusades* (New York: Macmillan, 1972), 163.

7 "It's Eisenhower," *New York Times* [hereafter *NYT*], July 13, 1952, E1.

Though nonpartisan and ostensibly apolitical, Eisenhower's military career proved to be a fertile environment for the development of political skills, on which his success in the armed forces was grounded, and which informed his conduct of the presidency. "There's no more active political organization in the world than the armed services of the United States," Eisenhower said in 1962. "As a matter of fact, I think I am a better politician than most so-called politicians."[8] Of his success within these hierarchical structures, Alan Brinkley writes:

> … Eisenhower won attention and respect not because he was particularly brilliant or charismatic but because he had great political gifts. He was adept at flattering without fawning, skilled at persuading without antagonizing. He was unfailingly discreet. He got along with everyone. Virtually no one disliked him.[9]

If his pre-presidential career won Eisenhower fame, then, it also did much to form him as a politician.

For political associates close to Eisenhower, his status as hero in the war that remained a key life experience for millions of Americans (and in which many had served) was the leading reason for his power as a political personality. Speaking of the 1952 campaign, Len Hall, who would serve as chair of the Republican National Committee (RNC) during the Eisenhower years, noted that when "the great hero" made an appearance, "people didn't just applaud … . When they applauded, they jumped up and down. I mean really, this was something different."[10] Herbert Brownell, a former RNC chair who would act as attorney general under Eisenhower, was similarly impressed by his political power. Brownell later described him as "the most highly regarded man in the world":[11]

> Oh, it was an absolutely magnetic personality so far as crowds were concerned. And they didn't care too much, you know, what he said or how

8 Steve Neal, *Harry and Ike: The Partnership That Remade the Postwar World* (New York: Scribner, 1991), 31.

9 Alan Brinkley, "A President for Certain Seasons," *Wilson Quarterly* 14, no. 2 (Spring 1990): 111.

10 Oral history interview with Leonard W. Hall by David Horrocks, May 19, 1975, Dwight D. Eisenhower Library, Abilene, Kansas [hereafter DDEL] (online at https://www.eisenhower.archives.gov/research/oral_histories/oral_history_transcripts/Hall_Leonard_478.pdf, accessed November 14, 2017), 12.

11 Newton, *Eisenhower*, 51.

> he said it. But he was a national hero of the first magnitude so that he had a ready audience. I think it was just an emotion, really an emotional sweep across the country that they were so glad to have a man of his background and caliber as a candidate that they accepted him.[12]

Although it was clear that the wartime service of this general-turned-politician definitively informed his popularity, more profoundly the reasons for Eisenhower's power as a political personality puzzled many contemporaries.[13] Moreover, this background was not straightforwardly an advantage for Eisenhower in a political culture that did not welcome military encroachment in civilian matters; in 1952, polls suggested that Eisenhower's identity as a "military man" was his greatest negative, mentioned as problematic by two in five of those who voted for his Democratic rival Adlai Stevenson, and even by almost one in five of his own voters, far outweighing unfavorable references to his lack of experience in government or politics.[14] "The popularity of President Eisenhower has got beyond the bounds of reasonable calculation and will have to be put down as a national phenomenon, like baseball," wrote James Reston of the *New York Times*, one of the era's foremost observers of Washington, in 1955. "The thing is no longer just a remarkable political fact but a kind of national love affair, which cannot be analyzed satisfactorily by the political scientists and will probably have to be turned over to the head-shrinkers."[15] In person – as the comments of Hall and Brownell suggest – Eisenhower's charisma was yet more striking. The crowd's enthusiasm for the president at a 1956 appearance impressed a foreign journalist so much that he remarked, "I haven't seen anything like this since Hitler."[16]

Certainly the fit between the politician and the political moment was strong; the new demands of the Cold War and the enlarged role in global affairs that accompanied its arrival aligned well with Eisenhower's biography in restoring and then keeping the peace, all the more so because Eisenhower sounded concerns about the need to avoid any "garrison state" in which Cold

---

12 Oral history interview with Herbert Brownell by Thomas Soapes, February 24, 1977, DDEL (online at https://www.eisenhower.archives.gov/research/oral_histories/oral_history_transcripts/Brownell_Herbert_EL.pdf, accessed November 14, 2017), 4.

13 Kenneth E. Morris and Barry Schwartz, "Why They Liked Ike: Tradition, Crisis, and Heroic Leadership," *Sociological Quarterly* 43, no. 1 (1993): 134-136.

14 Angus Campbell, Gerald Gurin, and Warren Miller, *The Voter Decides* (Evanston, Ill.: Row, Peterson, [1954]), 60-62.

15 James Reston, "Not a Political Movement but a Love Affair," *NYT*, September 11, 1955, E8.

16 Katie Louchheim, diary entry, July 17, 1956, folder "Journals Vol. 5 May–Dec. 1956," box 77, Katie Louchheim Papers, Manuscript Division, Library of Congress, Washington, D.C.

War preparedness absorbed too much money and wielded too much political influence.[17] In 1952, Eisenhower's promise to "go to Korea" in search of a solution to conflict there harnessed this advantageous political identity (a position that had appeal, somewhat paradoxically, to voters both who favored complete withdrawal and who supported escalation of the conflict), and the 1956 presidential election took place within a scarcely less turbulent international context (the Suez crisis, the Soviet invasion of Hungary), but more broadly the early Cold War ensured that the political salience of foreign policy remained high. As election day approached in 1956, polling for the Eisenhower campaign suggested that "the President's great strength was in his handling of foreign affairs" (and "[no] more than a slight knowledge of what the Administration had accomplished in four years on domestic problems").[18] In the words of Washington journalist Arthur Krock, for the public Eisenhower remained "the muscular guardian of peace."[19]

Eisenhower's military background – as a man of peace – aligned productively with his agenda for domestic as well as foreign policy. His administration sought domestic tranquility after the political turbulence of the New Deal and then the Fair Deal; Eisenhower saw the interest-group pluralism that harnessed the electoral strength of the Democratic Party coalition as hostile to the larger national interest, instead pursuing a vision that historian Robert Griffith labels "the corporate commonwealth."[20] In one of his first addresses on politics, delivered to the American Bar Association in September 1949, Eisenhower criticized in particular the state of capital-labor relations; a view of employers' and employees' interests as mutually exclusive was, according to Eisenhower, "distorted doctrine [that] is false and foreign to the American scene where common ideals and purpose permit us a common approach toward the common good." The direction for the United States to take, he said, was "down the middle of the road between the unfettered power of concentrated wealth

17 On the basis of their analysis of polling data, political scientists Angus Campbell, Gerald Gurin, and Warren E. Miller concluded, "Eisenhower, because of his background and experience, seems to have been perceived as a person peculiarly able to cope with the nation's international problems." Campbell *et al.*, *Voter Decides*, 58.

18 Morris Janowitz and Dwaine Marvick, *Competitive Pressure and Democratic Consent: An Interpretation of the 1952 Presidential Election*, 2nd edition (Chicago: Quadrangle, 1964), 47-48; memo, J.E. Bachelder and Gerard B. Lambert to Sherman Adams, October 29, 1956, folder "OF 138–C–4 (8)," box 712, Official File, Dwight D. Eisenhower Records as President (White House Central Files), DDEL.

19 Arthur Krock, "Eisenhower Triumphs on His Popular Image," *NYT*, November 11, 1956, 213.

20 Robert Griffith, "Dwight D. Eisenhower and the Corporate Commonwealth," *American Historical Review* 87, no. 1 (1982): 87-122.

on one flank, and the unbridled power of statism or partisan interests on the other."[21] When he won the White House, the quest for a "middle way" informed much of his domestic agenda, also tagged "modern Republicanism."[22]

But if the skills of a war hero and peacemaker seemed to address the nation's needs quite acutely during the 1950s, Eisenhower's other characteristics seemed no less important in helping to account for his appeal – often described as those of a "father figure."[23] In 1952 Harold Stassen, a former governor of Minnesota who would join the Eisenhower administration, noted that those personal strengths included "warmth of personality ... thoughtfulness of others [and] genuineness." Eisenhower was, furthermore, "one of the people" with a "humble beginning," as well as a "real man," according to Stassen.[24] James Reston saw Eisenhower as "a symbol of the atmosphere of the time: optimistic, prosperous, escapist, pragmatic, friendly, attentive in moments of crisis and comparatively inattentive the rest of the time."[25] Sidney Hyman, a political historian of the era, viewed Eisenhower as a father figure for the nation, or more precisely "a father-protector, the ultimate source of clemency and discipline" – offering reassurance in troubled times.[26] For Hyman, Eisenhower's emergence to eminence had peculiar characteristics, thus crafting the distinctiveness of his popularity. "Mr. Eisenhower was one of the very few men who came to the Presidency with his place in universal history already won. ... He was formed all of a sudden on Europe's field of battle – a victorious Supreme Commander sent by heaven to be the savior of nations," observed Hyman. "Here, if anywhere else in modern times, was a piece of Greek mythology come to life, this birth of a fully shaped hero."[27] Yet if Eisenhower's pre-political background equipped him with the highly unusual status of "an officer rocketed into world fame," in the words of contemporary political scientists Charles Thomson and

21 "Text of General Eisenhower's Address before Bar Association," *NYT*, September 6, 1949, 17.

22 For William Hitchcock, the idea of a 'middle way' creates a more profound connection between political image and political agenda, "for the key to Eisenhower's success lay in his ability to balance, in his own person and in his policies, the contradictions in American society," he writes. "People liked him because he seemed to embody so many virtues that they admired – even when these virtues were in tension with one another." Hitchcock, *Age of Eisenhower*, 245.

23 Tom Wicker, *Dwight D. Eisenhower* (New York: Times Books, 2002), 2.

24 Harold E. Stassen, memo, August 19, 1952, folder 28, box 120, series 6, Thomas E. Dewey Papers, University of Rochester Library, Rochester, New York.

25 Reston, "Not a Political Movement."

26 Sidney Hyman, "Absorbing Study of Popularity," *NYT* magazine, July 24, 1960, 24.

27 Hyman, "Absorbing Study," 7, 24.

Frances Shattuck, he also became a president whom "many people found ... somewhat less rigidly military than they had thought a Supreme Commander would be – a figure above the turmoil of politics and partisan qualities, who in his public distaste for sharp controversy and in his hate for petty misdoing fitted well the image of the benign yet judging father."[28]

It was not just his status as war hero, then, that Eisenhower's military background gave him as a political asset. His image would remain that of a non-political politician – a president above politics. Asked in 1954 by journalist Merriman Smith whether he saw himself as a politician, Eisenhower said that he did not, "[b]ecause I really think a man can be classed as a politician only after he has spent life in a political arena. But I can say, and I think without egotism, in many, many ways I will make smarter political decisions than a lot of guys who are pros – because they have gotten too used to the narrow quick advantage, rather than taking a look at the longer range."[29]

Still, his pre-presidential years were enmeshed in politics, if nonpartisan in nature; his lengthy career in the army had equipped him with political savvy long before he started work in Washington as Chief of Staff of the Army during the Truman administration. It was a strength that many contemporaries did not notice, encouraging them to interpret Eisenhower in the White House as inactive and disengaged. In his classic book about the modern presidency, *Presidential Power*, published in 1960, political scientist Richard Neustadt saw Eisenhower as falling short in exercising the "power to persuade" – in harnessing public prestige to demand action in Washington.[30] Yet historical analysis has evaluated Eisenhower much more positively than contemporary scholarship did, often finding him successful in exercising what political scientist Fred Greenstein calls "hidden-hand leadership" – orchestrating action by others in pursuit of a goal, while concealing his own role.[31]

The organizational skills that Greenstein explored rested on lessons learned in negotiating the complex bureaucracies of the army. Eisenhower's pre-presidential career also encouraged him to develop an administrative approach that involved extensive delegation and an elaborate and expanded

---

28 Charles A.H. Thomson and Frances M. Shattuck, *The 1956 Presidential Campaign* (Washington, D.C.: Brookings Institution, 1960), 1.

29 "Conversation with Merriman Smith 11/23/54," folder "ACW Diary November 1954 (2)," box 3, Ann Whitman Diary Series, Papers of Dwight D. Eisenhower as President of the United States (Ann Whitman File), DDEL [hereafter AWF].

30 Richard E. Neustadt, *Presidential Power and the Modern Presidents: The Politics of Leadership from Roosevelt to Reagan* (New York: Free Press, 1990).

31 Fred I. Greenstein, *The Hidden-Hand Presidency: Eisenhower as Leader* (New York: Basic Books, 1982).

staffing system to work on policy and to provide advice. Andrew Goodpaster, who was a White House staff secretary after working for Eisenhower at NATO, later observed, "Eisenhower, of course, was accustomed to a well organized headquarters" with a bureaucratized, careful handling of decisions and actions; he discovered that the White House lacked such order, a discovery that precipitated a series of changes to formalize these processes.[32] For speechwriter Emmet John Hughes, some of the ways that Eisenhower's military background influenced his presidential style were disadvantageous. "Nowhere did the lack of civil experience so betray itself," he wrote, "as in this system's cheerful assumption that, once the Chief Executive had pointed in a certain political direction, the full force of government would move in that direction, in concert as precise and as massive as battalions and divisions wheeling through field maneuvers."[33] But if Eisenhower's focus on systematized delegation and decision-making processes facilitated criticisms of an above-the-fray style, the result has more commonly garnered positive evaluations as successfully influential. "Eisenhower," writes political scientist John Sloan, "was a unique charismatic leader in that he was deeply concerned with organizational problems."[34] In doing so, he created a model that influenced later presidents, becoming – in the words of R. Gordon Hoxie – "the principal architect of the institutional Presidency."[35]

Eisenhower's use of the "hidden hand" also revealed an awareness of the value that the above-politics image offered, and more broadly his maintenance of the popularity that his pre-presidential career had created partly rested on an acute awareness of image management. Eisenhower would be the last president born in the nineteenth century, but he avidly and successfully embraced techniques of modern political communication, especially involving the new medium of television.[36] For example, the pioneering television ads screened by the 1952 Eisenhower campaign not only deployed the candidate's positive image as war hero, but also humanized it, so that, in the words of political scientist Robert Gilbert, "General Eisenhower's physical appearance, personal

32 Kenneth W. Thompson, ed., *The Eisenhower Presidency: Eleven Intimate Perspectives of Dwight D. Eisenhower* (Lanham, Md.: University Press of America, 1984), 65.

33 Emmet John Hughes, *The Ordeal of Power: A Political Memoir of the Eisenhower Years* (New York: Atheneum, 1963), 153.

34 John W. Sloan, "The Management and Decision-Making Style of President Eisenhower," *Presidential Studies Quarterly* 20, no. 2 (1990): 295-313 (quotation, 305).

35 Sloan, "Management and Decision-Making Style," 309.

36 Craig Allen, *Eisenhower and the Mass Media: Peace, Prosperity, and Prime-time TV* (Chapel Hill: University of North Carolina Press, 1993); David Haven Blake, *Liking Ike: Eisenhower, Advertising, and the Rise of Celebrity Politics* (New York: Oxford University Press, 2016).

mannerism, and personality were such as to project him on the TV screens as a grandfather figure, a healer, a thoughtful and wise leader who would provide the nation with steady guidance throughout the years of his presidency."[37] The pro-Eisenhower argument could thus rest on a simple slogan: "I Like Ike."

Enthusiasm for Eisenhower as a politician had surfaced soon after World War II, turning to serious contemplation of the war hero as a presidential candidate in 1948. Bipartisan in nature (one measure of the breadth of Eisenhower's popularity), this speculation was initially stronger on the Democratic side; Eisenhower's background and reputation inspired confidence in his presidential promise even when little was known of his political views. When Eisenhower acknowledged his Republican affiliation and entered party politics in advance of the 1952 presidential election, his candidacy kindled a personal movement of remarkable reach and longevity. Citizens for Eisenhower, which first mobilized support in the quest for the Republican nomination before acting as a candidate-centered organization reaching out particularly for non-Republican loyalists in the fall contest against Stevenson, claimed a membership of some two million Americans at its height in 1952. Surviving well beyond Eisenhower's "crusade" of 1952, the Citizens movement was resuscitated not only in 1956, but also during the congressional contests of 1954 and 1958. There were even abortive efforts to revive Citizens after 1960, as a way to prolong support of Eisenhower Republicanism.[38]

Eisenhower and his supporters saw the Citizens movement as an opportunity to deploy his personal popularity to boost the success of the Republican Party. The spectacular nature of Eisenhower enthusiasm was in deep contrast with the public standing of the party at large. Relegated to minority status during the Great Depression and the New Deal – when the Democratic Party's commitment to programmatic innovation in answer to the nation's socioeconomic challenges unlocked the support of an electoral majority – the Republicans still languished under an unfavorable image as the party of an elite, aloof from the problems of ordinary Americans. Seeing this disparity between the parties as unhealthy for democracy, as well as believing that the Democrats' "big government" agenda was damaging, Eisenhower – enjoying an image profoundly superior to that of his party – pursued a serious project to boost GOP fortunes. His engagement achieved such a level of seriousness even though partisan activity was, of course, entirely absent from his life as a soldier.

---

37 Robert E. Gilbert, "The Eisenhower Campaign of 1952: War Hero as Television Candidate," *Political Communication* 3, no. 3 (1986): 305-306.

38 Robert Mason, "Citizens for Eisenhower and the Republican party, 1951-1965," *Historical Journal* 56, no. 2 (2013): 513-536.

This was a project with two complementary facets; the first was ideological, involving a quest for the modern Republicanism of middle-way politics, which moderated the party's conservatism, and the second was organizational, involving an effort to recruit Citizens members to the Republican Party. It was assumed that a fusion between Citizens, seen as dedicated to the Eisenhower agenda, and the party would promote modern Republicanism, as well as equipping the party with an ample supply of grassroots activists to mobilize the vote. That agenda, as well as Eisenhower himself, seemed to possess such electoral promise. According to a 1957 Gallup poll of Republican voters, offered a choice between Eisenhower Republicanism and conservative Republicanism, nearly three quarters preferred the former and less than one fifth indicated a preference for the latter.[39]

As Citizens leader Peter Clayton put it, when planning for the campaigns of 1956, this project sought "to translate the enthusiasm which the Eisenhower name has created into a bigger, richer, Republican Party with a Republican president and a Republican Congress in office *long after Eisenhower leaves office*."[40] For Eisenhower's confidants and aides, the project's personalized dimension seemed important. Henry Cabot Lodge, who provided political advice to Eisenhower while acting as U.S. ambassador to the United Nations, told the president, after the 1956 elections, that the party "should as speedily as possible make itself over into your image" in order to "become the majority party in America."[41] Also in the aftermath of the 1956 elections, which offered a strong victory for Eisenhower but setbacks for many other Republican candidates, Walter Williams of Citizens underlined the imperative "to sell better than ever before the idea of tying the 'image of Eisenhower' to the Republican Party so that the public generally will come to accept the term, "Modern Republicanism," as being synonymous with the Party built in the 'image of Eisenhower.'"[42] Paul Hoffman, too, another Citizens leader, emphasized "the image of Eisenhower" as the essential characteristic for a revitalized party.[43]

---

39 Note of Gallup poll, March 24, 1957, folder "Republican Leaders, 1958," box 7, subseries 2, series 5, Jacob K. Javits Collection, Stony Brook University Libraries, Stony Brook, New York.

40 Letter, Peter Clayton to Frank [?], June 2, 1955, folder "Citizens for Eisenhower," box 32, Thomas E. Stephens Records, DDEL.

41 Memo, Henry Cabot Lodge to Dwight D. Eisenhower, November 7, 1956, folder "Lodge, Henry Cabot 1956 (1)," box 24, Administration Series, AWF.

42 Letter, Walter Williams to Dwight D. Eisenhower, November 14, 1956, folder "138-C Republican Party (3)," box 708, Official File.

43 Telegram, Dwight D. Eisenhower to Paul Hoffman, January 6, 1953, folder "Hoffman, Paul (5)," box 19, Administration Series, AWF.

Such image-rooted insights informed the campaigning of Citizens. For example, in 1956 its television ads rejected references to the party – much less popular than the president, of course – in favor of fostering "an emotional preference for Eisenhower and his principles, for Eisenhower the great leader, the great human being."[44] In 1954 and 1958, Citizens overcame the absence of Eisenhower from the ballots with the message that its goal was the election of Republican congressional candidates "who, of their own attributes, can be effectively and popularly associated with President Eisenhower's personal popularity and his dynamic and progressive program" (though Democratic politicians sometimes insisted that they offered better support to the administration's agenda than many congressional Republicans did).[45]

The Eisenhower image was powerful enough to buoy the president's popularity throughout his turbulent years in office, but it fell short in supporting his goal to boost the success of the Republican Party at large. Even as late as November 1958, following disappointing midterm results, Eisenhower told House Minority Leader Joseph W. Martin, Jr. of Massachusetts "that the need in the next two years is to bring the public, which still 'likes Ike,' to a full appreciation of the necessity for transferring this liking to the Republican party as an institution."[46]

Nevertheless, the results of these efforts were disappointing enough to cause Walter N. Thayer, a Citizens leader, to conclude in 1960 that "the Republican Party, for whatever reason, during the past eight years has not found the way to avail itself of the energy and enthusiasm these people have to offer."[47] Similarly, in early 1964, Eisenhower observed that the party "has been slow – and possibly too complacent – to recognize the value of and the need

---

44 Young & Rubicam, Inc., "Network Television for National Citizens for Eisenhower-Nixon: Proposed Policies and Budget," September 10, 1956, folder "Citizens for Eisenhower-Nixon (1)," box 10, Stephens Records.

45 "National Citizens for Eisenhower Congressional Committee: Statement of Policy and Objectives," September 27, 1954, folder "Political Files National Citizens for Eisenhower Congressional Committee Final Report, Part II, 1954," box 5, Political File, Thayer Papers; "The sober fact, of course, is that when the President denounces the Democrats as enemies of his program," said Adlai Stevenson in October 1954, "he must know that on many key measures – foreign trade, housing, health, the conduct of foreign relations – the Democrats were far better supporters than the Republicans." Gladwin Hill, "Stevenson Says G.O.P. Misrepresents Its 2-Year Record," *NYT*, October 10, 1954, 1, 44.

46 Bryce Harlow, memo for the record, November 19, 1959, folder "Staff Notes Nov. 1958," box 37, DDE Diary Series, AWF.

47 Letter, Walter N. Thayer to Richard Nixon, December 5, 1960, folder "Political Files Nixon, Richard M. 1955-64," box 7, Political File, Walter N. Thayer, III Papers, Herbert Hoover Presidential Library, West Branch, Iowa.

for adopting a doctrine of the center." He added that the failure to mobilize enough Republicans in support of his moderate vision was "[o]ne of the great disappointments of my eight years following 1953."[48] Polls suggested that in 1960 no more than three in ten Americans identified themselves as Republicans – unquestionably the Republican Party continued to languish in minority status.[49] The pursuit of the Eisenhower agenda did have some positive implications for the popular image of the Republican Party. No longer was the GOP seen as a threat to the achievements of the New Deal, a damaging association that had helped to explain the party's minority status. But the change in image was incomplete. Most Americans still saw Republicans as representing the party of socioeconomic privilege, whereas the Democrats were the party of the people.[50]

Regardless of the strengths and weaknesses of Eisenhower's quest for a middle way, and the accompanying effort to moderate the Republican Party, the project demonstrated how, from the start, this war hero with a nonpartisan and even apolitical image was, in one respect, a deeply and divisively partisan figure. In the battle for the presidential nomination of 1952, he was the candidate of the party's moderate wing, challenging the more conservative wing and its favored candidate, Senator Robert A. Taft of Ohio. Taft supporters seemed immune from the overwhelming enthusiasm that Eisenhower inspired as a leader, because of his connections with the Republican faction that they opposed. Harrison Spangler, an Iowa Republican who had acted as chair of the Republican National Committee between 1942 and 1944, argued to congressional Republicans that Eisenhower's background as a soldier left him ill-equipped to enter politics. "In these perilous times, we are confronted by aggression from abroad and immorality and fiscal collapse at home," he wrote to them. "To combat the forces which have brought us to this plight, our Party is called to rise above moves which many people at least will believe are dictated by mere political expediency and opportunism. Surely the Republican Party has among its leaders a statesman who has the qualifications and character which are demanded."[51]

48 Letter, Dwight D. Eisenhower to Walter N. Thayer, January 23, 1964, folder "Eisenhower, Dwight D. 1964," box 2, Political File, Thayer Papers.

49 Warren E. Miller and Santa A. Traugott, *American National Election Studies Data Sourcebook, 1952-1986* (Cambridge, Mass.: Harvard University Press, 1989), 81.

50 Campbell *et al.*, *American Voter*, 47.

51 Letter, Harrison E. Spangler to Thomas E. Martin, August 9, 1951, folder "Pre GOP Convention, Election, 1952 August, 1951," box 2, Vincent Starzinger Papers, Herbert Hoover Presidential Library, West Branch, Iowa.

This factional conflict had characterized the party's response to its descent to minority status during the Depression years; party moderates advocated what their critics derisively labeled a "me-too" strategy that stressed agreement with New Deal liberalism's goals (if differences with its methods and achievements), whereas party conservatives more fundamentally stressed disagreement with its acceptance of "big government." When in 1948 Thomas E. Dewey experienced a second defeat for the presidency, conservatives insisted Dewey's failure provided proof of the moderates' lack of electoral promise, arguing that their party should underscore difference with the Democrats in order to achieve progress at the polls.[52] Eisenhower's candidacy in 1952 restored momentum to the moderate side, denying Taft the Republican nomination for the presidency, which it is otherwise highly likely that he would have achieved. Despite the war hero's national popularity, indeed, the Eisenhower-Taft contest was finely balanced. It was resolved only at the party's national convention, because of the Eisenhower team's success in securing interpretations of party rules that favored the acceptance of their supporters, rather than Taft's, as convention delegates. This success – of party rules rather than of popular appeal – definitively gave the majority to Eisenhower.

Although Eisenhower's turn to party politics had a strongly factional dimension, its motivation connected with his biography of military service – and not only because, as Fred Greenstein notes, "he could afford to conceive of his presidency as a response to duty rather than an appeal to fame: his presidency was a postlude."[53] It was because Taft, anchored in a foreign policy tradition of non-interventionism, was skeptical of the emerging Cold War emphasis on networks of mutual security as the guarantor of global peace that Eisenhower had decided to acquiesce to those moderate Republicans who had been pushing him to run.[54] When Herbert Brownell visited Eisenhower at NATO's Paris headquarters to discuss his potential candidacy, Eisenhower stressed as crucial

52 See, for example, transcript of Republican National Committee meeting, January 26, 1949, folder "Transcript of Luncheon Session of Republican National Committee, Omaha, Nebraska," box 6, Hugh Scott Papers, Albert and Shirley Small Special Collections Library, University of Virginia, Charlottesville, Virginia; minutes, Republican Strategy Committee, December 13, 1949, in Paul L. Kesaris, ed., *Papers of the Republican Party*, part I: *Meetings of the Republican National Committee, 1911-1980* (Frederick, Md.: University Publications of America, 1986), series A, reel 9; transcript, RNC Policy Committee, January 18, 1949, in Kesaris, ed., *Papers of the Republican Party*, part I, series A, reel 9.

53 Fred I. Greenstein, "The Hidden-Hand Presidency: Eisenhower as Leader: A 1994 Perspective," *Presidential Studies Quarterly* 24, no. 2 (1994): 239.

54 William B. Pickett, *Eisenhower Decides to Run: Presidential Politics and Cold War Strategy* (Chicago: Ivan R. Dee, 2000).

his disagreement with Taft over the closeness of relations with Western European allies and over an internationalist approach to free trade – all central to the Cold War project of which he had been part. "It was only because of his interest in seeing the country turn its eyes outward and away from isolationism that caused him to seek the presidency," Brownell said later, "and he made that very clear."[55]

When Eisenhower entered the White House and Taft became majority leader of the Senate, the two found much more common ground on domestic matters between them than the bitter Republican contest of 1952 had suggested. Yet Eisenhower continued to see middle-way politics as responsive to an electoral imperative and the transformation of the Republican Party as important. "This party of ours has got to realize that they won't exist unless they become a party of progressive moderates," he commented to press secretary James Hagerty in late 1954. "If the right wants a fight, they're going to get it."[56]

Eisenhower consolidated the success against non-interventionism that he achieved in thwarting Taft's presidential bid by challenging more broadly this rebuke to bipartisan commitment to containment in the Cold War. Most notably, though not without difficulty, Eisenhower defeated the Bricker Amendment (the significance of which to conservative Republicans was symbolized through its introduction, by its sponsor John W. Bricker of Ohio, as Senate Resolution 1 in January 1953), designed to limit executive power in foreign policy. This was part of a larger process that helped Eisenhower to push congressional Republicans away from non-interventionism and toward internationalism.[57] Not without difficulty, too, Eisenhower saw the downfall by late 1954 of the anticommunist crusade that Wisconsin Senator Joseph R. McCarthy irresponsibly led against domestic subversion – making noise but failing to find real subversives.[58]

Eisenhower thus experienced some success in reforming the conservative approach to the Cold War – sometimes through what biographer Louis

55 Thompson, *Eisenhower Presidency*, 165.

56 Michael J. Birkner, "What Was Modern Republicanism?" *Register of the Kentucky Historical Society* 105, no. 3 (2007): 467.

57 Duane Tananbaum, *The Bricker Amendment Controversy: A Test of Eisenhower's Political Leadership* (Ithaca: Cornell University Press, 1988); Gary W. Reichard, *The Reaffirmation of Republicanism: Eisenhower and the Eighty-third Congress* (Knoxville: University of Tennessee Press, 1975).

58 David A. Nichols, *Ike and McCarthy: Eisenhower's Secret Campaign Against Joseph McCarthy* (New York: Simon & Schuster, 2017); Greenstein, *Hidden-Hand Presidency*, 187-201.

Galambos calls "Machiavellian moments," the art of which he had learned in the army.[59] Nevertheless, even though the skills of leadership, management, and organization that Eisenhower had developed in the army assisted him in many of the presidency's duties, this was not true for his larger role as party leader, in pursuing a vision for party revitalization. On the one hand, the looseness of GOP structures defied his military-informed approach to leadership; on the other, Eisenhower and his supporters were not able to deploy the strength of his own popularity in service of the party's transformation.[60] In remarks after the 1956 elections, when the president easily defeated Adlai Stevenson but Democrats retained control of Congress, Eisenhower tried to define his victory as an endorsement for modern Republicanism.[61] But many of those who had supported Taft viewed the pursuit of modern Republicanism with disappointment and even alarm. As Eisenhower put it in the spring of 1957, "he was forced down the throats of a lot of people in '52," according to the notes of a meeting in preparation for a press conference. "Some will never forget it. ... There is so much resentment, and those people will never give up."[62]

Just as conservative Republicans were largely aloof from Eisenhower enthusiasm in 1952, they remained skeptical of Eisenhower's middle-way project. Not only did Eisenhower fail to mobilize the more conservative members of his party in support of this "modernization," but his initiatives encouraged the development of a new conservatism which would prove more successful in securing intra-party support. A survey by the Republican National Committee of party leaders in the Midwest, for example, found that they identified Eisenhower personally as a key strength of the party, but many criticized his ideas. "Ike is strong on foreign relations," one respondent argued, "but weak on some domestic issues: (1) Compromising with socialistic matters; (2) Taking bad advice on domestic matters; (3) Could cut some spending." Another respondent viewed Eisenhower's leadership of the party rather more negatively:

---

59 Louis Galambos, *Eisenhower: Becoming the Leader of the Free World* (Baltimore: Johns Hopkins University Press, 2018), ix.

60 Irwin F. Gellman, *The President and the Apprentice: Eisenhower and Nixon, 1952-1961* (New Haven: Yale University Press, 2015), 232-233, 564.

61 Dwight D. Eisenhower, remarks, November 7, 1956, American Presidency Project, online at https://www.presidency.ucsb.edu/documents/radio-and-television-remarks-following-the-election-victory, accessed April 19, 2019; Craig Allen, "Eisenhower's Congressional Defeat of 1956: Limitations of Television and the GOP," *Presidential Studies Quarterly* 22 (1992): 57-71.

62 Notes of pre-press conference briefing, May 15, 1957, folder "May '57 Miscellaneous (2)," box 24, DDE Diary Series, AWF.

"We have no Republican Party as we knew it in the past. We have changed the label, yes, but the bottle is the same New[/]Fair Deal contents."[63]

Frustration with the Eisenhower record fueled the revitalization both of intellectual conservatism and of conservative Republicanism, both of which would achieve political influence over the coming decades. Emblematic of the former development was the launch in 1955 by William F. Buckley Jr. of *National Review*, a magazine animated by disillusionment with modern-Republican thinking and driven by the goal to refashion American conservatism in a more attractive form. William Rusher, who became *National Review*'s publisher in 1957, later underscored the significance of that disillusionment. "As a matter of fact, modern American conservatism largely organized itself during, and in explicit opposition to, the Eisenhower Administration," he wrote to Buckley in 1972. "Under your leadership."[64] Indeed, the election of 1956 divided the magazine's editors, some of whom concluded that abstention, designed to promote conservative control, was preferable to support for Eisenhower and his agenda. The non-voters included Buckley, who in an editorial shortly before election day attacked the administration for its "easy and whole-hearted acceptance of all that came before, of the great and statist legacy of the New Deal."[65] The politician who soon emerged as the leader of conservatism was Senator Barry Goldwater of Arizona, who first won election to the Senate in 1952 as an Eisenhower Republican, but whose 1960 book, *The Conscience of a Conservative*, was barely less critical of moderate Republicanism than of the Democrats' liberalism. Indeed, despite Eisenhower's success in challenging non-interventionism among conservatives, Goldwater helped to pioneer a new critique of containment – of its inadequacy against the communist threat.[66]

Rooted in his biography of military service, and forged most of all in the context of World War II, the Eisenhower image, then, proved to be a powerful advantage for Eisenhower as president and in particular as a leader who managed to maintain a reputation as above the partisan fray, even when engaging closely in political conflict. The way in which Eisenhower maintained

---

63 Public Opinion Polls, Survey Report, forwarded by Lou Guylay to Meade Alcorn, May 28, 1957, folder "Republican National Committee Poll, 8 Midwestern States (1957)," box 42, Howard Pyle Records, DDEL.

64 Letter, William A. Rusher to William F. Buckley, Jr., March 9, 1972, folder 5, box 121, William A. Rusher Papers, Manuscript Division, Library of Congress, Washington, D.C.

65 John B. Judis, *William F. Buckley, Jr.: Patron Saint of the Conservatives* (New York: Simon and Schuster, 1988), 144-146 (quotation, 145).

66 Barry Goldwater, *The Conscience of a Conservative* (Shepardsville, KY: Victor Publishing, 1960).

his popularity demonstrates not only the strength of that image, but also his success in understanding the nature of his political appeal and burnishing it. Nevertheless, the experience of the presidency shows the limitations as well as strengths of his image. Probably it was too much to expect that the hero of World War II could fully restore the public standing of the Republican Party – leading members of which on the conservative side anyway numbered among the more skeptical about Eisenhower. Instead, in tackling the challenges of war and peace during the 1950s, Eisenhower avoided a decline in personal popularity that usually accompanies such engagement with controversy. Moreover, he rethought many of the structures attached to the modern presidency in ways that were influenced by his pre-presidential career.

CHAPTER 8

"Like a Jackass in a Hailstorm": Lyndon Johnson, Vietnam, and the Upending of the American Century

Keith M. Finley

On 15 March 1965, Lyndon Baines Johnson (LBJ) stood before a joint session of Congress with an air of quiet dignity. The week prior to the oration Americans watched in horror as the spectacle of police violence against peaceful civil rights protestors in Selma, Alabama played out before them on the evening news. President Johnson planned on using this address not only to rally the nation in those divisive moments, but to also urge Congress to pass a sweeping voting rights bill that would complete the legislative assault against *de jure* segregation and its satellite institutions begun the year before. Although the famous address was penned by Johnson staffer Richard Goodwin, the president's history, ideas, and perspective permeated its content. In that moment, Johnson reached his finest hour as president. All the acrimony that would engulf his presidency over the war in Vietnam was in the future. No longer just a Stetson-wearing Texan or a slick political operator with a penchant for wheeling and dealing, he was a genuine national leader who engaged universal American truths. When Lyndon Johnson reached the point in his address where he uttered the words "we shall overcome" – a phrase synonymous with the civil rights struggle – few doubted that his crusade against voter discrimination would culminate in success.[1]

If Johnson's career ended in 1965, he would be remembered as one of the country's better presidents. His genuine concern for the poor and disenfranchised, in part, led him to the rostrum in 1965 but so too did his vaulting ambition which often guided the causes he championed. Johnson needed to win accolades as much as he needed to demonstrate to those who considered him an uncouth bumpkin that he had more common sense than anyone in the room. In 1965, still glowing from his landslide victory in the 1964 presidential

1 Lyndon Baines Johnson, *The Vantage Point: Perspectives of the Presidency, 1963-1969* (New York: Holt, Rinehart, and Winston, 1971), 160-167; Juan Williams, *Eyes on the Prize: America's Civil Rights Years, 1954-1965* (New York: Penguin Books, 1987), 278.

© KONINKLIJKE BRILL NV, LEIDEN, 2020 | DOI:10.1163/9789004422643_010

election, Johnson was at his absolute best. Shortly, the nation would see Lyndon Johnson at his worst. Tragically for a man who accomplished so much, it would be the negatives that stood out the most.[2]

Biographers have long grappled with the complex character of Lyndon Johnson. Journalist Robert Caro, who has written numerous volumes on the Texan, depicts him as an amoral politician who focused most of his efforts in pursuing greater degrees of power. Others such as historians Robert Dallek and more recently Randall Woods have presented more balanced accounts of the man that leave open the possibility, despite the Texan's penchant for crass power plays, that Johnson's actions might have served more than mere Machiavellian ends. The growing body of literature devoted to unraveling Lyndon Johnson's actions, personality, and character underscores the difficulty of pigeonholing this most complex of men. To truly understand the president from Texas it is necessary to start at the beginning, for the character traits that informed the actions of the man were forged while he was still a boy.[3]

Childhood associates of Lyndon Johnson have asserted that the only way to grasp his character and personality is to understand the Texas Hill Country, known for grinding poverty and backbreaking work, where he grew up. Lyndon Johnson was born on 28 August 1908 in the small town of Johnson City, Texas. It was there that he learned his earliest political lessons from his father Samuel Ealy Johnson Jr., who served in the Texas Legislature. Sam Johnson was an honest man who by all accounts fought against special interests and who could not be bought – a rare characteristic in the Texas State House in those days. In the cloistered isolation of the Hill Country, few options existed for enterprising young men save for public service. Young Lyndon Johnson had an excellent guide to that world. The father passed to the son a concern for the less fortunate, in part, because the Johnsons knew hard times too. Although the situation was never as dire as President Johnson liked to describe it, the family regularly struggled with finances. Despite these troubles, Sam Johnson remained an honest politician, refusing to use elected office as a conduit for wealth. For the son, the father's influence cast a long shadow. On the one hand, Lyndon Johnson learned that politicians were servants of the public interest.

2 "The Presidents. History's Judgment." *Time*, 13 April 1998, 106.

3 Robert A. Caro, *The Years of Lyndon Johnson: The Path to Power* (New York: Alfred A. Knopf, 1982); Caro, *The Years of Lyndon Johnson: Means of Ascent* (New York: Alfred A. Knopf, 1990); Caro, *The Years of Lyndon Johnson: The Passage of Power* (New York: Vintage Press, 2013); Robert Dallek, *Flawed Giant: Lyndon Johnson and his Times* (New York: Oxford University Press, 1999); Randall B. Woods, *LBJ: Architect of American Ambition* (New York: Free Press, 2006).

On the other hand, he discovered that the path of altruism, although paved with good intentions, often ended in poverty. Sometimes, as Johnson came to discover, one needed to take the best deal on the table and walk away or risk losing everything in a quixotic battle over ideals. As a result of these boyhood perceptions learned directly or indirectly from his father, pragmatism ran side-by-side with idealism in Johnson's political worldview. This strange duality shaped many of the political and personal decisions he made for the remainder of his life.[4]

Lyndon Johnson's mother also proved critical in developing his mature personality. One of Johnson's earlier biographers Doris Kearns Goodwin, who had unfettered access to the president as she worked on the book, got it right when she noted that Rebekah Baines Johnson's influence on her son was of paramount importance. The college educated Rebekah demanded excellence from Lyndon who, in turn, craved her adulation. Always seeking to improve her son's performance, she regularly withheld her affection in an effort to elicit from him a new, even better performance. Victories were not cherished for long as Rebekah withdrew in an effort to coax new triumphs. As a result of this carrot and stick approach to parenting, the adult Lyndon Johnson craved adulation and refused to rest on his laurels once success was achieved. Extrapolating from his experiences with his mother, Johnson believed that the affections of voters could only be secured through constant achievement. His thirst for praise and his idealistic streak coupled with his paranoia that America's intellectuals looked down on him drove his future actions. Johnson needed to not only outdo everyone to satiate his thirst for approval, he had to similarly prove to all that he was as smart and cunning as those with more impressive paper credentials.[5]

---

4 For some of the numerous works that address the early life of Lyndon Johnson see: Caro, *The Years of Lyndon Johnson: The Path to Power*; Caro, *The Years of Lyndon Johnson: Means of Ascent*; Paul K. Conkin, *Big Daddy from the Pedernales: Lyndon Baines Johnson* (Boston: Twayne Publishers, 1968); Robert Dallek, *Lone Star Rising: Lyndon Johnson and His Times, 1908-1960* (New York: Oxford University Press, 1991); Ronnie Dugger, *The Politician: The Drive For Power from the Frontier to Master of the Senate* (New York: Norton, 1982); Roland Evans and Robert Novak, *Lyndon Johnson: The Exercise of Power* (New York: New American Library, 1966); Doris Kearns, *Lyndon Johnson and the American Dream* (New York: Harper and Row, 1968); Merle Miller, *Lyndon: An Oral Biography* (New York: Putnam, 1980); Alfred Steinberg, *Sam Johnson's Boy: A Close-Up of the President from Texas* (New York: MacMillan, 1968); Irwin and Debi Unger, *LBJ: A Life* (New York: Wiley, 1999).

5 Doris Kearns, "Lyndon Johnson's Political Personality," *Political Science Quarterly* 91, no. 3 (Autumn 1976): 385-409; see also: Hyman L. Muslin and Thomas H. Jobe, *Lyndon Johnson The Tragic Self: A Psychohistorical Portrait* (New York: Plenum Press, 1991).

After graduating from Southwest Texas State Teachers College in San Marcos, Johnson went to work as an educator in the small south Texas town of Cotulla that he referenced in his famous "We Shall Overcome" speech. As that oration reached its climax, Johnson reminisced about his time in Cotulla where he first became aware of the painful legacy of racism in America as he glanced upon the forlorn faces of the Mexican American students he taught. Few of them could speak English and all of them were desperately poor. There Johnson encountered the insidious impact of class and race-based prejudices that impoverished many. As his public career blossomed, he made great use of that humble school house where he received an important education on the impact of discrimination in America – or at least this was how he wanted future historians to frame the experience.[6]

Following Cotulla, Johnson served a stint as a congressional secretary before winning election to the U.S. House of Representatives. By this point a clear pattern emerged in Johnson's behavior. Victories both big and small left him dissatisfied; he was always looking for the next obstacle to surmount – a fact that further reveals the impact of his childhood quest for affection. The drive for accolades fueled his ambition and instilled in him a mania for work. As Johnson observed about himself, "I have very strong feelings about work, when it is there to be done, I do it."[7] Once he entered the political arena, his ferocious work ethic would always be there, leading to a serious heart attack in 1955 while serving as a U.S. senator. Rather than slow the pace of his efforts, Johnson's health crisis heightened his sense of mortality by reminding him that men in his family had a history of dying young from heart ailments. Time was of the essence; he needed to act fast before the family's bleak medical history caught up with him. As senator, Johnson followed the surest path to power. Saddling up to powerful southern Democrats in the chamber such as Georgian Richard Russell and Virginian Harry Byrd, Johnson carefully plotted a course that would make him a household name as majority leader. Although often accused of being a wheeler and a dealer, he also earned a reputation as a man who got things done. Early in his Senate tenure, Johnson established himself as a work horse by funneling responsibility into his hands so that others came to him when they needed favors. From an ideological standpoint in the 1950s, Johnson appeared to be a man who was just as comfortable talking to conservatives as he was to liberals, prompting some to ponder whether he

6 Mitchell Lerner, "'Almost a Populist': Texas, the South, and the Rise of Lyndon Johnson," *Southwestern Historical Quarterly* 117, no. 3 (January 2014): 236-265; Woods, *LBJ*.

7 Johnson, *Vantage Point*, 425.

believed in anything except his own ambitions. Johnson, however, was far too complex to be judged by a simple liberal vs. conservative binary paradigm. He adapted to his circumstances by recognizing at this stage of his career that politics was the art of the possible and very rarely the art of the desirable. For Senator Johnson, it was far better to be a pragmatist and achieve some positive ends than it was to be an idealist and accomplish nothing. Minnesota politician Hubert Humphrey, who served with Johnson in the Senate before becoming his vice president, remarked regarding the Texan, "I always figured that he was a rather clever, adroit, astute pragmatist."[8] When Johnson exhibited strains of idealism it almost always came packaged with pragmatism. While in the Senate, Johnson cut many corners, trimmed his sails, and delivered an array of compromises. One such deal, the Civil Rights Act of 1957, although watered down, proved an enormous accomplishment, representing as it did the first civil rights law to pass in Congress since the Reconstruction Era. On the down side, the bill resulted in few tangible changes in the state of southern race relations. Regardless of the bill's limitations, Johnson took advantage of every opportunity to stress his role in the law's passage, thereby garnering national acclaim for orchestrating a compromise that got the proposal out of the Senate without a filibuster.[9] To his southern constituents who were less than thrilled with his achievement, Johnson emphasized the limited scope of the law, suggesting "this bill merely seeks to insure all Americans what we in Texas already possess [the right to vote]."[10]

When the Democratic Party's nominee John F. Kennedy tapped LBJ to be his vice presidential running mate in 1960, Johnson accepted the offer on the grounds that in the event of victory he could transform the office into something meaningful. Just the opposite occurred. In effect, Johnson went from being one of the most powerful men in America as the Senate's majority leader to the occupier of the largely ceremonial job of vice president which included

---

8 Transcript, Hubert H. Humphrey Oral History Interview I, 8/17/1971 by Joe B. Frantz, Internet Copy, LBJ Library.

9 Robert A Caro, *The Years of Lyndon Johnson: The Master of the Senate* (New York: Alfred A.Knopf, 2002); Gilbert C. Fite, *Richard B. Russell, Jr., Senator From Georgia* (Chapel Hill: The University of North Carolina Press, 1991); John A. Goldsmith, *Colleagues: Richard B. Russell and his Apprentice, Lyndon B. Johnson* (Washington, D.C.: Seven Locks Press, 1993); Ronald L. Heinemann, *Harry Byrd of Virginia* (Charlottesville: University of Virginia Press, 1996); For an in depth discussion of the Civil Rights Act of 1957 see: Keith M. Finley, *Delaying the Dream: Southern Senators and the Fight Against Civil Rights, 1938-1965* (Baton Rouge: Louisiana State University Press, 2008), 138-190.

10 LBJ to Margine S. Laidlaw, August 29, 1957, "Judiciary-Civil Rights-1957," Box 289, Senate Papers, LBJ Library.

few meaningful duties. More important, Johnson felt ostracized for lacking the refinement and Ivy League pedigree typical of most in Kennedy's inner circle. Always attuned to snubs by those who fancied themselves as his social betters, Johnson's insecurities mounted as he interacted with what he considered the administration's pretentious members. Those years as vice president were hard on Johnson, who was not accustomed to standing on the periphery while others made important decisions. Most reporters devoted little attention to Johnson during his three years as vice president, but for those who did his words shed light on what was to come. He was beginning to assume the role of champion for racial justice.

Johnson's circumstances had changed and like a chameleon he was changing too. Although his Texas birth made him 'southern' in the classic sense of the term, Johnson's upbringing happened in the Hill Country of that state which was far more western in its orientation, sharing little in common with plantation districts to the east. In contrast to the argument advanced in *The Indicted South* by Angie Maxwell, Lyndon Johnson's perception that he was somehow persecuted by "outsiders" rarely included a fealty to the region's peculiar history. The persecution he saw remained centered on him, tied especially to his lack of polish and to his San Marcos degree. Unlike Maxwell's prototypical southern politician who embraced a "siege mentality" and sought to turn back the clock to some idealized moment in the past, Johnson, as president, aimed to destroy the injustices of the South all of which were tied to that mythologized past. Johnson certainly identified as a southerner when expediency dictated, but his personal political rudder guided him beyond narrow parochialism.[11] Indeed, Hubert Humphrey recalled that Johnson stressed his non-southern credentials by making "it clear that he was [from the] southwest and a westerner, cowboy style rather than plantation style; it was a ranch house rather than a plantation."[12] Free for the first time as vice president from

11 Angie Maxwell, *The Indicted South: Public Criticism, Southern Inferiority, and the Politics of Whiteness* (Chapel Hill: The University of North Carolina Press, 2014); See also: Irving Bernstein, *Guns or Butter: The Presidency of Lyndon Johnson* (New York: Oxford University Press, 1996), 3-11; It is hard to imagine Johnson uttering things such as "until justice is blind to color, until education is unaware of race, until opportunity is unconcerned with the color of men's skins, emancipation will be a proclamation but not a fact," when he was just a politician from Texas. Lyndon B. Johnson, *A Time For Action: A Selection From the Speeches and Writings of Lyndon B. Johnson, 1953-1964* (New York: Atheneum Publishers, 1964), 127; William S. White, *The Professional: Lyndon B. Johnson* (Boston: Houghton Mifflin Company, 1964), 56. See also: Caro, *The Years of Lyndon Johnson: The Passage of Power*.

12 Transcript, Hubert H. Humphrey oral History Interview II, 6/20/1977 by Michael C. Gillette, Internet Copy, LBJ Library.

regional shackles and acting now as a national politician, Johnson expressed a devotion to the fight for racial equality that the former congressman and senator from Texas had never intimated in public. The tragic assassination of John Kennedy catapulted Johnson into the White House, granting the American people their first substantive glimpse of the transformed Texan.

Johnson hit the ground running, seeking to remain true to Kennedy's legacy while also forging a new path to cement his reputation. Assuming the role of caretaker and innovator, Johnson set his sights on some of the biggest legislative prizes left over from the New Deal. He was not going to sit idle as chief executive; he was going to lead.[13] In his first State of the Union address, he declared an "unconditional war on poverty," after which he put his staff to work on a bill that would serve as the opening salvo of his war.[14] At the same time, Johnson recognized the limitations of his efforts, noting "no single poverty program could reverse centuries of discrimination... There was no magic formula. We had to try a wide variety of approaches. Some worked better than others. Some failed completely. ... That was all part of the risk." Emphasizing the need for rapid action, he told one reporter, "we have to pull the drowning man out of the water and talk about it later."[15] The politician who was often accused of extreme pragmatism increasingly found himself asserting that politics was "the art of making possible what seems impossible."[16] Infused with a new sense of purpose, Johnson sought to make good on his grand visions for the country. His frenzied effort to outdo all previous presidents in terms of their legislative output struck no one who knew Johnson's need to win laurels as a surprise. Republican Senator George Aiken, who served with LBJ in the Senate, succinctly described the president: "Lyndon Johnson is an operator; he's a driver."[17] He had always been that way. Johnson's position as the head of the free world did not change his ceaseless need for acceptance or his elemental fear of losing support once he secured it.

To reach his lofty goals, Johnson expended prodigious amounts of his own energy and that of his staff to get things accomplished. Describing how it was to work for Lyndon Johnson, Special Assistant to the President Joseph Califano noted, "he barked orders at me over the phone at dawn and after midnight, in the formal setting of the Oval Office and as he stood stark naked brushing

13 Johnson, *Vantage Point*, 18.
14 Lyndon B. Johnson, *My Hope for America* (New York: Random House, 1964), 37-45.
15 Johnson, *Vantage Point*, 81.
16 Ibid., 461.
17 Transcript, George Aiken Oral History Interview, 10/10/1968 by Paige E. Mulhollan, Internet Copy, LBJ Library.

his teeth in his bathroom. I watched him laugh, swear, get angry, cry, get hurt, hurt others, dream, and achieve things most everyone thought was impossible." Working for Johnson entailed recognizing that one's term of employment extended beyond the hours of 9 and 5. Demonstrating his fixation on achievement, Johnson intended to push Congress as it had not been pushed since the New Deal.[18]

Revenue for his varied initiatives came from passing President Kennedy's stalled $11 billion tax cut bill that generated a considerable economic boom when passed in late February 1964. The much-anticipated cornerstone in the War on Poverty – the Economic Opportunity Bill – was unveiled in the spring of 1964 and featured an array of provisions including the creation of a Jobs Corps, the formation of the Head Start Program, and a federal loan system for those businesses willing to hire the chronically unemployed. Built into the law was a Community Action Program that idealistically promoted maximum feasible participation of the poor in shaping programs designed to benefit them. For Johnson, the bill represented at least a partial step toward the creation of the Great Society. The stated premise behind the War on Poverty proved simple. A country with vast wealth should be able to provide a decent standard of living for all its citizens. Johnson pressed the issue, asserting that the American poor "had no voice and no champion. Whatever the cost, I was determined to represent them. Through me they would have an advocate, and I believed, new hope."[19] Striking a classic Johnson pose that reflected his need for constant public affirmation, he was not going to tackle the plight of the poor in a small way – he was going to wage "war on poverty," and presumably through the passage of legislation he was going to destroy it. To explain the fight, Johnson turned to his youth and the lessons his father taught him regarding the evils of economic injustice, along with those lessons he learned as a teacher at the impoverished Cotulla school. As he sought additional solutions for American poverty, Johnson looked ahead to the upcoming 1964 election.[20]

---

18 Dallek, *Flawed Giant*, 46-71; Joseph A. Califano, Jr., *The Triumph and Tragedy of Lyndon Johnson: The White House Years* (New York: Simon and Schuster, 1991), 9; Frank Cormier, *LBJ: The Way He Was* (New York: Doubleday and Company, 1977); Patricia D. Witherspoon, "'Let Us Continue:' The Rhetorical Initiation of Lyndon Johnson's Presidency," *Presidential Studies Quarterly* 17, no. 3 (1987): 531-539.

19 Johnson, *Vantage Point*, 71.

20 Robert L. Branyan and R. Alton Lee, "Lyndon B. Johnson and the Art of the Possible," *The Southwestern Social Science Quarterly* 45, no. 3 (1964): 213-225. Carl M. Brauer, "Kennedy, Johnson, and the War on Poverty," *The Journal of American History*, 69, no. 1 (June 1982): 98-119; Dallek, *Flawed Giant*, 71-84; Randall B. Woods, *Prisoners of Hope: Lyndon B. Johnson, the Great Society, and the Limits of Liberalism* (New York: Basic Books, 2016).

The 1964 presidential contest, pitting Republican Barry Goldwater against Democrat Lyndon Johnson, was a study in contrasts. With Goldwater glorifying extremism, Johnson came across calm, dignified, and honest. Johnson carefully navigated the shoals in 1964 and said all the right things, including down-playing the severity of the problems in the Southeast Asian nation of Vietnam. While Johnson might have said what the American people wanted to hear, they would soon find out that he might not have been as honest as they had thought. When the dust settled, Johnson won 61 percent of the popular vote and a whopping 482 to 52 margin in the Electoral College. Ever the astute politician, Johnson noted that every day he was in office he was going to lose support. His conception of the inevitable loss of voter allegiance mirrored his experiences with his mother who withheld her affection once a past success grew stale. Johnson thus always found himself reaching for the next plateau in an effort to keep the applause going. Savoring the moment was not one of the president's strong suits.[21]

The pace of the work and the scope of the freshly elected president's agenda was stunning. His wife-Claudia 'Lady Bird' Johnson – who saw more of Lyndon than anyone else – suggested that her husband's success was tied to his willingness to push through barriers to achieve objectives. Echoing Mrs. Johnson's comments, Joseph Califano recalled, "Johnson could not stand for anyone to be beyond his reach or not working. He didn't like his cabinet members to leave Washington at all, even for short vacations or personal trips. … I learned fast that Johnson used every waking minute of every day."[22] Without question, those who fell into Johnson's circle were often used as pawns. One such individual was Special Assistant Walter Jenkins, who worked with the Texan for twenty-five years and was considered by many to be the chief of staff. During the 1964 presidential campaign, the forty-six-year-old aide was caught in an incriminating position in a Washington, D.C. YMCA bathroom well-known to law enforcement as a homosexual pick up spot just a few blocks from the White House. Making matters worse, the record revealed that Jenkins, who was married with six children, had been detained at the same restroom under suspicion of a similar transgression in 1959.

Johnson's response to the mid-October incident was characteristic. Rather than comfort his old friend, Johnson refused to answer questions regarding Jenkins. He left it to his staff to spin the episode as a case of exhaustion exacerbated by excessive drinking. Even more tragic was the fact that Johnson failed

---

21 Bernstein, *Guns*, 117-155; Dallek, *Flawed Giant*, 122-184; Robert David Johnson, *All the Way with LBJ: The 1964 Presidential Election* (Cambridge: Cambridge University Press, 2009).

22 Califano, *The Triumph*, 26-27.

to speak directly to Jenkins, choosing instead to employ his chief legal advisor Abe Fortas as a conduit to the beleaguered aide. The Johnson camp feared that Goldwater would pounce on the episode of "loose morals" to close the gap in the campaign. In the middle of the Cold War, when it was believed that homosexuals in positions of governmental power were especially vulnerable to blackmailing, Jenkins' arrest briefly sent Johnson's campaign into a panic. The kind and compassionate Lady Bird felt sympathy for Jenkins and wanted to immediately offer him a job at the KTBC television station she owned, an idea her husband promptly dismissed after considering the potential blowback in an election season. Ironically, Mrs. Johnson always maintained that there was no better person to have on one's side in a tough situation than her husband. Jenkins no doubt felt different. He became a campaign casualty in 1964 and collateral damage in the war on poverty.

Maintaining propriety, or at least the perception of it, was more important than consideration of a friendship that spanned decades. Johnson ultimately considered threats to his approval ratings of greater concern than his devotion to his faithful servant. When working with Johnson, you were in as long as you contributed to his success. Johnson's pragmatism, learned from the failings of his father, thus never disappeared and clearly shaped the outwardly idealistic rhetoric he adopted in his early presidency. Jenkins had to be removed because the incident would provoke public outrage, undermine LBJ's reelection bid, and permanently cease his upward political trajectory. Johnson's personal characteristics influenced and defined every aspect of his political career. For a politician who devoted all of his waking hours to his craft, no other alternative was possible. Jenkins, like most in Johnson's orbit, learned that the president could not escape the personal traits he had exhibited throughout his professional life.[23]

After the election, priority went to securing a health insurance program for the elderly. Through Medicare and Medicaid, the government would foot portions of doctor and drug bills for the aged and medical costs for the indigent. Johnson pitched his successful venture in health care in a manner that highlighted not just how beneficial the program would be for the elderly, but also how other chief executives starting with President Harry Truman had tried and

23 Michael Beschloss, *Reaching for Glory: Lyndon Johnson's Secret White House Tapes, 1964-1965* (New York: Simon and Schuster, 2001), 54-102; Clark Clifford, *Counsel to the President: A Memoir* (New York: Random House, 1991), 399-402; Eric F. Goldman, *The Tragedy of Lyndon Johnson* (New York: Alfred A. Knopf, 1969), 104-108, 249-252; Allen J. Matusow, *The Unraveling of America: A History Of Liberalism in the 1960s* (New York: Harper and Row, 1984), 146; Miller, *Lyndon: An Oral Biography*, 486-488.

failed to get Medicare through Congress. Ever in search of accolades he felt denied to him because of who he was, Johnson made sure the world knew it was he, not the kindly Truman or the Harvard educated Kennedy, who sealed the deal. Lyndon Johnson from the Texas Hill Country outsmarted them all. Successes for Johnson occupied but fleeting moments of his time. Before long, he was casting about in search of new accomplishments, new accolades, and new ways to demonstrate that he was ideally suited to hold the highest office in the land.[24]

Federal aid to elementary and secondary education in the form of $1.5 billion was also secured after being bottled up in Congress since Kennedy's presidency. One of the big stumbling blocks to passage of the original Kennedy proposal was southern concerns regarding any bill "which would give the Federal Government the slightest excuse or reason to impose a Federal policy on our system of education."[25] As the pressure to end segregation mounted in the first half of the 1960s, southerners viewed all signs of federal intrusion into local matters as a harbinger of integration. To counter this, Johnson went straight for the heart strings. Without federal assistance, he asserted "many American children would be doomed to inferior education, which presaged an empty future. Not only would those children suffer but so would their country."[26] Wrapping himself in the cloak of patriotism and portraying himself as champion of children's rights, Johnson explained that all school age youngsters should have access to a quality learning environment. Thanks to the influence of his college-educated mother, LBJ had developed an unbending belief that education was a panacea for numerous ailments, including poverty. Time would prove that no amount of funding and no amount of government control over education could solve the larger systemic shortfalls that limited achievement in the classroom. The same principle applied to the struggle for racial equality in America. No amount of legislating could undo decades of systematic

---

24 Vaughn Davis Bornet, "Reappraising the Presidency of Lyndon B. Johnson," *Presidential Studies Quarterly* 20, no. 3 (1990): 591-602; Dallek, *Flawed Giant*, 195-203; Robert H. Wilson, Norman J. Glickman, and Laurence E. Lynn Jr., eds. *LBJ's Neglected Legacy: How Lyndon Johnson Reshaped Domestic Policy and Government* (Austin: University of Texas Press, 2015); Julian E. Zelizer, *Lyndon Johnson, Congress, and the Battle for the Great Society* (New York: Penguin Books, 2015); Oral history transcript, Arthur Krim, interview 2 (II), 5/17/1982, by Michael L. Gillette, Internet Copy, LBJ Library.

25 Richard B. Russell (hereafter cited: RR) to Grantland Barnes, 24 March 1961, Box 186, Folder 19, Richard B Russell Collection, Richard B. Russell Library, University of Georgia, Athens (hereafter cited: Russell MSS).

26 Johnson, *Vantage Point*, 207, 104.

discrimination.[27] Lyndon Johnson, a devotee of both the healing power of legislation and of education, tackled the matters head on, believing that force of will could move mountains. He sought to accomplish what all who came before him failed to achieve. If he managed to cure the most pressing of the nation's ills, Johnson reckoned he could secure for himself the respect he long felt denied to him. No target proved as important as racial injustice in America.

At the start of his presidency, Johnson observed with regard to civil rights that "there was no question in my mind as to what I would do. I knew that, as President and as a man, I would use every ounce of strength I possessed to gain justice for the black American."[28] Johnson would bring his strong personality to bear in securing passage of the revolutionary Civil Rights Act of 1964 and the Voting Rights Act of 1965. These legislative battles were no sure thing, forcing Johnson to expend a lot of political capital to see them pass. Some of his former Senate colleagues from the South such as Alabama Senator John Sparkman were initially optimistic regarding LBJ's new role as chief executive, observing that the Texan was "the kind of President we need in these difficult times. I believe moreover that he is a friend of the South."[29] Floridian Spessard Holland added, "although I may not agree with him on every issue, I have known him for many years and believe he still stands by his convictions."[30] Looking back after several major civil rights defeats, Johnson's close friend and former Senate colleague Richard Russell, who led the southern opposition against civil rights in the chamber, offered harsher words: "it is frightening to see the lengths to which this Administration and the Congress will go in their efforts to grant special privileges to a small group at the expense of the white people of the South."[31] Regarding Johnson, Russell noted, "I hope that he will soon shake off the extreme left-wingers who surround and advise him and rely more on his own thinking."[32] If Russell expected Johnson to make such a change he was mistaken, as his friend and former protégé went on to accomplish more in the field of civil rights than any of his predecessors, except

27 Hugh Davis Graham, *Uncertain Triumph: Federal Education Policy in the Kennedy and Johnson Years* (Chapel Hill: The University of North Carolina Press, 1984).

28 Johnson, *Vantage Point*, 157.

29 John Sparkman (hereafter cited: JS) to Lela Mae Goodson, 29 April 1964, 18-E-9, Box #25, No Folder, John Sparkman Collection, W.S. Hoole Special Collections Library, University of Alabama, Tuscaloosa (hereafter cited: Sparkman MSS).

30 Spessard Holland to R.E. Williams, 1 April 1964, Box 808, Folder 28, Spessard Holland Collection, Claude Pepper Library, Florida State University, Tallahassee.

31 RR to Newton Wilcox, 22 June 1965, Box 32, Folder 3, Russell MSS.

32 RR to James M. Aiken, 15 May 1965, Box 33, Folder 5, Russell MSS.

maybe Abraham Lincoln, who oversaw the northern victory in the Civil War that ended slavery in America.

Despite his stirring public pronouncements regarding civil rights, Johnson might have hinted to some that he was uncomfortable with Black leaders taking their discontent to the streets. Senator Sparkman, for one, observed in the days following the Bloody Sunday episode in Selma, "the President stated to me that his Administration aides had strongly urged King to stop demonstrations, but King apparently feels himself bound only by laws with which he agrees."[33] Whether or not Johnson simply told Sparkman what he thought the Alabama Senator wanted to hear was not clear at the time. A few days later, in his "We Shall Overcome" speech, Johnson advanced another narrative in which he noted that America's Black population had waited long enough for justice, indicating in a very public manner that the civil rights protests were both necessary and proper.

As a politician, LBJ sought common ground. He ingratiated himself to others, pulling them into his web by subtly and not so subtly pressuring them. A political realist, Johnson never pushed politicians to vote outside of the interests of their constituents, but when wiggle room existed, Johnson would bring the full weight of the "Johnson Treatment" to bear in trying to sell his perspective. The "Treatment" as described by journalists Rowland Evans and Robert Novak involved the president buttonholing a politician and letting loose an avalanche of information, all the while invading the personal space of his quarry, creating what they called a "hypnotic experience" that "rendered the target helpless." Based on the Evans and Novak model, politicians determined to stand up to Johnson withered under the onslaught and became another vote for one of LBJ's prized pieces of legislation. Not all sources are in agreement regarding the tactic, however.[34]

A careful examination of the recollections of the politicians who knew Johnson best reveals that the famed "treatment" was more media symbol than political substance. At root, Johnson was a pragmatic thinker. He knew that certain politicians, especially those within his party, were open to suggestion.

---

33 JS to R.C. Bonds, 12 March 1965, 67-A-959, Box 1, Folder 13, Sparkman MSS.

34 Bernstein, *Guns*, 43-81, 214-244; Dallek, *Flawed Giant*, 111-121, 211-221, 322-329; Sylvia Ellis, *Freedom's Pragmatist: Lyndon Johnson and Civil Rights* (Gainesville: University Press of Florida, 2013); Evans and Novak, *Exercise of Power*, 104; Nick Kotz, *Judgement Days: Lyndon Baines Johnson, Martin Luther King Jr., and the Laws that Changed America* (Boston: Houghton Mifflin Company, 2005); William E. Leuchtenburg, *The White House Looks South: Franklin D. Roosevelt, Harry S. Truman, Lyndon B. Johnson* (Baton Rouge: Louisiana State University Press, 2005), 297-338.

Hubert Humphrey related that Johnson was an "unbelievable man in terms of sizing people up, what they would do, how they would stand under pressure, what their temperament was."[35] In short, Humphrey considered LBJ a "psychiatrist" who used all of the tools of persuasion in his considerable arsenal to bring doubting politicians in line. Much has been made of Johnson's physical presence, especially his 6-foot 3.5-inch frame, which prompted Republican Senator Everett Dirksen to remark, "physically Lyndon Johnson is a very impressive person. You put him in an average room and he shows up exceedingly well."[36] According to the journalists who popularized the "treatment," Johnson used his "impressive" frame to lean into and touch people in his efforts to win favor. Although this physical intimidation has been widely reported, many of Johnson's contemporaries did not consider presidential groping a form of coercion. Democratic Senator Earle Clements of Kentucky perceived the physical touching allegedly associated with the "treatment" differently, suggesting "he [Johnson] would do that by nature, even though he wasn't trying to outwardly persuade you. That was just kind of his nature."[37]

If Clements is to be believed, Johnson had a different sense of personal space and felt comfortable embracing and caressing others regardless of the nature of his audience or the content of the conversation. Indiana Democrat Birch Bayh took things even further by suggesting the treatment "may be overplayed; it was never used on me."[38] Joining Bayh in downplaying the tactic was fellow Democrat James Eastland of Mississippi, who noted he "never felt any" White House pressure during Johnson's presidency.[39] Politicians on the other side of the aisle expressed similar sentiments. Republican Thomas Kuchel of California, for example, observed that he received no direct pressure from the president because Johnson "respected the fact that it would be difficult for a Republican to vote for a Democratic issue."[40] In short, the evidence suggests that the much vaunted "Johnson Treatment" was less commonly deployed, or

35 Transcript, Hubert H. Humphrey Oral History Interview I, 8/17/1971 by Joe B. Frantz, Internet Copy, LBJ Library.

36 Transcript, Everett Dirksen Oral History Interview I, 5/8/1968 by William S. White, Internet Copy, LBJ Library.

37 Transcript, Earle C. Clements Interview, 10/24/1974 by Michael L. Gillette, Internet Copy, LBJ Library.

38 Transcript, Birch Bayh Oral History Interview I, 2/12/1969 by Paige E. Mulhollan, Internet Copy, LBJ Library.

39 Transcript, James Eastland Oral History Interview I, 2/19/1971 by Joe B. Frantz, Internet Copy, LBJ Library.

40 Transcript, Thomas Kuchel Oral History Interview, 5/15/1980 by Michael Gillette, Internet Copy, LBJ Library.

at least far less overtly so, than has often been reported. Far from aggressively attempting to assert his will over others, Johnson carefully selected his targets. Southern patriarchs such as James Eastland were too powerful to be manipulated and were thus left alone, as were most Republicans who sometimes found Johnson's mannerisms "irritating."[41] The president knew not to expend his energy on those ideologically opposed to his agenda. He instead focused his efforts on those amenable to changing their positions if presented with the proper persuasion and patriotic appeals. Johnson remained who he had always been, even as the mechanisms of power available to him had greatly increased. In this way, the shadow of Sam Johnson, whose idealism without pragmatism led to his financial ruin, and Rebekah Johnson, whose demands for ever greater achievements instilled in her children an insatiable drive for success, shaped the president's vision, agenda, and even his interaction with the people in his orbit. His pragmatism enabled him to achieve the legislative victories he so desperately coveted; yet these same personality traits would lead him down the path of his greatest failures.

Despite his civil rights achievements, Johnson's presidency will also be remembered for the paroxysms of urban violence that plagued the nation in the second half of the 1960s. His administration would see the Watts Riots and similar racial disturbances engulfing American cities such as Newark and Detroit. For those inclined to believe that LBJ coddled minority groups and was reaping what he had sown, the explosions in American cities provided ample grist for their mill. Georgia Senator Richard Russell, for example, commented in the wake of the Watts Riots that enactment of sweeping civil rights proposals such as the one passed in 1964 "would not begin to satisfy the supposed beneficiaries. Unhappily, this prediction has already borne out."[42] Johnson could not believe what he was seeing and felt betrayed by the very people he had done so much to help. Considering his less than sanguine assessment of voter loyalty, Johnson should not have been too surprised that something negative had quickly followed one of his great achievements. Even with the important legislative advances of the 1960s, the problems of economic discrimination were still there, cemented in residential lines that bills such as the Open Housing Act of 1968 did little to alleviate. Adding to the mounting discord in America was the war in Vietnam that simmered quietly on the backburner before it started to boil over. Criticism from all angles picked up,

41 Transcript, George A. Aiken Oral History Interview, 10/10/1968 by Paige E. Mulhollan, Internet Copy, LBJ Library.

42 RR to Katharine Haynes, 13 July 1965, Box 32, Folder 3, Russell MSS.

prompting Johnson to offer a characteristically colorful anecdote at a 1966 Democratic Party dinner in which he indicated that as president he often felt "like a jackass in a hailstorm," assailed from all directions but powerless to escape.[43] Once Johnson set his sights on Vietnam, domestic matters took on secondary importance. The criticism against his leadership that he referenced in 1966 was nothing compared to what would follow. The incredible momentum of his early presidency that witnessed several landmark legislative successes came to an abrupt end.[44]

When Johnson became president, 16,000 American troops were stationed in Vietnam as advisers. When he left office, over 500,000 service personnel were in country and over 30,000 Americans had died in the conflict. It was a war that before it ended would exhaust America financially and produce civil disobedience that verged on civil insurrection. The conflict transformed America's vision of itself and others' perception of the U.S., while also underscoring a fundamental reality often overlooked in Washington: not every nation wanted to be like the United States. Johnson had long believed that the people of Southeast Asia would become firm allies if America poured financial resources into the region and, in effect, undertook a spending spree there on par with the one introduced by FDR during the New Deal.

Speaking before the United Nations General Assembly in December 1963, President Lyndon Johnson waxed poetic about the many programs that Franklin Roosevelt initiated to lift America out of the Great Depression, including things such as water and soil conservation efforts, electrification projects, and massive public works initiatives. Next, Johnson noted that America and similarly wealthy countries needed to ensure that the impoverished nations of the world experienced the same rewards by sharing their riches.[45] Viewing foreign policy through the prism of the Cold War, Johnson offered a simple formula for global peace–export the blessings of America which in his mind were synonymous with New Deal-style programming to everyone and the world would come around. LBJ correctly deduced that many developing nations would benefit from American financial assistance; where he miscalculated was in his belief that hydroelectric dams and improved agri-

43 Robert L. Hardesty, *The LBJ the Nation Seldom Saw* (San Marcos: Southwest Texas State University, 2003).

44 Bernstein, *Guns*, 379-425; Califano, *The Triumph*, 207-226; Dallek, *Flawed Giant*, 221-226. 405-418; Leuchtenburg, *White House*, 338-346. Matusow, *Unraveling of America*, 360-375; James T. Patterson, *The Eve of Destruction: How 1965 Transformed America* (New York: Basic Books, 2012).

45 Johnson, *Time for Action*, 159-160.

cultural methods would by default make a nation democratic. This belief left him blissfully ignorant of the profound cultural differences that separated his worldview shaped in the Texas Hill Country from the outlook of a poor rice farmer in South Vietnam.

More than just a failure to grasp cultural distinctions plagued the president. Johnson assumed command in the middle of the Cold War. He had been in Washington when it was learned that China had fallen to the communists during the presidency of Harry Truman. From that point forward, Johnson became a prisoner of the "us vs. them" approach to foreign policy in which the world's complexity was forced within Cold War strictures pitting the U.S. against the U.S.S.R. Remembering the bitter interrogation of Truman officials concerning the loss of China, Johnson sought a path, any path, that would lead either to victory or at the very least to a salvageable situation that permitted America to pull its commitment from South Vietnam without losing face. Johnson hoped that a massive infusion of combat personnel outfitted with the latest military technology would force concessions from North Vietnam. Force of will helped Johnson smash through legislative walls. He hoped that force of arms would break down the enemy in Vietnam, securing both peace and praise.

As American involvement escalated, Johnson stressed that he made decisions about Vietnam after careful consideration of advice from countless experts. "I was going to do what had to be done to protect our interests and to keep our promises," Johnson asserted.[46] Despite a plethora of recommendations from others, Johnson's foreign policy approach was his alone, a fact that ultimately proved deleterious. He was no longer working in the political milieu in Washington where he was an expert; he was operating on a global stage with actors he did not know and could not cajole. Lyndon Johnson's full term as president began with one of the greatest electoral mandates in U.S. political history, yet ended with the emergence of the so-called credibility gap in which the president was accused of obscuring how poorly things were going in Vietnam, all the while failing to offer the military a useful measure of success in the conflict save for the vague injunction to "nail the coonskin to the wall" – LBJ's way of saying "win." War always prompts protests, yet the backlash Johnson experienced over Vietnam appeared to him to extend beyond "the bounds of

46 Politicians such as Republican John Tower of Texas remember frequently being asked by Johnson to stop by the White House to discuss the situation in southeast Asia. Tower remembers Johnson earnestly soliciting opinions from trusted politicians regardless of party in an effort to get things right in Vietnam. Transcript, John Tower Oral History Interview II, 9/22/1971 by Joe Frantz, Internet Copy, LBJ Library. Johnson, *Vantage Point*, 68.

reasonable debate and fair dissension." In fact it was the anti-war protestors who Johnson observed "prolonged the war, prevented a peaceful settlement on reasonable terms, encouraged our enemies, disheartened our friends and weakened us as a nation."[47] As Johnson saw it, raucous protests at home emboldened the enemy, providing them with not only the will to resist but also with the assurance that American resolve was weak. Johnson certainly recognized that Americans desired peace. He simply failed to bring it about. The man who proved so adept at reading his fellow Americans utterly failed in his ability to read his foreign adversaries. All the traits he learned as a child and honed as a politician were of little use in the global arena. As his customary routes to success failed, Johnson cast about for answers completely out of his element. Numerous overtures emanated from Washington in the 1960s seeking a cessation of the fighting only to be summarily dismissed by North Vietnam. The locus of options available to the president got smaller as his commitment in Vietnam grew and as the resolve of his opponent strengthened. As 1968 dawned, Ho Chi Minh's communists were planning to capitalize further on sagging American enthusiasm with a bold military stroke aimed at the towns and cities of South Vietnam.[48]

The 31 January 1968 Tet offensive shocked everyone, coming as it did after glowing forecasts that the war was nearly won. The fallout from that event prompted LBJ to bow out of the presidential election that year, so he could focus on ending the war. Despite the backlash, the Tet offensive which proved so devastating to the Johnson administration ultimately ended in military defeat for the North Vietnamese. As for the decline in American morale that it precipitated, Johnson blamed the media for "a great deal of emotional and exaggerated reporting of the Tet offensive in our press and on television. The media seemed to be in competition as to who could provide the most lurid and

47 Johnson used the 'coonskin' metaphor often in his career. He used it to exhort his staff to work harder and he obviously used it in relation to Vietnam as his way of urging the military on to victory. Stanley Karnow, *Vietnam: A History* (Middlesex, Penguin Books, 1984), 459, 490, 515; George C. Herring, *LBJ and Vietnam: A Different Kind of War* (Austin: University of Texas Press, 1994); Johnson, *Vantage Point*, 530.

48 David M. Barrett, "The Mythology Surrounding Lyndon Johnson, His Advisers, and the 1965 Decision to Escalate the Vietnam War," *Political Science Quarterly* 103, no. 4 (1988): 637-663; Bernstein, *Guns*, 379-425, 471-521; Dallek, *Flawed Giant*, 221-226, 340-399, 405-418; George Herring, *The War Bells Have Rung: The LBJ Tapes and the Americanization of the Vietnam War* (Charlottesville: University of Virginia Press, 2015); Herbert Y. Schandler, *Lyndon Johnson and Vietnam: The Unmasking of a President* (Princeton: Princeton University Press, 1977); Brian VanDeMark, *Into the Quagmire: Lyndon Johnson and the Escalation of the Vietnam War* (New York: Oxford University Press, 1995).

depressing accounts."[49] Long-time Johnson associate and one-time presidential press secretary George Reedy opined regarding Johnson's love/hate relationship with the news media, "as far as he was concerned, the press was to be kept ignorant of policy until he was able to trumpet it, in some overwhelming thing… [W]hen he got in the White House I think that he felt that a president was entitled to have everything that he thought and said and did completely secret until he was ready to announce it."[50] His handling of press relations would come back to haunt him, especially as his administration shifted from the War on Poverty to the war in Vietnam. The media firestorm that followed the Tet offensive only furthered Johnson's distrust of the press, just as it undermined popular faith in the Commander in Chief. Johnson's reservations regarding the media were tied directly to his omnipresent fear that public approval might be removed from him. His combative response to the primary mechanism for shaping public opinion – the nation's media outlets – proved consistent with Johnson's general outlook. Johnson wanted positive forecasts in conjunction with headlines that touted his record, not negative reporting that might sway voters against him. This expectation alienated the press that he desperately needed when the wheels started to come off of his presidential steamroller. As president, the glare of the media was omnipresent, undermining Johnson's ability to shape the thrust of news features as he had once done as a senator. Instead of growing into the office by coming to terms with the expectations of the nation's chief executive, Johnson gradually withdrew from his obligation to the fourth estate.[51]

As for allegations that he lied about his intentions in Vietnam, Johnson claimed that deception never entered into the equation. He did not want a significant troop commitment in Vietnam while he was still fulfilling the remaining time left in Kennedy's term. He waited to make that decision until after the

---

49 Johnson, *Vantage Point*, 384. Interestingly enough, the mastermind of North Vietnam's victory Vo Nguyen Giap observed that the clear collapse of American support for the war following TET provided the communists with a much needed morale boost. The NVC realized that they no longer needed to win; they just needed to outlast the Americans. Vo Nguyen Giap, *How We Won the War* (Philadelphia: Recon Publishers, 1976).

50 Oral history transcript, George E. Reedy, interview 25 (XXV), 8/7/1990, by Michael L. Gillette, LBJ Library Oral Histories, LBJ Presidential Library, Internet Copy, LBJ Library.

51 Califano, *The Triumph*, 253-272; David Culbert, "Television's Visual Impact on Decision-Making in the USA, 1968: The Tet Offensive and Chicago's Democratic National Convention," *Journal of Contemporary History* 33, no. 3 (1998): 419-449; Michael Mandelbaum, "Vietnam: The Television War," *Daedalus* 111, no. 4 (1982): 157-169; George D. Moss, *Vietnam: An American Ordeal*, 6th Edition (New York: Routledge, 2010); Peter C. Rollins, "The Vietnam War: Perceptions Through Literature, Film, and Television," *American Quarterly* 36, no. 3 (1984): 419-432.

election. His 1964 victory, as LBJ saw it, was not a mandate regarding American involvement in Vietnam, only a decision concerning the type of leader who would direct action there. The American people did not want a trigger-happy Goldwater threatening a nuclear holocaust, they wanted Johnson's reasoned approach to the situation. From members of Congress to the Joint Chiefs of Staff, blame for the failure in Vietnam was widely shared. During his presidency, Johnson's decisions on most issues – especially popular ones – were his alone. On this most critical issue of his administration, Johnson professed that dozens of individuals helped him reach the decision that standing firm in South Vietnam was essential. By deflecting the blame onto others, Johnson hoped to stem the tide of his fast-declining approval ratings. Johnson would never admit that his desire to win praise and not be the first American president to lose a war, coupled with his inability to read the mood of foreign leaders as he effectively read those of American politicians, drove Johnson to repeatedly misstep in Vietnam. Had he pulled the plug early in his presidency he might have faced a brief backlash, but, in the long term, he would have spared the nation one of the more divisive episodes in its history. That Johnson never considered an immediate and unilateral withdrawal a viable option underscores the restrictive impact his personality had during his presidency. The very same traits that helped him triumph in the domestic realm ensured his stumbling in the global one.[52]

History has not been kind to the president from Texas. Once he decided to escalate the war in Vietnam, Johnson unknowingly set in motion the forces that would undermine his legacy. His decisions are not surprising, considering he came of age politically during the Cold War. Ideas such as containment were not just abstract notions for him, they were reality. Unless the Vietnam domino was saved from communist clutches, other Southeast Asian nations would follow and he would be accused of falling asleep at the wheel, as Truman had been with China. Being in control of the most powerful military force on earth certainly clouded his sense of the possible. Clark Clifford, who advised Johnson throughout his presidency on foreign policy and served as secretary of defense following the resignation of Robert McNamara in 1968, opined regarding America's approach in Vietnam, "we were constrained by the fact that our South Vietnamese allies were corrupt, inefficient,

52 Larry Berman, *Lyndon Johnson's War: The Road to Stalemate in Vietnam* (New York: W.W. Norton and Company, 1989); Dallek, *Flawed Giant*, 494-530; George Herring, *America's Longest War: The United States and Vietnam, 1950-1975* (New York: McGraw-Hill Higher Education, 2013); Johnson, *Vantage Point*, 116-120.

and poorly motivated. This was critical: in the final analysis, American objectives in Vietnam depended more on the capabilities of our allies in Saigon than on our own efforts."[53] By the time members of the administration came around to this idea, it was already too late. Once massively committed to a ground war in Vietnam, Johnson could not simply pull the plug on the operation as reports from the field grew less sanguine. He instead believed that the weight of America's firepower and resources would break the back of his opponents in Vietnam. Johnson, like all occupiers of the Oval Office, was a product of time and place. His scope of experience included World War II, a conflict in which the strength of American arms knew no limitations. He naturally conflated the experience of that war with the one in Vietnam and jumped into the fray with certainty that things would go America's way.[54]

Summarizing his administration, Johnson proudly noted, "when we made mistakes, I believe we erred because we tried to do too much too soon, and never because we walked away from a challenge."[55] Lyndon Johnson was committed to the enactment of a sweeping agenda that included the eradication of poverty and racial injustice. Later in his administration he took things even further by pushing for the renewal of the nation's aging cities, the preservation of America's wilderness areas, and the imposition of legislation that was designed to make all Americans safer. At the same time he launched the legislative flood that rivaled Franklin Roosevelt's New Deal, Johnson was making commitments to dramatically escalate America's involvement in Vietnam, embroiling the country in a war that would help topple his administration. President Johnson discovered the hard way that his lifelong habit of trying to secure greater laurels than everyone around him came at a terrible price. Johnson's shortcomings stem, in part, from the quintessentially American characteristic of boundless optimism born in a land blessed with seemingly limitless resources. Indeed, LBJ was the last of America's leaders who governed with the absolute certainty that the United States was a country that could win any war and solve any problem. As a result of his policies both foreign and domestic, which were clearly a product of his Texas-sized dreams and personality, President Lyndon Johnson ensured that the so-called "American Century" would end with far less optimism than it began.

---

53 Clifford, Clark, *Counsel to the President*, 404.

54 Warren I. Cohen and Nancy Bernkopf Tucker, eds., *Lyndon Johnson Confronts the World: American Foreign Policy, 1963-1968* (New York: Cambridge University Press, 1994); Frank E. Vandiver, *Shadows of Vietnam: Lyndon Johnson's Wars* (College Station: Texas A&M Press, 1997).

55 Johnson, *Vantage Point*, 566.

After he left the White House, Johnson observed that he had been unfairly treated. He perceived this bias throughout his public career as each rung he climbed up the political ladder brought with it increased scrutiny and criticism. Until the end of his days, Johnson asserted that the "metropolitan press of the Eastern seaboard," harped on "my style, my clothes, my manner, my accent, and my family" without cessation.[56] No matter how hard he pushed, no matter how many achievements he had secured, he felt unfulfilled and underappreciated. The personality traits that catapulted him to the highest office in the land also brought him to the nadir of his popularity as his failed war in Vietnam, in conjunction with what he considered unfair media coverage, led to his abrupt withdrawal from the political arena. As he entered a very brief post-presidential period that ended with his death on 22 January 1973, LBJ thought little about all the things he had accomplished. He was too busy dwelling on how he had fallen short.

56 Johnson, *Vantage Point*, 94.

CHAPTER 9

The Perfect Storm: Richard Nixon and the Office of Telecommunications Policy

Kathryn Cramer Brownell

In 1974, after serving as the inaugural director of Richard M. Nixon's newly formed Office of Telecommunications Policy (OTP), Clay T. Whitehead worried about the state of television. Known informally as the country's 'television czar,' he had dedicated the past four years to revamping communications policies in the country. He was optimistic about the future of new technologies, notably satellite, cable television, and computers. But he feared that Americans had little understanding of the "corporate and governmental forces" behind the dominant medium that so fundamentally shaped their lives.[1] Over the past two decades, public relations agencies popped up across the political landscape, teaching politicians how to communicate with television (for a hefty fee, of course). Over the past five years, journalists, like Joe McGinniss who penned the best-selling exposé on Nixon's 1968 advertising campaign *The Selling of the President*, revealed to the public the details of these political communication strategies that manipulated images on television screens. Yet little knowledge existed on how television actually functioned and how it had become a "creation of government." Whitehead saw this behind-the-scenes role of government policy in shaping "commercial efforts," "regulatory attitudes," and public engagement with television as harnessing the real power in American society and he was committed to changing public narratives and policies toward both established and emerging communication technologies.[2] Working for the Nixon administration over the past five years, he had the platform and authority to do so.

His efforts were short lived, however. By 1978, under President Jimmy Carter, the OTP lost its policy-making authority, public prominence, and eventually its funding as it merged into the National Telecommunications and Information Administration in the Department of Commerce. As the Watergate scandal

1 Draft 1, "Introduction." Folder- Drafter Chapter 1 from 1974 book, Box 50, Clay T. Whitehead Papers (CTWP), Library of Congress, Washington D.C.

2 Book outline, Folder- CTW Book introduction outline, n.d. Box 50, CTWP.

© KONINKLIJKE BRILL NV, LEIDEN, 2020 | DOI:10.1163/9789004422643_011

unfolded, policymakers and the public began to view the office as just another pawn in the president's war against the media. OTP staffers quickly fled the sinking ship of the Nixon administration, with few individuals willing to salvage its remains under Ford and Carter. But thirty years later, Whitehead and his former colleagues looked back on their time at the OTP as the "gathering storm" that paved the way for the "transformation of television" and American society more broadly at the end of the twentieth century.[3] He firmly believed that by crafting policies that promoted competition and the free market to challenge broadcasting's monopoly, the OTP launched dramatic economic, technological, and political changes in the media landscape. But the telecommunications storm itself required one other element – the person whose policy agenda and governing approach ultimately allowed the OTP to have a dramatic impact in the short time it existed: President Richard Nixon.

The OTP existed for less than eight years, but it generated national attention and sparked controversy by embodying the personality of Richard Nixon. The OTP agenda frequently reflected Nixon's complicated relationship with the press that had shaped the highs and lows of his political trajectory, and in turn, the public perception of OTP's function was shaped by Nixon's well publicized vendetta against the Fourth Estate. As a result, studying the ways in which television transformed American democracy during the Nixon era requires an understanding of how the personal politics of the president shaped and were shaped by cultural attitudes, technological pressures, and the executive bureaucracy itself.

Over the course of his political career, Richard Nixon became known, and at times feared, for his hostility toward the mainstream media. The image of a scowling Nixon at press conferences captured his personal paranoia about media biases against him as well as his persistent political battle with the press to control his image. During his presidency and in the decades since his resignation, journalists and scholars have documented how Nixon built an enemy list of 'unfriendly' reporters, whom he punished by excluding them from traveling with the president, harassing them with the IRS, and even attempting to censor them through the courts.[4]

---

3 These are the chapter titles that Whitehead wrote out in his manuscript draft. This research and the book outline can be found in Box 50, CTWP.

4 William E. Porter, *Assault on the Media: The Nixon Years* (Ann Arbor: University of Michigan Press, 1976). David Greenberg, *Nixon's Shadow: The History of an Image* (New York: W.W. Norton, 2003); Louis W. Liebovich, *Richard Nixon, Watergate, and the Press* (Westport: Praeger, 2003); Mark Feldstein, *Poisoning the Press: Richard Nixon, Jack Anderson, and the Rise of Washington's Scandal Culture* (New York: Picor, 2011).

What began as a personal vendetta against reporters became central to how Nixon governed. He infamously assailed against journalists for "kicking him around" in the press conference that followed his 1962 gubernatorial defeat in California. In his mind, the reason he had lost that campaign (and the 1960 presidential one before it) was not simply biased media coverage, but lack of coverage. If the press is against a candidate, complained Nixon, "give him the shaft, but also recognize if they give him the shaft, put one lonely reporter on the campaign who will report what the candidate says now and then."[5] These sentiments shaped the very function of the OTP and the policies about expanding media diversity and access that emanated from it. As a result, White House staffers like Whitehead had an unprecedented opportunity to turn Nixon's hostility toward the media into a policy platform that transformed the economic, social, and political assumptions that had undergirded the broadcasting industry for over four decades.

While previous presidents had dismissed telecommunications policy as insignificant, Nixon did not. The 37th president believed deeply that postwar broadcasting policies had propped up the authority of his opponents, so he saw communications policy as a tool to dismantle their political power. The result was a 'perfect storm' in which the president's personal beliefs about media bias, his career battling broadcast reporters, and his political quest to undermine the liberal establishment met with newfound institutional support for the telecommunications industry and young staffers eager to transform the status quo of the media landscape.

Over the past decade, Richard Nixon has captured the attention of historians for the ways in which his divisive and controversial presidency ushered in political polarization that broke down the post-World War II liberal consensus and paved the way for the nation's rightward shift. He articulated a cultural populism that tapped into the growing grassroots conservative mobilizations in the suburbs of Atlanta, Phoenix, and southern California and gave a national voice to the 'Silent Majority.' Over the past decade, political historians have argued that Nixon did not invent the GOP's 'Southern Strategy,' rather he capitalized on activism and ideological shifts begun at the local level.[6] Biographers, on the other hand, have contended that Nixon did not just benefit from

5 Gladwin Hill, "Nixon Denounces the Press as Biased," *New York Times*, November 8, 1962, 1.

6 See for example, Lisa McGirr, *Suburban Warriors: The Origins of the New American Right* (Princeton: Princeton University Press, 2002); Matthew Lassiter, *The Silent Majority: Suburban Politics in the Sunbelt South* (Princeton: Princeton University Press, 2007); Elizabeth Tandy Shermer, *Sunbelt Capitalism: Phoenix and the Transformation of American Politics* (Philadelphia: University of Pennsylvania Press, 2015).

a divided America. Rather he led a drive to bring the South and the Sunbelt into the Republican Party and ushered in the modern era of distrust in government and ideological fracture.[7] These narratives frequently begin with Nixon's youth, exploring how his exclusion from Ivy League networks, which his political rival John F. Kennedy navigated with such ease, bred a deep resentment of the 'Eastern Establishment' that never accepted him. Many have used a psychological element to examine his paranoia – of the press, academia and other enemies planning his demise – concluding that his inner demons overran his political brilliance as he used any means necessary to wage war against his opponents, something the Watergate scandal exposed.

Biographical accounts frequently ignore the broader cultural, social, and institutional environment in which presidents operate, just as studies of these landscapes frequently allude to the person in the most powerful political office as merely an outside actor in driving political change. Recent scholarship on the presidency, however, has pushed for a "third way" to more effectively bridge these two approaches and integrate the president into American political history.[8] The Office of Telecommunications Policy – a policy-making entity, a public relations operation, and a bureaucracy developed by the president – provides an opportunity to examine the intersection between the personal and the broader cultural environment and institutional structures in which Richard Nixon operated.

Though a small office in the White House, the OTP gained national attention and influence as a player in Nixon's battle against broadcast television in particular. As a result, a team of communications policymakers transformed the White House into a platform to promote competition and diversity as a solution to Nixon's deeply held belief about the media bias that had attempted to undermine his political career. While the connection between partisanship and policymaking turned the OTP into a "pariah" among executive agencies, it also allowed staffers to challenge strongly held assumptions about the economic structures, political role, and social responsibilities of the television in-

7 For a historiographic overview of Nixon biographies, see Iwon W. Morgan, "Nixon Biographies," in *A Companion to Richard M. Nixon*, ed. Melvin Small (Hoboken, NJ: Blackwell Publishing, 2011). More recent biographies continue to emphasize the role of Nixon in creating these political divides. See: Rick Perlstein, *Nixonland: The Rise of a President and the Fracturing of America* (New York: Scribner, 2009); Evan Thomas, *Being Nixon: A Man Divided* (New York: Random House, 2016); and John Farrell, *Richard Nixon: The Life* (New York: Doubleday, 2017). For an overview of "psychobiographers," see Greenberg, *Nixon's Shadow*, 232-269.

8 Brian Balogh and Bruce Schulman, *Recapturing the Oval Office: New Historical Approaches to the American Presidency* (Ithaca: Cornell University Press, 2015).

dustry.[9] Under Nixon's administration, the personal combined with broader technological and cultural changes in media to make the presidency – not Congress, the Courts, or the Federal Communications Commission – a major policy player in shaping the institutional structure and function of the media in American political life.

Since its founding, the United States has undergone dramatic changes in communications technology that have put pressure on the government to make political decisions about media's content and economic structure.[10] From the newspapers of the Early Republic to the telegraph and telephone of the nineteenth century to the explosion of radio and film in the twentieth century, the government has actively subsidized certain technological developments, regulated its content, and encouraged or limited its expansion.[11] Because radio and then television used airwaves policymakers categorized as 'public,' the federal government took an active role in establishing the rules for producing and distributing content over the airwaves during the twentieth century.[12] But, it was Congress that shaped regulatory legislation, not the president. The Radio Act of 1927 encouraged a system of commercial sponsorship to develop for radio and delegated authority to an independent regulatory body, the Federal Radio Commission.[13] The 1934 Federal Communications Act, which created the more permanent Federal Communications Commission, continued policies that allowed a corporate and monopolistic structure to undergird the development of radio and then television as long as programming also served the public interest.

Unlike other New Deal regulatory commissions that gained the public trust, the FCC earned a reputation for incompetence at best and corruption at worst.[14] The FCC was overwhelmingly made up of political appointees from both sides of the aisle with a vested financial and professional interest in

9 Francis E. Rourke and Roger E. Brown, "Presidents, Professionals, and Telecommunications Policy Making in the White House," *Presidential Studies Quarterly* 25, no. 2 (Spring 1996): 539-549.

10 Paul Starr, *The Creation of the Media: The Political Origins of Modern Communications* (New York: Basic Books, 2002).

11 Richard R. John, *Spreading the News: The American Postal System from Franklin to Morse* (Cambridge: Harvard University Pres, 1998); Richard R. John, *Network Nation: Inventing American Telecommunications* (Cambridge: Belknap Press, 2015).

12 Starr, *The Creation of the Media*; Michele Hilmes, *Radio Voices: American Broadcasting, 1922-1952* (Minneapolis: University of Minnesota Press, 1997).

13 Rourke and Brown, "Presidents, Professionals, and Telecommunications Policy Making in the White House," 541.

14 James Baughman, *Television's Guardians: The FCC and the Politics of Programming, 1958-1967* (Knoxville: University of Tennessee Press, 1985).

national network corporations – Columbia Broadcasting System (CBS), National Broadcasting Company (NBC), and then later American Broadcasting Company (ABC). FCC regulatory policies allowed the 'Big Three' television networks to gain a monopoly over the airwaves during the post-World War II era. National broadcasters convinced their friends at the FCC of the benefits of the network affiliation system and developed economically lucrative contracts with local broadcasters who then gained access to 'high quality programming' in exchange for airing content from that particular network.[15] Elected officials benefited from news coverage of their activities in Washington, which local broadcasters related to constituents in their efforts to promote local programming and educate listeners and viewers on public affairs. As a result, close collaboration between broadcasters, congressional leaders, and the FCC created a favorable regulatory environment that benefited both congressional representatives eager to stay in the public eye of constituents on television and the broadcasting industry, which experienced little competition in exchange for this positive coverage.

As concerns about the inadequacy of partisan appointments to meet Cold War technological challenges grew, ideas for a telecommunications office in the executive branch took shape. For example, in 1962 John Kennedy's foreign policy face-off with the Soviet Union over the potential placement of missiles in Cuba revealed the "inadequacy of [a] government communications system."[16] Soon after, the National Security Council discussed ways to establish a unified communications network to facilitate Cold War decision-making. Not until the end of Lyndon Johnson's presidency, however, did a task force on communications policy that went beyond defense concerns form. Headed by the undersecretary of state for political affairs, Eugene V. Rostow, this committee pushed for a more prominent telecommunications office in either the Department of Commerce or Transportation. Because it submitted its report just after Nixon won the 1968 election, Johnson left it to his successor to grapple with its lengthy recommendations. After two decades of White House dismissal of telecommunications issues, Richard Nixon took action, and his deep and transformative experiences with the media itself shaped the structure and mission of what would become the Office of Telecommunications Policy.

---

15 Charles Ponce de Leon, *And That's The Way It Was: A History of Television News in America* (Chicago: University of Chicago Press, 2015).

16 This particular incident is related in the history of the OTP in Charles C. Joyce, Jr. "Ad Hoc Review Group for Organization for Telecommunications within the Executive Branch," Feb. 9, 1976. Folder- Federal Regulatory Reform- Office of Telecommunications Policy Study, Box 20, Edward C. Schmults Papers, Gerald R. Ford Library (GRFL), Ann Arbor, Michigan.

Richard Nixon had a different relationship with the television industry than his predecessors. Lyndon Johnson's wife had $7 million invested in broadcasting and radio stations, and both John F. Kennedy and Dwight Eisenhower had close friendships with broadcasters, frequently turning to them for advice on media strategy.[17] In fact, the postwar period emerged as a time of professional collaboration between the elite men who ran American politics and those men who reported on their activities. Even as broadcasting networks expanded their newsrooms, deference to 'official' sources in Washington and a respect for the Cold War consensus shaped the news agenda, ultimately bolstering the prestige, prominence, and values of the postwar establishment and its belief in the importance of government intervention abroad and at home.[18]

Richard Nixon's rapid rise to national prominence relied on his ability to capitalize on anticommunist politics and the television environment that contributed to the growing idea of 'Cold war consensus' that this powerful communications medium promoted.[19] As a newly elected congressman, his prominent place accusing former diplomat Alger Hiss of betraying national security interests relied on the powerful use of staged media investigations that served as a Cold War 'morality tale' on the dangers of communist subversion. In launching his subsequent senatorial campaign, he learned how to fight dirty and engage in California's unique style of "media-driven performative politics" to take down his opponent, former actress Helen Gahagan Douglas, by using the powerful accusation that she was "pink down to her underwear," a line that stunned, and stuck.[20] He then catapulted to the forefront of Republican politics, securing a place as Dwight Eisenhower's running mate two

17 On Lady Bird's holdings see: Baughman, *Television's Guardians*, 138-139. On Eisenhower and Kennedy's relationship with broadcasters and their role in advising them in political campaigns, see: David Greenberg, *Republic of Spin: An Inside History of the American Presidency* (New York: W.W. Norton, 2016), 276-354.

18 On the social networks that bound together this professional network, see Kathryn McGarr, "'We're All In This Thing Together': Cold War Consensus in the Exclusive Social World of Washington Reporters," in *Media Nation: A Political History of the News*, eds. Bruce Schulman and Julian Zelizer (Philadelphia: University of Pennsylvania Press, 2017), 77-95. See also the criticism of this world by conservatives in: Nicole Hemmer, *Messengers of the Right: Conservative Media and the Transformation of American Politics* (Philadelphia: University of Pennsylvania Press, 2016).

19 Greenberg, *Nixon's Shadow*.

20 On California's unique style of media-driven performative politics, see, Jonathan Bell, *California Crucible: The Forging of Modern American Liberalism* (Philadelphia: University of Pennsylvania Press, 2012), Kathryn Cramer Brownell, *Showbiz Politics: Hollywood in American Political Life* (Chapel Hill; University of North Carolina Press, 2014). On the 1950 Senate campaign, see Greg Mitchell, *Tricky Dick and the Pink Lady: Richard Nixon vs. Helen Gahagan Douglas: Sexual Politics and the Red Scare* (New York: Random House, 1998).

years later. When accusations that he had accepted bribes threatened to derail his ascendency, he turned to television. In a powerful speech broadcast across the country, he opened his checkbook to the American public, celebrated his wife Pat's "sturdy" Republican cloth coat, and vowed that he would keep his dog Checkers that a political supporter had sent him because his daughter Trisha loved him so much. Viewers' enthusiasm following the address secured his place on the Republican ticket.[21]

Nixon's political success depended on mastering television, but in his presidential bid in 1960, he stumbled before a challenger even more media savvy: John F. Kennedy. Nixon assailed his opponent that year for being superficial, flashy, and using "cheap publicity" to dominate headlines.[22] He firmly believed that Kennedy's close friendship with journalists, reporters, and Hollywood entertainers gave him an unfair advantage in the election. The television debates, which Nixon would later blame for his electoral defeat that year, again crystalized Kennedy's superior media operation. Two years later, his bitterness toward the press exploded in what he bitterly declared would be his "last press conference."

Nixon's animosity toward the press fueled two developments that would later shape both his presidency and the broader media environment in which he operated. First, he became obsessed with controlling his public image as he remade himself into a 'New Nixon' and relaunched another presidential bid in 1968. During this campaign, he surrounded himself with a team of media advisors, including advertising executive Harry Treleaven, the fiery speechwriter Patrick Buchanan, and the savvy television producer Roger Ailes, who all reinforced the message that "he didn't lose in 1960, [his] tinker-toy" television operation did.[23] So he built an impressive team of advertisers, entertainers, and pollsters dedicated to making people "like him."[24] But positive portrayals of Nixon also hinged on preventing the circulation of negative stories about him or discrediting accounts of his opponents. Clouding his campaign and then his presidency in secrecy, Nixon attempted to control the stories disseminated about his presidency just as he attempted to bully, threaten, and cajole journalists who wrote stories that challenged this carefully crafted narrative his team constructed.[25]

21 Greenberg, *Nixon's Shadow*, 31-35.

22 Brownell, *Showbiz Politics*, 188-207.

23 Memo from Bill Gavin to Len Garment, Re: Nixon notes, Folder Bill Gavin 2 of 3, box 69, Name File box 3 of 29, 1968 Campaign File, Len Garment, WHCF, Richard M. Nixon Presidential Library, Yorba Linda, California.

24 Joe McGinniss, *The Selling of the President, 1968* (New York: Trident Press, 1969).

25 For a discussion of Nixon's spin machine, see Greenberg, *Republic of Spin*, 397-402.

More broadly, Nixon saw the mainstream media as central to the dominance of the broader 'Eastern Establishment' in American politics and culture. Rooted in New York City and Washington D.C., the broadcasting industry had gained immense power in shaping the national agenda. Nixon felt that this collaboration between media and political insiders had derailed his career as an 'outsider.' The bitter president claimed to represent those other individuals outside the establishment, the 'Silent Majority' in the South, West, and Midwest whose voices and perspectives had been squashed by the elite on the East coast. By directing funds for programs like the National Endowment for the Humanities away from New York and to the heartland or by using housing policies to fracture the Democratic labor coalition, 'Tricky Dick' used public policy to wage war against the political establishment.[26] Nixon also worked to reshape the bureaucracy. Linking liberalism's enduring power to the bureaucrats who served in the federal government, Nixon quickly brought loyal Republicans into positions of power. While not unusual for presidents to staff their own White House with dedicated party members, Nixon took it a step further. He attempted to fill the ranks of the Justice Department, the Treasury Department, and the Office of Management and Budget with Republicans that did not just agree with him ideologically, but professed personal loyalty to the president.[27] For Nixon, political power depended on staffers willing to bend the law at times to serve the president's war against the 'Establishment.'

Nixon's obsession with the media and his quest to remake government institutions shed essential light into the short but effective operations of the Office of Telecommunications Policy. Moreover, it explains the contradiction that the president who attempted to personally censor the press more than any of his predecessors would also be the one to reshape the media landscape to pull back government regulations and expand First Amendment rights to encourage more voices on the airwaves. Clay Whitehead argued that Nixon "understood and cared more about [communications policy development] than anybody on his White House staff."[28] Three years after Nixon's resignation, Whitehead maintained that the president constantly lamented the "sad state of nationally controlled television around the country," and that when "faced

26 Bruce Schulman, *The Seventies: The Great Shift in American Culture, Society, and Politics* (Boston: Da Capo Press, 2001), 23-52.

27 Michael Koncewicz, *They Said No to Nixon: Republicans Who Stood Up to the President's Abuses of Power* (Oakland: University of California Press, 2018).

28 "The Whitehead Years," *Cablevision*, March 28, 1977. News clipping in folder- Communications Reform- OTP, Box 36, Domestic Policy Staff- Simon Lazares' 1976 Campaign Transition File, Jimmy Carter Presidential Library (JCPL), Atlanta, Georgia.

squarely with policy issues," notably how to grapple with satellite technology and cable television, Nixon "would come down on the side of less government control over the media at least in part for principle, and in part because he realized very explicitly that government controls over media would be used much more effectively by a liberal president who followed him in office than could be used by him or a conservative."[29]

Formed in 1970 as part of a congressional bill to reorganize the White House bureaucracy, the OTP was initially tasked with overseeing spectrum management responsibilities – the same concern that began discussions of such an office during the early days of the Cold War. But via executive order, Nixon expanded the OTP functions to include policy decisions on how the media landscape should operate as an economic, social, and political entity.[30] Moreover, the order clearly articulated the organization's mission to not just advise the president on telecommunications but to also "assure that the executive branch views are effectively presented to the Congress and the Federal Communications Commission on telecommunications policy matters." Under his administration, the OTP took on significant and controversial issues, like an Open Skies Policy for satellite development, the Fairness Doctrine, the Prime Time Rule, broadcast license renewals, and regulations for cable television. And it did so by capitalizing on Nixon's broader governing strategy: directly challenging perceived 'enemies' and identifying the political bias inherent in current policies that the president believed had strengthened the liberal establishment at his expense. The future of television dominated the attention of OTP policy discussions in ways that would directly target the existing economic structure of the broadcasting and telephone corporations on the coasts and benefit both Richard Nixon and entrepreneurs in Middle America.

And yet, the push for the OTP came not from Nixon or his close circle of advisors, but from a young, smart White House staffer – Clay Whitehead – ultimately illuminating how bureaucrats themselves could capitalize on the president's personal biases to pursue their own goals. Before joining Nixon's campaign in 1968, Whitehead had a pedigree that included a B.S. and M.S. in

29 "The Whitehead Years," *Cablevision*, March 28, 1977.

30 Executive Order 11556- Assigning Telecommunications Functions, September 4, 1970. http://www.presidency.ucsb.edu/ws/?pid=105884. See also discussion of the OTP's history under Nixon in: Charles C. Joyce, Jr. "Ad Hoc Review Group for Organization for Telecommunications within the Executive Branch," February 9, 1976. Folder- Federal Regulatory Reform- Office of Telecommunications Policy Study, Box 20, Edward C. Schmults Papers, GRFL.

electrical engineering and a Ph.D. in management from Massachusetts Institute of Technology as well as experience as a research analyst at Rand Corporation. Whitehead quickly proved both his ability and his loyalty when he took the lead on crafting policies for the satellite industry in 1969. In these early months of the Nixon administration, Whitehead saw an opportunity to inject a new economic model of competition into an industry that had shown great promise to revolutionize the transfer of information across the country through the skies, rather than through wired terrestrial connections. Moreover, his solution hit at the economic power that national broadcast corporations had secured over the past two decades.

The idea of monopoly had shaped the development of television: national networks had protection from competition to encourage investments into programming and developing new technology to improve television. Unsurprisingly then, telephone and television monopolies quickly saw satellites as an opportunity to expand their control of information by developing what they called the "technical and operational design of the pilot system." However, Whitehead did not want to continue the dominant policies that would advance corporate monopoly – whether by broadcasting networks or AT&T. Why not, argued Whitehead, use this moment to "stimulate a more vigorous and innovative" model of competition that would "minimize the regulatory impediments to technological and market innovation" and "use this approach as a wedge to encourage more vigorous and innovative competition among communications organizations"?[31]

By opening the door to other businesses, notably cable operators eager to find ways to go around broadcast and telephone corporations to transmit programming, Whitehead's 'Open Skies' proposal used the White House as a platform to challenge the mutually beneficial arrangement between the FCC and the industries it regulated.[32] ABC and NBC executives reminded Whitehead of the technological achievements ushered in by their companies since the Radio Act of 1927 by allowing the private sector to develop technologies. But while they advocated for private capital to flourish rather than government-owned satellites, the proposals also celebrated the accomplishments of a "bifurcated setup with a few dedicated satellites operated by one or two industries" to establish a system that would provide "a degree of competition."[33] Although they

31 "Domestic Satellite Policy Working Paper," July 8, 1969. Folder- Domestic Affairs, 1969-1970. Box 4, CTWP.

32 White House statement by Clay Whitehead, August 19, 1969. Folder 8- Telecommunications Industry replies to letters, Box 16, CTWP.

33 Letter from Leonard Goldenson to Clay Whitehead, September 16, 1969. Folder 8-Telecommunications Industry replies to letters, Box 16, CTWP.

argued that this would "obviate" a monopoly, Whitehead worried how it would ultimately replicate the oligopoly that gave the the 'Big Three' such economic power in broadcasting.

Later, Whitehead would recall that the industry-proposed plan to run the satellite system as a monopoly corporation "wasn't a great way to preserve private enterprise" and he argued that if "we're even going to have competition in the communications business, we have to start it with this new technology."[34] So he pushed to get the White House on board to offer up an alternative, opening up bids for a variety of companies to submit plans to build and operate satellite receivers. It worked, and new businesses – including a variety of cable companies and even a small electronics company like Scientific-Atlanta – got involved in the domestic satellite industry.[35]

The lessons of the 'Open Sky' policy were stark: a telecommunications advisor could help politicians match their political philosophy with technological developments and no longer would they have to rely on the status quo simply because they did not have the technological knowhow. While the details of this policy shift for the satellite and television industry would take several years to firm up with profound implications down the road, Whitehead's work immediately encouraged Nixon to establish the Office of Telecommunications Policy. Formed in the fall of 1970 with Whitehead at its helm, the OTP reported directly to the president, explicitly seeing its mission to design new policy options outside those crafted by the FCC and Congress.

The OTP began under a glimmer of hope and a cloud of suspicion. During a time of dramatic technological change and growing frustrations with the limits of network television on both the left and the right, a range of individuals and industries were eager for a more coherent government policy in the fields of cable television, public television, satellites, data transmission, and computers.[36] But Nixon's opponents also understood the deep resentment the new

34 Taped Conversation between Tom Whitehead, Brian Lamb, and Henry Goldberg n.d. (2003?) Folder- Interviews- Box 60, CTWP.

35 Parson, *Blue Skies*, 328-333.

36 On the left especially, civil rights activists sought to challenge local news portrayals of protests in the South, see Steven D. Classen, *Watching Jim Crow: The Struggles over Mississippi TV, 1955-1969* (Durham: Duke University Press, 2004). On the right, conservatives challenged the liberal bias in media since the 1950s, gaining more visibility and recognition in the 1960s, as Hemmer, *Messengers of the Right* argues. In "Blue Skies and Strange Bedfellows," Thomas Streeter explores the debates among progressives, liberals and conservatives that formed in hope that new technology could solve urban decline, failures in the New Deal state, and debates about media access across the spectrum. These studies, however, frequently reinforced one another, creating a 'common consensus' among this coalition.

president had toward the media industry and feared he may use the power of the Executive Branch to strangle the free press.[37] After all, a vocal attack on 'media bias' and a secretive effort to control the flow of information from the White House defined his first term.[38] For Nixon, the OTP became another tool to pursue his campaign to transform media institutions. For OTP staffers, this campaign became a way to publicize the deeper social and political implications of the economic inequalities begot by network monopoly and to cut through the technical jargon that had prevented political discussions of more competitive alternatives.

In November of 1972, the president won a landslide victory to launch his second term as president. As Nixon began reorganizing his staff to implement the mandate he felt he had received by winning every state except Massachusetts, OTP economist Bruce Owen penned an analysis of how to conquer the problem of 'network power' the administration and the country faced. Titled "Project BUN," or "Break Up Networks," Owen's report contained a powerful indictment about the economic, political, and social problems that emerged from the fact that "three national networks dominate television."[39] Viewers had only three options for news and entertainment programming, and advertisers had only three potential clients for access to consumers. The result: national networks had enormous economic power. But the political and social implications were also profound, argued Owen, because of the networks' "ability to control the flow of information and of ideas to the people." The power to "mold public opinion" that Owen described in the report's introduction would have worried any top Nixon advisor and the president himself, as they spent extensive time and resources monitoring news coverage and devel-

37 For more on the launch of the OTP and the debate surrounding it, see Kathryn Cramer Brownell, "'Ideological Plugola,' 'Elitist Gossip,' and the Need for Cable Television," in *Media Nation: A Political History of the News*, eds. Bruce Schulman and Julian Zelizer (Philadelphia: University of Pennsylvania Press, 2017). For the controversy OTP sparked, see Rourke and Brown, "Presidents, Professionals, and Telecommunications Policy Making in the White House" and James Miller, "The President's Advocate: OTP and Broadcast Issues," *Journal of Broadcasting & Electronic Media* 26, no. 3 (1982): 625-639.

38 Spiro Agnew frequently led the attack against campaign against the networks, see Matthew Pressman, "Objectivity and its Discontents: The Struggle for the Soul of American Journalism in the 1960s and 1970s," in *Media Nation*, eds. Schulman and Zelizer (Philadelphia: University of Pennsylvania Press, 2017), 96-113. H.R. Haldeman worked to implement a tight restriction over information; on his efforts to follow Nixon's obsession over the 'PR' efforts see H.R. Haldeman, *The Haldeman Diaries: Inside the Nixon White House* (New York: G.P. Putnam's Sons, 1994).

39 Bruce Owen, "Project BUN," Folder 8- Project BUN, Box 36, CTWP.

oping a sophisticated polling operation. The solution: policies that promoted cable television as a direct competitor to broadcast (rather than maintaining its restricted development merely as an ancillary arm of the industry as the FCC had for two decades), encouraged new networks, and loosen the ties between affiliates and national networks.

The report highlighted the problem of media bias and proposed solutions to the problem of 'network power' in ways that appealed directly to Nixon. For example, cable television promised diversity on the dial and promoting the medium's growth with a free market approach fit the atmosphere of deregulation that had started to grow in the Republican Party. Presidential support of its development, which the OTP concluded "was coming anyway," would "get the President associated with its future in a positive way."[40] But the pursuit of these long-term policies of economic competition and diversity, noted the report, might also allow for a short term opportunity to strong-arm the content of news program deemed "liberally biased" – a tactic that fit into Nixon's immediate goals of combating the growing tide of criticism against his administration. Calling "punitive punishment" against the networks "counterproductive," the BUN report instead urged action that combined a broad commitment to "broadcast freedom" with a "clear signal that things can get rough in other areas if there isn't more exercise of management responsibility over programming and news." The author of Project BUN, Bruce Owen, cared deeply about the economic implications of the network monopoly, and the bulk of the report discussed the nuances of fiscal options to solve this issue. Whitehead concurred, but focused his efforts on how competition could drive new technological innovations. Both OTP staffers, however, took advantage of Nixon's media outlook – or perhaps his media obsession – to frame these policy shifts in White House briefs and public speeches that highlighted the need for "less biased TV news" and the problem of "elitism" in network programming.[41]

Consider for example the speech for which Whitehead would become famous (or infamous, depending on one's perspective) that launched the public relations component of Project BUN. At the end of December, Whitehead traveled to Indianapolis with a well-planned and diligently crafted speech to local broadcasters. With the White House's direct encouragement and feedback on the speech, Whitehouse assailed the political problems of the network con-

---

40 Ibid.

41 See for example the talking points and one-page brief that followed the 11-page discussion of Project BUN.

trol and bias.[42] He blasted national news programs for betraying the trust of television viewers who tuned into the program for information and facts and instead found reporters who confused "sensationalism with sense" and dispensed "elitist gossip in the guise of news analysis." By claiming that programs were filled with "ideological plugola," the speech explicitly linked the OTP to the president's war against the media and deeply worried reporters who feared that Nixon's second term would intensify efforts to censor and bully the press. Some would go as far to depict Whitehead as the "reincarnation of Joseph Goebbels" – the notorious Nazi propagandist.[43] On the other hand, it captured the praise of conservative commentators. James Kilpatrick observed that Whitehead "had come to replace Vice President Agnew, who has turned demure in recent months, in the Administration's great body contact game with badgering the TV networks."[44] Television host of the show *Firing Line*, conservative icon William Buckley, invited Whitehead on his show and professed his admiration for the phrase "ideological plugola."[45] Whitehead generated media attention on his subsequent whirlwind of public speeches and the president personally congratulated him on how he "was handling his job, particularly with respect to the problem of the networks and broadcasting."[46]

These controversial speeches led many to believe that Whitehead had climbed the ranks of the White House, which was simultaneously experiencing turnover in top personnel due to the Watergate scandal, to become Nixon's new media attack dog. And yet, before leaving the White House, Whitehead publically broke with the president about funding for the Corporation for Public Broadcasting – a fight that made the front page of the *New York Times* and

---

42 Remarks of Clay Whitehead, Director of Office of Telecommunications Policy at the Sigma Delta Chi Luncheon, Indianapolis, Indiana, December 18, 1972. Folder: Speech- Indiana Broadcasters Association, December 18, 1972, Box 42, CTWP. For more details on the planning of the speech and its reception, see, Brownell "'Ideological Plugola,' 'Elitist Gossip,' and the Need for Cable Television."

43 "Free Cable TV," January 19, 1974, news clipping on Whitehead and the OTP collected in: folder- Cable television and regulation- 2, Box 21, Frederick Lynn May Collection, GRFL.

44 News clipping, James Kilpatrick, "Whitehead off Base in Attack on TV Industry," *The Evening Star and Daily News*, December 26, 1972. Folder: Speech- Indiana Broadcasters Association, December 18, 1972, Box 42, CTWP.

45 Transcript, *Firing Line*, (taped February 1, 1973 and aired February 16) with guest Clay Whitehead. Southern Educational Communications Association, Hoover Institution Library and Archives, Stanford University, Stanford, California.

46 Memorandum: Meeting with the President, February 5, 1973, H.R. Haldeman, Charles Colson, and Clay T. Whitehead. Folder 6- Memoranda and other misc. documents, Box 31, CTWP.

led to Whitehead's resignation – and he submitted a policy report proposing cable television legislation that surprised observers in both the cable and broadcasting industry for its balance and objectivity.[47] Suspicious commentators speculated that these final actions, which were "notable for their lack of political mischief," were just Whitehead's last-ditch effort to rebuild his reputation before entering the private sector.[48]

But these efforts in fact revealed that Whitehead and the OTP were not simply Nixon's pawns. Rather, Whitehead and his staffers capitalized on Nixon's personal antagonism toward the media to change the policy conversation and usher in alternative political approaches to regulation that would later transform the television and satellite industries. Over the next year, amidst the Watergate scandal, the OTP became demonized as another example of presidential bullying. And yet, this "presidential jawboning," cable industry advocates argued, also constituted the first time that government envisioned a landscape in which distribution and programming competitors could challenge the prominence of the broadcasting industry.[49] The next year, the expansion of new media outlets like Ted Turner's Atlanta-based superstation or the pay cable channel Home Box Office (HBO) offered newfound diversity on television screens via companies that were notably not owned by the dominant television corporations.

The OTP used Nixon's media obsession, which permeated White House policy discussions and built a wall of hostility between the press and the president, as an opportunity for new policies to launch the 'Information Age.' In fact, following Nixon's resignation, broadcasters attempted to use Nixon's 'anti-media' legacy to stall legislative reforms the OTP introduced, notably the attempt to deregulate cable television. The thesis, former OTP staffer Brian Lamb explained in a column for *CATV*, "has been that the Republicans want cable to grow so audiences will be fractionalized, profits will suffer, and cutbacks in news and public affairs will result." The former Nixon aide called the thesis a "ballyhooed charge" and was hopeful that a congressional report prepared by the Democratic chairman of the House Subcommittee on Communi-

47 Whitehead discusses this conflict with Nixon in "The Whitehead Years," *Cablevision*, March 28, 1977.

48 These particular quotes come from Les Brown, "Whitehead and Cable TV Plan," news clipping, January 21, 1974. This news clipping is part of a collection of media responses to the Cabinet Committee on Cable Television Report in: Folder- Cable Television and Regulation-2, Box 21, Frederick Lynn May Collection, GRFL.

49 Sol Schildhause, "memorandum on the Cabinet Committee on Cable Communications," January 16, 1974, Box 3, folder 10- Memorandum 1967-76, Sol Schildhause Collection, Barco Library, Denver, Colorado.

cations would dispel the "charges of Republican political motivation" behind cable reform.[50]

The thesis is not complete "ballyhoo," but it is incomplete. Whitehead would later admit to an "uneasy alliance" that formed between Nixon and OTP staffers, arguing that his "biggest fights were with the White House staff and the president," not the broadcast industry that he frequently attacked.[51] Both sides were committed to dismantling the power of communications monopolies, but for very different reasons. However, they agreed that cable deregulation, satellite competition, and the break-up of the AT&T monopoly would create freedom of entry for more competitors, which would be good for consumers. They launched research and initiatives to do this, and increasingly, more politicians across the political spectrum concurred. In fact, when debating the OTP's future, the Ford administration explicitly worried about its image as a "politically motivated enemy of the nation's broadcast television industry," and his economic advisors concluded that the abolition of the OTP was necessary as "part of post-Watergate house cleaning."[52] His administration encountered surprise resistance and "unexpected negative reaction from congressional and private sources" that prevented its attempt to eliminate the OTP in 1976, however. Even the Carter administration struggled with the question of what to do with the organization. The debate centered on the belief that media policy was significant enough to warrant a place in the White House to help navigate new areas of communications technology, but there remained a "fear" that media policy efforts would be seen as a "Nixonian" effort to "meddle in affairs of broadcasting."[53]

The persistence of the OTP as an embattled organization through these two presidential administrations sheds insights into how the personal motivations of a president can shape institutions and policies, as well as broader cultural attitudes and ideas of power. Nixon's presidency ingrained in American political life the essential role of 'spin' in winning campaigns and governing.[54] It also popularized a form of media politics that immediately began to reshape

50 Brian Lamb, "Broadcasters Won't have the Political Football to Kick Around Anymore," *CATV*, February 2, 1976, 4.

51 "The Whitehead Years," *Cablevision*, March 28, 1977.

52 Charles C. Joyce, Jr. "Ad Hoc Review Group for Organization for Telecommunications within the Executive Branch," February 9, 1976. Folder- Federal Regulatory Reform- Office of Telecommunications Policy Study, Box 20, Edward C. Schmults Papers, GRFL.

53 This specific discussion of "Carter's Plans for the OTP" appears in a newsclipping from *Television Digest*, January 3, 1977. However, broader concerns about what to do with the OTP are in: Folder, OTP, Box 5, Barry Jagoda Papers, Jimmy Carter Presidential Library.

54 Greenberg, *Republic of Spin*; Brownell, *Showbiz Politics*.

party mobilization during the 1970s and contributed to political realignment itself.[55] These ideas translated into the very operation of the bureaucracy as well. Unlike his predecessors, whose concerns about telecommunications policy were couched in views of national security and defense, Nixon saw it as a tool to amass personal political power and promote his governing agenda.

Once Nixon's OTP established an alternative for the growth of the commercial satellite industry and then cable television, congressional representatives increasingly saw the direct benefits of more affordable and accessible media for them to navigate personally the growing need for television in American politics. During the 1950s and 1960s, those elected officials that cared about broadcasting policy overwhelmingly supported broadcasters; after all, they were important political allies who could use their news programming and influence to maintain a connection between elected officials and constituents. Most lawmakers, however, simply allowed the FCC to act and never challenged or questioned the structures that gave such power to the three networks. But the OTP pierced holes in the accepted logic of network monopoly, demonstrating how communications systems could operate through competition rather than a regulated monopoly. The Ford administration understood what a central role the White House could play in providing an alternative to the regulatory policies that had shaped political institutions since the New Deal. "There is considerable recognition that the regulatory process tends to be self-reinforcing, and that external pressures are needed to open new policy options, to advocate appropriate legislative changes, and to afford the President staff assistance in proposing and evaluating policies and legislation," explained a background memo on the functions of the OTP.[56]

This recognition of the powerful role of media as an institution in American politics made Whitehead's mission to expose the "corporate and government" forces shaping television programming resonate even after Whitehead resigned and the organization ceased to exist. In fact, reforming media policy increasingly became a focal point for political activism on the left and the right.[57] Nixon's OTP combined the definition of "telecommunications" as a

---

55 Kathryn Cramer Brownell, "Watergate, the Bipartisan Struggle for Media Access, and the Growth of Cable Television," article forthcoming from *Modern American History*.

56 Charles C. Joyce, Jr. "Ad Hoc Review Group for Organization for Telecommunications within the Executive Branch," February 9, 1976. Folder- Federal Regulatory Reform- Office of Telecommunications Policy Study, Box 20, Edward C. Schmults Papers, GRFL.

57 See for example: Allison Perlman, *Public Interests: Media Advocacy and the Struggles over U.S. Television* (New Brunswick: Rutgers University Press, 2016); Hemmer, *Messengers of the Right*; Brian Rosenwald, *Talk Radio America: How an Industry Took Over a Political Party that Took Over the United States* (Cambridge: Harvard University Press, 2019);

"network" or a "science of technology" with the emerging field of "communications" which increasingly meant spin and public relations.[58] Ford and then Carter would attempt to make the science of technology distinctive from the political use of technology, but Nixon's OTP showed how interrelated these items were. Perhaps Nixon and then the OTP went away, but the philosophy he and its staffers advanced remained.

Brownell, "Watergate, the Bipartisan Struggle for Media Access, and the Growth of Cable Television."

58 Charles C. Joyce, Jr. "Ad Hoc Review Group for Organization for Telecommunications within the Executive Branch," February 9, 1976. Folder- Federal Regulatory Reform- Office of Telecommunications Policy Study, Box 20, Edward C. Schmults Papers, GRFL.

CHAPTER 10

Hellhounds on the Campaign Trail: Region, Religion, and Manhood in Jimmy Carter's Race for the White House

Maarten Zwiers

1 Introduction: Presidential Campaigns as Precursors

"My name is Jimmy Carter, and I'm running for President." The audience at the Democratic National Convention in New York roared after their candidate spoke the opening sentence of his acceptance speech. The same words had marked the beginning of Jimmy Carter's long road to Madison Square Garden. They now heralded the start of an even greater effort: the campaign for the White House. "It's been a long time since I said those words the first time," the former governor of Georgia continued, "and now I've come here after seeing our great country to accept your nomination."[1] On his journeys across the nation, Carter had sensed the American people wanted change. He presented himself as the candidate who would run an open government that did not operate in secrecy. Carter incorporated theologian Reinhold Niebuhr's ideas about love and justice in his speech. He also talked about faith. "We feel that moral decay has weakened our country, that it is crippled by a lack of goals and values, and that our public officials have lost faith in us." This atmosphere of negativity did not characterize the true spirit of the United States, Carter argued. "We want to have faith again," he exclaimed. "We want to be proud again. We just want the truth again… It is time for the people to run the government, and not the other way around."[2]

In 1976, the United States indeed seemed ready for change. The trauma of Vietnam and the scandals of the Nixon presidency had severely weakened public trust in the federal government. The people were looking for new lead-

1 Jimmy Carter, "Acceptance Speech: Our Nation's Past and Future," in Committee on House Administration (hereafter CHA), *The Presidential Campaign of 1976* (hereafter PC 1976) (Washington: United States Government Printing Office, 1978), I: 347-352. See also Peter G. Bourne, *Jimmy Carter: A Comprehensive Biography from Plains to Postpresidency* (New York: Scribner, 1997), 333-336.

2 Carter, "Acceptance Speech," 347-352.

© KONINKLIJKE BRILL NV, LEIDEN, 2020 | DOI:10.1163/9789004422643_012

ership.[3] At first sight, Jimmy Carter hardly seemed the man who could bring the U.S. back on track. If career politicians like Lyndon Johnson, Richard Nixon, and Gerald Ford had not been able to form strong, effective governments, how could a little-known peanut farmer and one-time governor of a Deep South state put the country back on the road to decency and respectability? "Jimmy who?" was a standard response when Americans were asked about the Democratic candidate. Even his own mother could not hide her disbelief when she heard about her son's presidential plans. When Carter told her at the end of 1974 that he was going to run for president, she asked: "president of what?"[4]

But when the campaign started, Jimmy Carter transformed his relative obscurity from a disadvantage into an asset. By occupying a place outside the political establishment, he effectively portrayed himself as the right man to clean out the White House. "I am not from Washington, I do not hold public office, and I am not a lawyer" soon became one of Carter's trademark lines.[5] Most biographers agree that the 'outsider image' was one of the main reasons why he won, although they have interpreted Jimmy Carter's integrity differently. Some even consider his identity as the uncorrupted Christian farmer a hoax. Patrick Anderson, Carter's speechwriter during the 1976 campaign, warned that we should forget "the big smile. That was a disguise. I imagined him living deep in a cave; you could barely see his eyes gleaming in the shadows."[6] Peter Bourne, who also played an important role in the Carter campaign, presented a far more positive image of the Democratic candidate. "In particular, his faith led him to strive for the same objectives by whatever means were at hand while he was in Georgia, as president, and after he left office," he wrote. "Throughout his career, Carter was guided by a consistent set of values and beliefs." According to Bourne, these values and beliefs were firmly grounded in Reinhold Niebuhr's theological philosophy: "The sad job of politics is to bring justice to a sinful world."[7]

During the past decades, scholars have attempted to present a more nuanced view of Jimmy Carter's political persona. Political scientist Betty Glad

---

3 Kenneth E. Morris, *Jimmy Carter: American Moralist* (Athens and London: The University of Georgia Press, 1996), 208-209; Bruce Schulman, *The Seventies: The Great Shift in American Culture, Society, and Politics* (New York: The Free Press, 2001), 121-123.

4 Quoted in Bourne, *Jimmy Carter*, 251.

5 Ibid., 250.

6 Patrick Anderson, *Electing Jimmy Carter: The Campaign of 1976* (Baton Rouge and London: Louisiana State University Press, 1994), 165.

7 Bourne, *Jimmy Carter*, 508.

stressed his ambition and a strong desire to win as the main traits that delivered him the presidency. But she also noted his enigmatic character, calling him "a puzzling figure."[8] The Carter campaign was not about a coherent program, but about the candidate's personal characteristics. Sociologist Keith Morris asserted: "The political term for the vision that Carter failed to articulate is *ideology*... The 'personal touch' was in fact the essence of the Carter campaign."[9] Republican candidate Gerald Ford described his opponent's campaign program as fuzzy. Carter himself preferred to call it populism, a set of beliefs he defined as an elusive mix of conservatism and liberalism. In an interview with *U.S. News & World Report*, he explained how his acceptance speech in New York was "designed to show that I derived my political support, my advice and my concern directly from people themselves, not from powerful intermediaries or representatives of special interest groups."[10] This strategy of presenting himself as a man of the people and in the meantime avoiding divisive issues enabled Jimmy Carter to rally voters behind him. "Carter established a broad based appeal by selling himself as both a liberal and a conservative, straddling issues with the agility of a tightrope walker," journalist Kandy Stroud observed.[11] In a more recent analysis of Carter's 1976 campaign, historian Zachary Lechner made a similar observation, claiming that his "brilliant merging and wielding of imagined southern culture promised a set of useful, albeit abstract, tools for cultural, social, and political rehabilitation." According to Lechner, Carter's "personality and message found a receptive audience of Americans worn down by the political and cultural tumult of the 1960s era."[12]

These studies generally try to explain *how* a Deep South politician was able to win a presidential election, just a decade after the dismantling of Jim Crow. The organization of a presidential campaign can also be an effective indicator of the winning candidate's ensuing White House politics, however. After all, during the campaign candidates will make promises they will (at least partly) try to turn into policy as chief executive. Moreover, many campaign

---

8 Betty Glad, *Jimmy Carter: In Search of the Great White House* (New York and London: W.W. Norton & Company, 1980), 18.

9 Morris, *Jimmy Carter: American Moralist*, 237, 238. Emphasis in original.

10 Jimmy Carter, "Interview with *U.S. News & World Report*, September 13, 1976," in CHA, *PC 1976*, I: 734-735.

11 Kandy Stroud, *How Jimmy Won: The Victory Campaign from Plains to the White House* (New York: William Morrow and Company, Inc., 1977), 425-426.

12 Zachary J. Lechner, *The South of the Mind: American Imaginings of White Southernness, 1960-1980* (Athens: The University of Georgia Press, 2018), 137, 160.

staffers receive White House jobs after victory, thus ensuring some continuity between the management and style of the campaign and the conduct of the presidential administration. As such, strengths but also weaknesses are transferred from the campaign trail to Pennsylvania Avenue. In the case of Jimmy Carter, many scholars search for explanations why such an ambitious, promising, and intelligent outsider failed to deliver as president.[13] According to historian Jeff Bloodworth, answers to this quandary "can be found in an examination of his presidential race."[14] Although major structural and international problems plagued the Carter presidency, like stagflation and the energy crisis, White House personalities also explain why his administration ran into trouble. These individuals had occupied key positions in the campaign. Specific ideas about religion and manhood, connected to their southern upbringing, surfaced during the campaign and subsequently determined Jimmy Carter's years in the White House.

2 The Making of a Southern Man

Many of the traits that characterized the campaign and administration of Jimmy Carter can be traced back to his childhood years. James Earl 'Jimmy' Carter Jr. was born on October 1, 1924, in Plains, Georgia. When he was three years old, the Carters moved to Archery, a small community three miles west of Plains. Father James Earl Carter Sr. started a successful farm and a commissary in the family's new hometown. He soon became a respected community leader. In his campaign autobiography, Jimmy Carter wrote how his "life on the farm during the Great Depression more nearly resembled farm life of fully two thousand years ago than farm life today."[15] In comparison to many other farmers during the 1930s, however, the Carter family did relatively well. They benefited greatly from the New Deal programs introduced by President Roosevelt – James Earl Carter made good money on enclosing open pastures and in 1937 he was appointed one of the directors of the local Rural Electrification Administration (REA).[16]

---

13 See for example Julian E. Zelizer, *Jimmy Carter* (New York: Times Books, 2010), 6.

14 Jeffrey Bloodworth, "Jimmy Carter's 1976 Presidential Campaign," in *A Companion to Gerald R. Ford and Jimmy Carter*, ed. Scott Kaufman (Chichester: John Wiley & Sons, 2016), 230.

15 Jimmy Carter, *Why Not the Best? The First Fifty Years* (1st edition 1975; Fayetteville: The University of Arkansas Press, 1996), 5.

16 Bourne, *Jimmy Carter*, 21-34; Glad, *Jimmy Carter: In Search of the Great White House*, 30.

In spite of the profits he made on federal programs, Carter Sr. soon became disillusioned with the New Deal.[17] As a businessman, he increasingly started to dislike the governmental interference of FDR's programs. At that point, James Earl Carter, like many other conservative Georgians, pledged their allegiance to Governor Eugene Talmadge. Talmadge was an archetypical southern demagogue and the political rallies of 'The Wild Man from Sugar Creek' were extremely popular events. During these all-day barbecues, Talmadge railed against the presumed dark forces that oppressed the simple farmer: the power structure in Atlanta, the federal government, and Blacks. Although he campaigned as a populist, appealing to the vote of the white working class, his programs in fact favored the businesses of men like James Earl Carter. Carter Sr. treated his African American workers with some respect, but he remained an arch-segregationist until his death. "He was quite conservative," Jimmy Carter described his father, "and my mother was a liberal, but within our family we never thought about trying to define such labels."[18]

The liberalism of Jimmy's mother Lillian contrasted sharply with the conservatism of her husband. It made her an outsider in southern society. She had trouble conforming herself to the standards of white womanhood in the South. Lillian Carter liked to go out, play cards, and have a sip of bourbon now and then. As a nurse in a small town, she catered to the needs of both Black and white. The people in Archery liked James Earl Carter's eccentric wife, although they never really accepted her as one of their own. "I never had close friends," she said. "I was never running in and out of people's homes. Small-town people can sometimes be afraid of independent minds."[19] Her family tied her to Archery, but when her children had grown up and after her husband died of cancer in 1953, she decided to join the Peace Corps. 'Miss Lillian' was sent to the small town of Vikhroli, just outside Mumbai, where she worked as a nurse for two years. When she returned to Plains in 1968, she told her daughter Gloria, "If it weren't for leaving home again, I'd spent the rest of my life in India – I'm still torn between this life and my life there."[20]

---

17 According to Peter Bourne, James Earl Carter, Sr., "like many other farmers, became disillusioned when in an effort to raise commodity prices the Agricultural Adjustment Administration (AAA) called for farmers to slaughter their pigs and plow under the cotton they had planted." See Bourne, *Jimmy Carter*, 36-37.

18 Carter, *Why Not the Best?*, 10; Morris, *Jimmy Carter: American Moralist*, 34-35; Corey T. Lesseig, "Talmadge, Eugene," in, *American National Biography*, eds. John A. Garraty and Mark C. Carnes (New York and Oxford: Oxford University Press, 1999), 283-284.

19 Quoted in Glad, *Jimmy Carter: The Search for the Great White House*, 31.

20 Quoted in Bourne, *Jimmy Carter*, 173.

Jimmy Carter also seemed to be torn – between the liberal nonconformity of his mother and the stern, masculine austerity of his father. In his memoirs, Carter described how he looked up to his father. "Even more than Mama, because I worked with him and observed his daily activities, my father was the center of my life and the focus of my admiration when I was a child."[21] Jimmy Carter enjoyed living in rural southwest Georgia. His boyhood primarily revolved around hunting, fishing, and swimming in the river. But he also had chores on the farm. Father believed in hard work and he expected his children to follow his example. "I never even considered disobeying my father, and he seldom, if ever, ordered me to perform a task," Carter remembered. He "simply suggested that it needed to be done, and he expected me to do it… he was a stern disciplinarian and punished me severely when I misbehaved," sometimes with the whip.[22] Carter Sr. could be jovial at times, and although he fulfilled his paternalist duties as community leader and major employer (every Fourth of July, he organized a big barbecue for the Black families that worked for him), he could also be quite dictatorial. James Earl Carter wanted absolute control, not only over his children, but also over his farm and his business.[23]

When Carter Sr. died, Carter Jr. went back to Plains to succeed his father. Just a year before his death, James Earl Carter had been elected to the state legislature with the help of the Talmadge machine. At first, Jimmy was hesitant about going to Plains and take over his father's farm. He had a budding career in the Navy and his wife Rosalynn did not want to return to Georgia. But Carter's roots and family obligations eventually drew him back to his hometown. "[He'd] come from this little town in Plains, Georgia, and it was almost like a medieval idea," one of Jimmy Carter's friends in the Navy, Bill Lalor, recalled. "One man, his father, was responsible for all the souls in Plains, Georgia. Without his father, those people were not going to have any means to live."[24] Not everybody was happy with Jimmy's return, however. Billy Carter was "mad as hell" that his older brother was going to run the family business, although he eventually accepted the prerogatives of the oldest son. "Finally, I decided to hell with it. Let Jimmy run the warehouse. He could [do] it without me."[25] Shortly thereafter, Billy left for Parris Island to join the Marine Corps.

21 Jimmy Carter, *An Hour Before Daylight: Memories of a Rural Boyhood* (New York etc.: Simon & Schuster, 2001), 122.
22 Jimmy Carter, *Why Not the Best?*, 10.
23 Bourne, *Jimmy Carter*, 26; Glad, *Jimmy Carter: The Search for the Great White House*, 29-31.
24 Quoted in Glad, *Jimmy Carter: The Search for the Great White House*, 67.
25 Quoted in Bourne, *Jimmy Carter*, 86.

Jimmy Carter quickly assumed the role of the new patriarch of Plains. He did not have extensive knowledge about the farming business, but he was an eager learner, and he consulted numerous books and talked to agricultural experts about running a successful peanut plantation. Soon, the Carter farm was a booming enterprise and Jimmy became more involved in different community organizations. He joined the Lions Club, headed the community development committee, and was appointed to the county school board. "He was always the leader of everything he got into," family friend John Pope described Carter during that period, "and he would give it a lot of time that most people wouldn't."[26] Up until then, religion did not yet play a prominent role in Carter's life. Although his family regularly attended the Plains Baptist Church, the first priority was his business. Not until the mid-1960s did he realize that his faith was not very deep. "I never really had committed myself to God," he confessed. "My Christian beliefs were superficial. They were primarily based on pride."[27] The main reason why he turned to Christ during that particular period was one of the first major setbacks in his quest for leadership: the defeat in the Georgia gubernatorial election of 1966.

Jimmy Carter was raised in the Baptist Church, but both his mother and father were at best nominal Christians. "It wasn't too much with us," Miss Lillian said. "The church is the center of everything in a small town... it was just more of a habit to go to church."[28] When Carter entered the Navy, he visited church irregularly. Upon his return to Plains he followed the religious pattern of his parents. Like his father, Jimmy taught Sunday school and became a church administrator, but he was not an evangelical in the strict sense of the word. Peanuts and public jobs were more important to Carter.[29] Politics also drew his attention. He was elected state senator in 1962, after a heated race that led to the defeat of incumbent Homer Moore, an unreconstructed representative of the old order. But despite his ascendancy as a businessman and politician, Jimmy Carter also discovered that the road to success is sometimes paved with failure. In 1966, he ran a well-organized campaign for the governorship. When the votes rolled in on September 15, however, Carter lost the primary to liberal candidate Ellis Arnall and right-wing zealot Lester Maddox, the ax-wielding racist from Atlanta who eventually won.

Now that Carter was no longer involved in state politics, he could devote his time to other things. He focused on turning his seed business into a suc-

26 Quoted in ibid., 90.
27 Quoted in Morris, *Jimmy Carter: American Moralist*, 157.
28 Quoted in Bourne, *Jimmy Carter*, 31.
29 Carter, *Why Not the Best?*, 77.

cessful enterprise. Just a month after his defeat in the elections, he also started campaigning for the next gubernatorial election of 1970, not intending to lose again.[30] Above all else, however, he rediscovered religion. Jimmy's sister Ruth Carter Stapleton played an important role in his renewed faith. Ruth was a successful evangelist, with a large following in the U.S. and across the world. In 1978, she even converted *Hustler* editor Larry Flint to evangelical Christianity.[31] For Jimmy, Ruth's visit seemed to come at the right time. In a 1976 interview with *The Washington Post*, he talked about the conversations they had while walking in a pine orchard on the family farm in Georgia. "I realized that my own relationship with God, with Christ, was very superficial… I came to realize that my Christian life, which I had always professed to be pre-eminent, had really been a secondary interest in my life." But his conversion was neither a miraculous experience, nor a prioritization of religion over politics. Ruth believed her brother's willingness "to give up his god (politics) was commitment enough." Jimmy retorted: "Ruth may have had an impression, but that's actually not right." Moreover, his rediscovery of Jesus was "not a profound stroke of miracle. It wasn't a voice of God from heaven… It wasn't mysterious."[32] From a titular Christian, Carter turned into an evangelical Baptist who journeyed to the North in 1968 to spread the Gospel there.[33]

3 Born-Again Politics in the New South

Carter combined his new vocation as born-again missionary with the game of politics. Between 1966 and 1970 he traveled across his home state, shaking hands with thousands of voters and telling them he was again running for governor. This second bid was more successful. His victory in the 1970 election even drew the attention of *Time*, which put a drawing of Carter on the cover in the spring of 1971. Judging from the picture on the front of the magazine, the new governor could have been one of JFK's brothers. It was an indication that

30 Ibid., 99.

31 Bourne, *Jimmy Carter*, 168; Rudy Maxa, "Hustling for the Lord; Larry Flynt's Pilgrimage Began over Supper with Ruth Carter Stapleton and Won't End Till There Is Peace on Earth," *The Washington Post*, January 8, 1978, 11.

32 Ruth Carter Stapleton quoted in Myra McPherson, "Carter's Sister: Healing the Wounds of the Inner Child," *The Washington Post*, March 21, 1976, A12; Jimmy Carter quoted in ibid. and in Jules Witcover, "1967 Event Gave Carter 'Inner Peace,'" *The Washington Post*, March 21, 1976, A6. See also Glad, *Jimmy Carter: The Search for the Great White House*, 331.

33 Bourne, *Jimmy Carter*, 175-176.

Americans started to look at the South from a different perspective. Carter's 1970 triumph signaled an important regional change; Dixie was whistling a different tune and the new governor of Georgia was whistling it the loudest. "Throughout the South, there are signs that the region is abandoning the fateful uniqueness that has retarded its development and estranged its people," *Time* reported. "William Faulkner's South – heavy with ghostly Spanish moss, penumbral myths and morbid attachment to the past – is giving way to a South that has discovered it does not need fable to shore up its pride or the past to cloud its future." Atlanta, "the city too busy to hate," was the perennial symbol of modern Dixie. The city had become a bustling business community and its skyscrapers gave it the epithet of "The Southern city of the future."[34]

Although Carter and other New South governors represented a changing region, they were also children of its past. In the same issue of *Time*, Carter was described as "both product and destroyer of the old myths. Soft-voiced, assured, looking eerily like John Kennedy from certain angles, Carter is a man as contradictory as Georgia self, but determined to resolve some of its paradoxes."[35] During the 1970 gubernatorial election, the candidate from Plains had run a well-coordinated populist campaign. The blue-collar workers were his people, he claimed: "These are my folks… I convinced the average working man and woman that I was their friend, that if I was elected, I would understand their problems." The peanut became the preeminent Carter symbol. Campaign commercials showed Carter working on his farm, while a voice-over said: "Jimmy Carter knows what it's like to work for a living… Can you imagine any of the other candidates working in the hot August sun? No wonder Jimmy Carter has a special understanding of the problems facing everyone who works for a living. Isn't it time someone spoke up for you?"[36]

Carter's appeal to the white working class vote also had dubious aspects, however. Although he never lapsed into overt race baiting, he did not shun the support of right-wing southerners either. He went to Washington to ask the endorsement of Richard Russell, a Jim Crow senator from Georgia, leader of the Southern Caucus, and co-author of the defiantly segregationist Southern Manifesto. Shortly before the 1966 election, Jimmy had in fact told the *Atlanta Constitution* he was a Russell Democrat. Ironically, Carter's opponent, former governor Carl Sanders, was viewed as the liberal in the 1970 primary elections. In contrast with the peanut farmer from Plains, Sanders was a cold and aloof

34 "New Day A'Coming in the South," *Time*, May 31, 1971, 14-20.
35 Ibid.
36 Bourne, *Jimmy Carter*, 189.

person, whose campaign slogan ("Carl Sanders ought to be governor again") attested to his arrogance. Carter effectively portrayed his rival as the man in the ivory tower, while he was the populist alternative.

This stance increasingly linked him to fellow southern populist George Wallace, who had run an extremely racist campaign during the Alabama gubernatorial elections held in the same year. Carter reminded the electorate that as governor, Sanders had refused to let Wallace talk to the state legislature or private groups. "I was a member of the Georgia Seedmen's Association," Jimmy Carter stated. "At the last minute, Governor Sanders sent us word that he would not allow Governor Wallace to speak on Georgia property. I don't think it is right for Governor Sanders to try to please a group of ultra-liberals, particularly those in Washington, when it means stifling communications with another state."[37] Another Carter TV commercial showed a decadent party at a country club where the fat cats were supposedly raising money for their candidate, Carl Sanders. "People like us aren't invited... We're too busy working for a living," the voiceover said. "Vote for Jimmy Carter, our kind of man, our kind of governor." The phrase "our kind of man" was directly copied from George Wallace's gubernatorial campaign.[38]

The dichotomy between Old South and New South became a prominent theme in the 1976 presidential elections. Carter wanted to show the American people that he was a southerner who had left the past behind and who had improved his state, both economically and on the issue of race relations. He estranged a lot of Georgia whites when he told them the Jim Crow era was really over. This was not a false commitment; Carter worked hard to pull his state out of its strangling history of poverty and bigotry. But at the same time he also tried to appease segregationists, for instance when he drafted an antibusing amendment together with George Wallace and Republican Winfield Dunn of Tennessee. During the gubernatorial election, critics often accused Carter of being unclear on these pivotal issues. The candidate himself had no qualms about this. He presented himself as a fighter for the common man, who did not adhere to any ideology but the voice of the people. In his campaigns for both the governorship and the presidency, Carter's image as the fair and uncorrupted outsider was the most important element and the Bible the main source of inspiration. "That Jesus was a social revolutionary and a populist who presented peaceful but brazen challenge to both the Roman rulers and

37 Quoted in Glad, *Jimmy Carter: The Search for the Great White House*, 130.

38 Bourne, *Jimmy Carter*, 190. For an overview of the 1970 elections, see Bourne, *Jimmy Carter*, 180-199, and Glad, *Jimmy Carter: The Search for the Great White House*, 127-140.

the Jewish elite was something that Jimmy understood and appreciated," Peter Bourne summarized Carter's views on politics.[39]

Since the 1970 gubernatorial bid, two men formed the core of Jimmy Carter's campaign staff: Hamilton Jordan and Jody Powell. Jordan, who was born in Albany in southwest Georgia, was a University of Georgia graduate and had served in Vietnam. He grew up in a political family and enjoyed the game of politics; Jordan did not mind pulling a couple of dirty tricks if it was going to deliver him the elections. He was important in setting up a grassroots organization (run from a bait shop in the Georgia countryside) that supported Carter in the race for governor and in winning the confidence of the rural white vote. Jordan's brother-in-arms Jody Powell was born in Vienna, only 25 miles northeast of Plains. He studied political science at Emory, where he wrote a thesis on southern populism and George Wallace. Carter's style somehow reminded him of the Alabama politician, and he joined the Carter team in 1969. When Carter was elected governor, Powell became his press secretary, a role he would fulfill for the next ten years. Both Jordan and Powell were extremely loyal to their candidate, although the latter probably was the most dedicated staffer Carter ever had.[40]

4 Hellhounds on the Campaign Trail

Carter's idea to run for president of the United States came shortly after the 1972 Democratic National Convention. The changed rules for the Democratic primaries, the war in Vietnam, and the escalating scandal around Watergate greatly enhanced the chances for an outsider like Jimmy Carter. The people on the governor's staff saw opportunities, but they also realized there was a long road ahead. Campaign worker Peter Bourne drafted a memo to Carter that concluded no southerner "has captured the presidency because he has not been willing to take the drastic step away from traditional southern politics." During the subsequent Thanksgiving holidays, Hamilton Jordan wrote a 70-page handbook, partly based on Bourne's ideas, which formed the groundwork of the Carter campaign for the primary and presidential elections. He stressed that every effort should be made "to court Wallace and gain his friendship and trust... I would hope you might gain his support if he saw in your candidacy

39 Bourne, *Jimmy Carter*, 179, 212-213.

40 Anderson, *Electing Jimmy Carter*, 47. On Hamilton Jordan and Jody Powell, see also Bourne, *Jimmy Carter*, 185-186; Glad, *Jimmy Carter: The Search for the Great White House*, 124-126.

an extension and continuation of his earlier efforts." By Christmas 1972, Jimmy Carter had made up his mind: he was going to run for the White House.[41]

The outsider image of Carter was primarily based on his southern background. References to his peanut farming business were readily made. A massive outpouring of campaign literature that stressed the rustic simplicity of the candidate from Georgia descended on the American people. On October 1, 1975 (Carter's fifty-first birthday), his autobiography *Why Not the Best? The First Fifty Years* was published by Broadman Press, an "inspirational literature" house located in Nashville. It was the epitome of everyman ideology. The book gave an account of Carter's rural background, his life in the Navy, and the accomplishments of his tenure as Georgia governor. *Why Not the Best?* answered two basic questions: "Can our government be honest, decent, open, fair, and compassionate? Can our government be competent?" According to Carter, both questions could be answered in the affirmative, as long as politicians would listen to the American people. He was going to do just that. Moreover, he was the right man for the job. "I am a Southerner and an American," he wrote in the introduction to his book. "I am a farmer, an engineer, a father and husband, a Christian, a politician and former governor, a planner, a businessman, a nuclear physicist, a naval officer, a canoeist, and, among other things, a lover of Bob Dylan's songs and Dylan Thomas's poetry."[42] Carter's book was populist literature at its best; it had something for everybody, and it offended nobody, except for the money-grubbing business elite and the supposedly heartless politicians in Washington.

Although Jimmy Carter devoted only two lines to his conversion experience in the book, spirituality was an important characteristic of his campaign. According to Bourne, there was only one theme: "faith in Jimmy Carter and the sense of hope he sought to inspire in the American people."[43] In 1976, many of Carter's fellow citizens were on a quest for inner peace. Some of them found it in the esoteric teachings of New Age, but most mainstream Americans started to practice a religion that was closer to home: evangelical Christianity. Protestant church attendance rose only nominally during the 1970s, but the shifts between nominations was remarkable. While mainline churches such as the Presbyterians and the United Methodists experienced a rapid membership drop, evangelical congregations were booming. In 1978, nearly 25 percent of the U.S. population considered itself evangelical. Only eight years later, this

41 Bourne, *Jimmy Carter*, 230-236.

42 Carter, *Why Not the Best?*, 1-2.

43 Bourne, *Jimmy Carter*, 344.

number had risen to 32 percent. Televangelists such as Jimmy Swaggart and Oral Roberts became national celebrities and Hal Lindsey's *The Late Great Planet Earth* (about the Apocalypse in a nuclear age) was the decade's best-seller. In an interview with National Religious Broadcasters on October 9, 1976, Jimmy Carter talked about this new mood of spirituality in America: "there was an article written in *New York* magazine by Richard Reeves who pointed out that the country was looking for some spiritual commitment and that one of the reasons that I had been successful in my early primary campaigns was because some people looked on me as a realization of their spiritual hopes."[44] Nonetheless, there were still enough Americans who were not attracted to evangelicalism. The fears of those voters needed to be allayed.

In numerous interviews, Jimmy Carter tried to show the American people he was a committed Christian, not a fundamentalist zealot who took every word in the Bible literally. He also emphasized his belief in the complete separation of church and state. "I've never let my religious convictions orient my decisions on a political matter and never have tried to use the strength of my political office to force my convictions on somebody else… So there will be no problem in my life as President in keeping separate religion and government," Carter told Roy Blodgett in an interview with *Liberty* magazine.[45] Though these interviews made clear that evangelical religion should be seen as a source of moral strength and not a political doctrine, both Jimmy Carter and his press secretary Jody Powell considered it necessary to do some talks about Carter's religious background with magazines that were not directly related with issues of faith. "Carter, always reaching out to new audiences, always being the Good Shepherd in search of the one strayed member of the herd, talked to *The New York Times*, and *The Washington Post*, and the network correspondents, and a host of magazine writers," journalist Jules Witcover wrote.[46] Robert Scheer of *Playboy* was one of them.

For three months, Scheer joined the Carter campaign and interviewed the candidate numerous times. The two men did not get along well.[47] Jimmy Carter saw the interviews as a way to express his religious views to an audience

---

44 Jimmy Carter, "Religion and the Presidency: Interview with National Religious Broadcasters, October 1976," in CHA, *PC 1976*, II: 973. Religious revivalism in the United States: Schulman, *The Seventies*, 92-93.

45 Jimmy Carter, "The Church and the State: Interview with *Liberty* magazine, September/October 1976," in CHA, *PC 1976*, II: 975-976.

46 Jules Witcover, *Marathon: The Pursuit of the Presidency, 1972-1976* (New York: The Viking Press, 1977), 527.

47 Anderson, *Electing Jimmy Carter*, 111.

that did not have a strong identification with evangelicalism. But Scheer's goal was to unmask the Georgia peanut farmer and expose what was really going on inside his head. In the end, the *Playboy* journalist won this psychological battle. When the final interview session had ended, Carter walked Scheer to the porch of his house in Plains. In a final effort to convince the reporter he was just as sinful as the average American (and without realizing Scheer's tape recorder was still running), Carter gave a short sermon about pride. He then admitted he "had looked on a lot of women with lust" and had "committed adultery in [his] heart many times." But that did not mean he was going to berate men who really cheated on their wives. After all, it was not up to him to "condemn someone who not only looks on a woman with lust but who leaves his wife and shacks up with somebody out of wedlock. Christ says, don't consider yourself better than someone else because one guy screws up a whole bunch of women while the other guy is loyal to his wife."[48]

Hamilton Jordan referred to the more eccentric elements of Jimmy Carter's faith as the 'weirdo factor,' which could estrange an important part of the electorate. The interview exposed it in full glory. On September 10, *Playboy* editor Barry Golson called Jody Powell to tell him that he and Bob Scheer were going to talk about it on the *Today* show the next morning. Scheer had agreed to send Powell a copy of the interview before the magazine would be available to the public, which was handed out to the press when the Carter campaign hit New Jersey and Pennsylvania on a whistle-stop tour on September 11. Powell tried to downplay the issue of his boss talking about "screwing" and "shacking" in the context of the Holy Bible. A reporter who had not read the entire piece asked Carter's press secretary where the word "screw" appeared in the article. "Somewhere in the shack, I guess," he responded. Other journalists asked about the repercussions the interview would have on the elections. "Well, I'll suppose you'll have some Republican committeewoman stand up somewhere and scream, 'Screwers out of the White House,'" Powell replied. "Other than that, not much."[49]

But Powell and Carter had more to worry about than Republican committeewomen. Carter's carefully crafted image as a morally pure man was shattered because of his obscene language. Many evangelical Christians in the South (Carter's bedrock constituency) were enraged by the *Playboy* interview. "I am highly offended by this," fundamentalist pastor W.A. Criswell of the First

---

48 Jimmy Carter, "Interview with *Playboy* Magazine, November 1976," in CHA, *PC 1976*, II: 939-964.

49 Quoted in Stroud, *How Jimmy Won*, 355. See also Bourne, *Jimmy Carter*, 346.

Baptist Church in Dallas said. "I think he's mixed up in his moral values, and I think the entire church membership will feel the same way. The whole thing is highly distasteful."[50] Jimmy Carter quickly realized the interview was not going to have the effect he had hoped for. Instead of reaching a broader audience by articulating his views on religion in common man's language, he was now seen as a perverse southern preacher with a foul mouth. According to an October 25 Gallup poll, only five percent of Americans who had heard about Carter's controversial statements in *Playboy* had a more positive view of Carter; sixteen percent were less favorably inclined toward the Democratic candidate.[51] "Jimmy Carter's 'Playboy' article and his stand on the Vietnam traitors most certainly do not reflect the beliefs and leanings of Mississippi's God-fearing conservatives," an angry female voter from the Mississippi Delta town of Greenville expressed, also condemning Carter's plan to pardon Vietnam War draft resisters.[52]

In the meantime, the campaign started to fall apart. It must have been distressing for Carter; as farmer, state senator, and governor, he had always strived for complete domination, but now his presidential efforts began to swirl out of control. Partly, this had to do with the delegation of tasks among campaign staff. Jim King, a former aide to Teddy Kennedy, scheduled flights and kept Carter happy. Hamilton Jordan was the man who ran the rest of the show. Patrick Anderson would later state he had "been in Mexican whorehouses that were better organized than the Carter campaign."[53] Another problem was Carter's disintegrating image as the man who would never tell a lie. After a brief visit to Texas, where he had to apologize to Lady Bird Johnson for calling her husband a liar in the (by then notorious) *Playboy* interview, Carter convened a meeting with the reporters active on the campaign trail. When he asked them how he could regain his momentum, they told him he should stop making misleading statements. Some of them also questioned how Jimmy Carter was going to be a moral leader for the country when he could not even

50 Quoted in Witcover, *Marathon*, 567.

51 George H. Gallup, *The Gallup Poll: Public Opinion 1972-1977* (2nd ed., Wilmington: Scholarly Resources, Inc., 1979), II: 889. To the question "Have you heard or read about the comments Jimmy Carter made in an interview with *Playboy* magazine?" 72 percent answered "yes" and 28 percent answered "no."

52 Lillian Haik to James O. Eastland, September 22, 1976, in File Series 3, Subseries 1, Folder: Politics – Jimmy Carter – 1976, in James O. Eastland Collection, Archives and Special Collections, J.D. Williams Library, University of Mississippi.

53 Quoted in Bourne, *Jimmy Carter*, 345. Peter Bourne wrote on the same page that Anderson "was close to the mark."

control his own campaign workers, who represented the rowdy side of the Deep South.

The image of the South Carter wanted to stress was his hometown in Georgia, not the 'helluvafella' traditions Jody Powell and Hamilton Jordan represented.[54] During the campaign, Plains turned into Jimmy Carter World, a quasi-theme park where his 'real' character could be discovered. This was the place where he shoveled peanuts and taught Sunday school. You could meet Miss Lillian there, or good old boy Billy, who was running the gas station in town. To a certain extent, the Carter family resembled the honest, decent, hardworking people of *The Waltons*, an immensely popular TV series during the seventies.[55] Plains was supposed to be a schoolbook image of the benevolent South, a southern version of Main Street, U.S.A. But beneath the veneer of the Protestant work ethic and the simple faith of Plains, Georgia, lay a deeper, darker South that was also part of the Carter campaign. It was Powell and Jordan's South of southern rock, hypermasculinity, and a reactionary anti-establishment attitude. Patrick Anderson gave a vivid description of Carter's confidantes when he compared them with the staff of vice-presidential candidate Walter Mondale. "And then there were Jody and Ham, looking like a couple of rawboned, narrow-eyed South Georgia thugs. There was always a hint of violence in them," Anderson wrote. "Bob Scheer captured it in *Playboy* when he described a time a car passed Jody too close and he roared 'You fucking asshole!' and gave chase until his wife calmed him."[56]

The differences between Carter's standpoints and the attitude of his staffers were sometimes striking. While Jimmy and Rosalynn supported the Equal Rights Amendment (ERA), Powell and Jordan were extremely uncomfortable with women having top positions on the campaign team. Carter's rhetoric about faith and morality contrasted sharply with the drinking, the profanities, and the lusting of his staff. While Carter tried to show the American people he was a normal Christian, Hamilton Jordan kept mocking his Baptist beliefs as the 'weirdo factor,' thus undermining the credibility of the man he was supposed to be supporting. "Especially for those reporters who had joined the campaign after Carter became the front-runner and had little direct interaction with the candidate, what they saw in dealing with the staff cast serious

54 For the helluvafella tradition, see for instance Ted Ownby, "Freedom, Manhood, and White Male Tradition in 1970s Southern Rock Music," in *Haunted Bodies: Gender and Southern Texts*, eds. Anne Goodwyn Jones and Susan V. Donaldson (Charlottesville: University Press of Virginia, 1997), 371.

55 Lechner, *The South of the Mind*, 144-145.

56 Anderson, *Electing Jimmy Carter*, 68.

doubts upon the sincerity of the lofty public statements Carter was making on race, religion, the role of women, honesty, and other moral issues," Peter Bourne observed. "This skepticism was inevitably conveyed, often subtly to the reading and viewing public."[57] It further undermined the image of Jimmy Carter as the devout southern outsider who would bring decency and faith back to America.

The cooperation between the Carter campaign and old-time segregationists also indicated how the Old South was still very much part of the Georgian's attempt to become president. In the battleground state of Mississippi, Carter's team tried to enlist the support of U.S. Senators James Eastland and John Stennis, two powerful Democratic politicians who had consciously fought desegregation in the 1950s and 1960s.[58] Patt Derian, a civil rights activist with deep knowledge of the political situation in Mississippi and deputy director of the Carter-Mondale campaign, strongly objected to this decision. "IT IS THOROUGHLY INCONSISTENT WITH THE BASIC PREMISES OF THIS CAMPAIGN to name a bunch of unreconstructed segs (Governor excepted), all white men, all men who have obstructed every Democratic Party effort for alieviation [*sic*] of poverty, disease and denial of citizen rights to head the Jimmy Carter Campaign in the state," she blasted.[59] Derian's protests apparently did not have much effect, because Eastland put his political machine in Mississippi to work for Carter. Frank Moore, Carter's deputy campaign director for the southeastern states, later acknowledged Eastland's critical contribution in carrying Mississippi for the Democratic ticket. "Governor Carter and I are both aware of how important Mississippi was to the final victory and the role that Senator Eastland played in that victory," he wrote Eastland's friend John Farese in December 1976.[60]

Winning Mississippi was of the utmost importance for Carter, because by November his commanding lead over Gerald Ford had virtually evaporated. Although he won the presidential election, the victory margin was razor thin:

57 Bourne, *Jimmy Carter*, 316.

58 The senators had different political styles, but a similar segregationist agenda. See Maarten Zwiers, "Good Cop, Bad Cop: Segregationist Strategies and Democratic Party Politics in Mississippi, 1948-1960," *The Southern Quarterly* 54, no. 1 (Fall 2016): 29-52.

59 Patt Derian to Tim Kraft, Phil Wise, and Jim Free, no date, "State File: Mississippi" folder, Box 217, Records of the 1976 Campaign Committee to Elect Jimmy Carter, Jimmy Carter Presidential Library, Atlanta, Georgia (hereafter JCPL).

60 Frank Moore to John B. Farese, December 22, 1976, "Senate Correspondence, 1977 – Eastland, Ford, Garn [O/A 4865]" folder, Box 61, Records of the Office of Congressional Liaison, JCPL.

Carter received only 50.1 percent of the votes. Historian Leo Ribuffo argued that Carter's religiosity delivered him the White House. He was the first Democratic candidate who received the support of the Southern Baptist constituency since Harry Truman in the elections of 1948.[61] As a representative of the rising Sunbelt and as an evangelical Christian in an era characterized by a new search for spirituality, the former Georgia governor was able to constitute an eclectic coalition of Southern Baptists, urban liberals, and mainstream voters that gave him the slim majority to win the presidency. Carter ran a populist campaign that focused on his own persona. After the intense partisan battles between liberals and conservatives of the preceding years, his message of hope, decency, and faith brought a refreshing non-ideological approach to U.S. politics.

But Carter's highly personal campaign also brought problems. Without taking a clear stand on the issues, Carter was often accused of being fuzzy. He also had trouble upholding his image as the honest farmer from the New South. Carter was often seen as a juggler: Kandy Stroud called him a "tightrope walker," while Patrick Anderson labeled the campaign "a high-wire act. Our man was up there in the spotlight with no net below him, dancing about, turning his daring flips, leaping to the left, bobbing to the right, dazzling the crowd but forever threatening to tumble into the void."[62] At the start of the race, the constructed image of Carter drew many voters into the Democratic camp. As Election Day came near, however, Carter's personal assets became more of a burden than an advantage. He blundered in the *Playboy* interview, estranging an important part of his most faithful following and raising the question how sincere his religion was. The good old boys on his campaign team even made matters worse. While Carter talked about his accomplishments as New South governor, his honesty, and his religious compassion, his staffers were hitting on women, used foul language, and showed an arrogant disrespect toward more liberal Democrats. Moreover, Plains did not turn out to be the pastoral town of a born-again Dixie. A few days before the election, Carter's Baptist church refused membership to four African Americans, including civil rights

61 Leo P. Ribuffo, "God and Jimmy Carter," in M.L. Bradbury and James B. Gilbert, eds., *Transforming Faith: The Sacred and the Secular in Modern American History* (New York etc.: Greenwood Press, 1989), 146. Ribuffo wrote: "According to a Gallup poll conducted in October, ten percent of voters were unimpressed by Carter's faith, 20 percent were impressed, and 70 percent reported no effect… A majority of evangelical Protestants voted Republican, as was usually the case, but Carter won by cutting the margin from 7.2 million in 1968 to 3.2 million."

62 Stroud, *How Jimmy Won*, 435; Anderson, *Electing Jimmy Carter*, 3.

activist Clennon King.[63] Moreover, George Wallace continued to be an important background presence throughout the campaign. He had endorsed Jimmy Carter as presidential candidate and Carter himself attributed his slim victory in Mississippi (which delivered him the presidency) to the Alabama governor. "We owe him a lot," he said.[64] Wallace explained how his race baiting during the 1970 gubernatorial elections had made him an unsuitable candidate for the presidency. "I had to do things – say things to get elected in Alabama, that made it impossible for me to ever be President," he told ABC newsman John Snell on the night of Carter's election.[65] Carter had said similar things in his race for the governorship, but after he got elected, he turned his state on the road to racial reconciliation.

5 Conclusion: The Duality of the Southern Thing

Jimmy Carter's presidential campaign consistently operated on two levels. Region and religion were central to both. The first level was the candidate's public image. During the months preceding the elections, Carter presented himself as the man who would never tell a lie, who would bring faith back to America, and who would base his policies on the wishes of the people. Although he confessed that religion was a central part of his life, Carter did his best to discard the widely held stereotype of the Southern Baptist Church as an institution filled with evangelical zealots. Instead, he talked about the translation of brotherly love into social justice. Secondly, Carter had to counter widespread skepticism about his regional background. Although the South was slowly moving into the American mainstream, many non-southerners still had their doubts about a southern candidate running for president. Jimmy Carter tried to show voters he represented the New South, where racism, economic backwardness, and bigotry had no place.[66]

But beneath all the idealism, the Carter campaign also had a more sinister side that sporadically surfaced during the election and more openly thereafter – the second level of the campaign. Carter made faith central to his bid

63 Wayne King, "Carter's Church Upholds Its Policy by Refusing to Admit Four Blacks," *New York Times*, November 1, 1976.

64 Quoted in Bourne, *Jimmy Carter*, 355.

65 Quoted in Dan T. Carter, *The Politics of Rage: George Wallace, the Origins of the New Conservatism, and the Transformation of American Politics* (2nd ed., Baton Rouge: Louisiana State University Press, 2000), 459.

66 Lechner, *The South of the Mind*, 138-143.

for the presidency, but he carefully avoided the more fundamentalist elements of his religion that could alienate voters who were not evangelical. Besides his sometimes-erratic religious views, Carter's identity as a southerner also proved to be more complicated than he wanted voters to believe. On the one hand there was Jimmy, the smiling peanut farmer who had not been tainted by the corruptive influences of Washington power politics. On the other, there was the southern planter-politician who always wanted to be in control and had catered to the segregationist Wallace vote. Even if Jimmy Carter was as sincere and transparent as he presented himself to the public, a huge discrepancy existed between his own image and the personalities on his campaign staff. Hamilton Jordan and press secretary Jody Powell embodied many of the stereotypical characteristics of the redneck South, two "tough-talking South Georgia shitkickers" who represented an "undercurrent of malice" in the campaign.[67] Peter Bourne agreed with this portrayal, although he was more nuanced in describing the good old boys network that was a dominant factor in Carter's team. "With all of their pluses, Jordan and others also brought into the campaign the dark side of the South, a regional inferiority complex reflected as resentment and paranoia," Bourne wrote.[68]

The regional inferiority complex noted by Bourne and others involved in the 1976 race forms a useful framework to explore Carter's failures as president. Different scholars have studied such a complex as an expression of southern identity, for instance Sheldon Hackney, who wrote about a 'siege mentality.'[69] A more recent attempt to explain southern culture (and white southerners' behavior) is Angie Maxwell's *The Indicted South: Public Criticism, Southern Inferiority, and the Politics of Whiteness.* Maxwell demonstrates how a regional inferiority complex is central to white southern identity. Outside criticism on southern institutions and southern culture more broadly triggers this complex, which results "in a collective about-face, often characterized by retreat or denial." According to Maxwell, "public criticism and a common experience of inferiority has contributed to white southern conservatism and homogeneity, which has survived and prospered with dogged perseverance." Feelings of inferiority and a compensating drive for recognition and superiority are closely interconnected, Maxwell argues. She also sees links between outside public criticism and manhood in the South. The nature of southern masculinity makes white men from the region "all the more susceptible, perhaps, to

---

67 Anderson, *Electing Jimmy Carter*, 67.

68 Bourne, *Jimmy Carter*, 337.

69 Sheldon Hackney, "Southern Violence," *The American Historical Review* 74, no. 3 (Feb. 1969): 924.

developing an inferiority complex," resulting in an intense drive to prove their male superiority and defend the social system they represent.[70] Such a mechanism also shaped the Carter campaign. Behind its New South rhetoric about faith, change, and redemption, a deeply rooted sense of inferiority connected to manhood and religion lurked that eventually came to dominate his years in the White House.

The Carter campaign thus was an inherently paradoxical event. The candidate's sincere faith and Jeffersonian ideals constantly had to compete with his regional background and the reactionary, hypermasculine attitude of his campaign staff. The public was attracted by the former, but feared the latter. Both sides were also part of Jimmy Carter's personality; Patrick Anderson called it the Mama side and Daddy side. "To a great extent, it was Carter's Mama side, the colorful, diverse, different, I'll-never-tell-you-a-lie, I-see-an-America side that won him the election," he claimed. "But after the election was won, the Daddy side took over with a vengeance."[71] The Carter administration increasingly became the domain of the so-called Georgia Mafia led by Powell and Jordan, who were both very distrustful of everything liberal. These men "had been plucked by Carter from towns in the Georgia backwoods no more than 40 miles from Plains, and programmed for total loyalty to Jimmy," *Rolling Stone* reporter Joe Klein observed. "He had taken up all of their adult lives. There were no other allegiances possible... or even fathomable."[72] As president, Carter fell into old habits, demanding absolute control of all issues that were related to the executive office, milling over details while losing sight of the big picture.[73] On July 15, 1979, with the country in a deep recession, the president decided it was time to tell the Americans they were in a deep crisis of confidence.

Voters did not want to hear that. They had elected Carter because his religious creed was a message of hope and a promise to restore honesty and decency in U.S. politics, not because they wanted a dour Baptist preacher in the White House who told them how the nation had lost its faith. In spite of the dismal reputation of the Carter administration however, his 1976 campaign has been important in a number of ways. First of all, it demonstrated that an evangelical candidate who made no secret of his faith could be elected to the

70 Angie Maxwell, *The Indicted South: Public Criticism, Southern Inferiority, and the Politics of Whiteness* (Chapel Hill: University of North Carolina Press, 2014), 6, 24.

71 Anderson, *Electing Jimmy Carter*, 166.

72 Joe Klein, "Hamilton Jordan and Jody Powell: The White House Whiz Kids," *Rolling Stone*, May 19, 1977.

73 See for example Stuart E. Eizenstat, *President Carter: The White House Years* (New York: St. Martin's Press, 2018), 56.

highest office in the nation. Secondly, his victory was a sign that the South had lost its stigma. On the night of the election, while the votes in Mississippi and Hawaii were still being counted, Carter's campaign workers from the South understood Jody Powell when he told them: "We have waited more than a hundred years for this moment. We can wait a few minutes more."[74] The white South might have lost the Civil War and suffered through Reconstruction, but a victory for Carter constituted redemption for Powell and his companions.

In 2001, the Drive-By Truckers, a rock band from Alabama, released its album *Southern Rock Opera*. The eighth track, titled "The Three Great Alabama Icons," recounts the stories of three notorious legends from the state: Lynyrd Skynyrd singer Ronnie Van Zant, football coach Paul William 'Bear' Bryant, and Governor George Wallace. Most of the song is about Wallace's political career, especially his conversion from outspoken segregationist in the 1960s to a politician catering to the Black vote in the 1980s. The Truckers labeled it 'the duality of the southern thing,' suggesting that the reality of the region's culture is often more complex than it appears at first sight.[75] A similar dualistic dynamic explains the behavior of Carter and his team. The generally accepted image of Carter as the good southerner stems from his carefully crafted campaign persona that delivered him victory in the 1976 presidential election. But a closer look at that race also reveals how the personalities that dominated the campaign already foreshadowed the troublesome relationship of the Carter administration with politics inside the Beltway. "There was an innocence, and an arrogance, about the idea that you could run the country with your Atlanta statehouse team," historian Roger Wilkins recounted.[76] Once victory in the election was secured, the Carter White House turned into a closed-off compound inhabited by southern men who desperately wanted to prove their superiority over the Washington establishment. Such personal feelings had a detrimental effect on Carter's ambitious presidential agenda.

74 Quoted in Bourne, *Jimmy Carter*, 355.

75 Patterson Hood, "The Southern Thing," recorded 2001, track 8 on *Southern Rock Opera*, Lost Highway Records, compact disc. See also Rien Fertel, *Southern Rock Opera* (New York: Bloomsbury Academic, 2019), 57-63.

76 "People and Events: The 'Georgia Mafia,'" PBS, accessed May 14, 2019, https://bit.ly/2EchCnf.

CHAPTER 11

Will the Real Trump Please Stand Up? Donald Trump's Elusive Persona

Jelte Olthof

Among the countless ways in which Donald Trump has promoted himself over the decades – including a vodka brand, a university, the Miss Universe pageant, and *The Apprentice* – none better captures the essence of his self-fashioning than his 2007 performance on WrestleMania. Sponsored by the World Wrestling Entertainment (WWE), the show's main feature was the so-called 'Battle of the Billionaires' between wrestlers representing Donald Trump and WWE-chairman Vince McMahon. The loser would have his head shaved by the winner. The match included a segment where Trump himself joined in the fight by body-slamming McMahon to the ground and punching him repeatedly in the face, while the crowd roared. The show ended with a grinning Trump shaving McMahon's scalp and subsequently being kicked in the stomach by the referee. The bizarre and sensational plot appealed to Trump's sense of showmanship and according to WWE-script writer Court Bauer, Trump was "game to do it all."[1]

The 'Battle of the Billionaires' was a smashing success that broke ticket sales for WWE[2] and forms a shorthand for everything Trump stands for. First, it was great promotion. McMahon and Trump had known each other since the late eighties, when Trump had brought WWE to Atlantic City to promote Trump Plaza casino.[3] For Trump, WrestleMania was a way to promote his supposed wealth – including a segment where he showered the audience with (mostly fake) money. Second, the event involved Trump's talent for self-depreciation by staking his famous comb-over coupe on the fight. Finally and most importantly, the world of professional wrestling with its fake and scripted fights is a perfect analogy for the way Trump operates. As David Brooks pointed out

1 Quoted in: Michael Kranish and Marc Fisher, *Trump Revealed. The Definitive Biography of the 45th President* (London: Simon & Schuster, 2016), 262.

2 Aaron Oster, "Donald Trump and WWE: From 'WrestleMania' to the White House," *Rolling Stone*, February 1, 2016, http://www.rollingstone.com/sports/features/donald-trump-and-wwe-how-the-road-to-the-white-house-began-at-wrestlemania-20160201.

3 Oster, "Donald Trump and the WWE."

© KONINKLIJKE BRILL NV, LEIDEN, 2020 | DOI:10.1163/9789004422643_013

in the *New York Times*, professional wrestling is akin to politics in that "it is perceived as fake and real at the same time" and what matters is "not so much who wins or loses, or whether you are good or evil, but the aggressiveness by which you wage each mano-a-mano confrontation."[4] Trump felt right at home here. "He knew how to read the crowd and manipulate them," said Bauer, who wrote the script for the 'Battle of the Billionaires.' Trump's famed wealth never formed an obstacle to his ability to identify with average Americans, but rather formed the *means* by which he connects with them. "Donald talks blue-collar," Bauer observed, "but he has the world. He's been selling people on that dream for a long time."[5]

The 'Battle of the Billionaires' is a prime example of Trump's brand of populism which casts him, a multi-billionaire real estate developer with an Ivy League education, as the hero and voice of ordinary Americans. Trump's undeniable ability to channel the grievances of millions of American voters earned him the nickname 'blue-collar billionaire' – a term first floated by Don Jr. and Jerry Falwell Jr. and eagerly adopted by the candidate.[6] For Trump, framing himself as a blue-collar billionaire is a way to bridge the gaping gap between his platinum-gold lifestyle and the modest background of many of his supporters. It allows him – son of a multi-millionaire who worked with his father's company since the late 1960s – to tap into the powerful narrative of rags to riches that presidential candidates since Andrew Jackson have invoked to boost their electoral prospects.[7] Trump, of course, cannot tout an impoverished family background, but this does not stop him from self-identifying with it. This type of self-fabrication certainly is not new – it was, after all, at the core of Barack Obama's 2008 campaign[8] – but with Trump it verges on the brink of fantasy. Trump may talk 'blue-collar,' but he never lived it. Though Fred Trump raised his kids to be hard-working 'killers,' Donald grew up in a suburban villa in Jamaica Estates and was driven to school in his father's Cadillac. Fred made his kids deliver newspapers to teach them the value of money

4 David Brooks, "Donald Trump Isn't Real," *The New York Times*, February 2, 2016, https://www.nytimes.com/2016/02/02/opinion/donald-trump-isnt-real.html.

5 Quoted in: Kranish and Fisher, *Trump Revealed*, 262.

6 Jon Delano, "Donald Trump Jr. Refers To Dad As 'The Blue Collar Billionaire' During Pittsburgh Campaign Stop," accessed July 14, 2017, http://pittsburgh.cbslocal.com/2016/09/14/donald-trump-jr-refers-to-dad-as-the-blue-collar-billionaire-during-pittsburgh-campaign-stop/; Republican National Convention, *Jerry Falwell Jr.'s Full Speech at 2016 Republican National Convention*, 2016, at 03:10, https://www.youtube.com/watch?v=m4ziZVeuj9w.

7 Jill Lepore, "Bound for Glory: Writing Campaign Lives," *The New Yorker*, October 20, 2008, http://www.newyorker.com/magazine/2008/10/20/bound-for-glory.

8 David Remnick, *The Bridge: The Life and Rise of Barack Obama* (London: Picador, 2010), 253.

and hard work, but unlike other paperboys, Donald would be chauffeured in a limousine whenever it rained or snowed.[9]

Trump's 'blue-collar billionaire' WWE-performance demonstrates his uncanny ability for self-fashioning. While image is important to all politicians, for the 45th president of the United States it appears to be the only thing that counts. To talk about Trump's personality, in other words, one first has to plow one's way through the web of lies, bravado, and bluff that he has spun around his public persona in over half a century. In a way, Trump's unlikely credentials as a bankrupt businessman, celebrity, and reality TV-star prepped him for 21st century politics, since it taught him the value of personality, which helps explain his unlikely victory in the 2016 election.

While structural causes play an important role in explaining Trump's elevation to the White House, his personality certainly was important to his victory as well. Trump has succeeded so well in self-creation that the 'real' Trump has become an elusive entity. Trump, I will argue, is the ultimate political performer who has succeeded in creating a public persona on the basis of bluff and bravado. As president, he effortlessly switches between being presidential and politically incorrect, and his 'real' personality remains elusive. The only thing Trump consistently defends is his own persona – attacking, suing, and threatening anyone who challenges his image. My aim in this chapter is not to expose the 'real' Donald Trump, but instead to demonstrate how the 45th president employed self-fashioning to create a public persona of a blue-collared billionaire that resonated with American voters in the 2016 election and has defined his time in office so far. In what follows, I will first sketch Trump's approach to self-fashioning and the type of public persona that he has created for himself since the late 1960s. In the course of this argument I will demonstrate how Trump's self-fashioning defies the traditional Aristotelian conception of ethos and draws on more recent rhetorical theories of persona to explain how the Trump phenomenon works. Finally, I will discuss why Trump's elusive persona is inherently problematic in politics in general and particularly for the role and function that the framers of the Constitution envisaged for the U.S. presidency.

1 Trump's Ethos and Persona

While Hillary Clinton certainly was more experienced and qualified, Trump won the framing competition by turning out to be a master rhetorician. As

9 Michael D'Antonio, *Never Enough: Donald Trump and the Pursuit of Success* (New York: St. Martin's Press, 2015), 39.

Bonnie Dow noted after the election, "one explanation for Trump's unexpected victory is that voters were attracted to who he was and how he presented himself as much as or more than what he said. The same can be said for Clinton's lack of appeal for those same voters."[10] Though lacking substance and detail, Trump's policies were recognizable and clear (the border wall, Muslim-ban, tough on China). The Clinton campaign, by contrast, spewed out vast quantities of technocratic policies,[11] but left unaddressed that, despite her decades in the political limelight and countless public performances, few Americans felt they actually knew her.[12] Clinton clearly understood this – as she noted in her DNC-acceptance speech: "I get it that some people don't know what to make of me" – yet seemed unable to overcome it.[13] While Clinton lacked a clear public persona, persona was basically what Trump offered his voters.

For many commentators and scholars seeking to explain the 2016 election, it marked the triumph of the politics of emotion. Whether they called it populism, economic nationalism or otherwise, the gist of the argument is that a disgruntled section of the electorate made their discontent know by electing the outrageous outsider over the tedious technocrat.[14] In 2016, the argument goes, *pathos* – the appeal to emotion – triumphed over the rational arguments of *logos*. This line of reasoning is superficial and problematic. By reducing the alienation of a large class of Americans with the political establishment to a matter of 'feelings,' this explanation denies the legitimacy of the discontent and dismisses it as a mere opinion. More importantly, reducing the 2016 election to just anger misses the mark. As Dow notes, the 2016 election "was more about persona than prose," and thus transcends the logos/pathos dichotomy and necessitates a turn toward the third rhetorical proof: *ethos*.

10 Bonnie J. Dow, "Taking Trump Seriously: Persona and Presidential Politics in 2016," *Women's Studies in Communication* 40, no. 2 (2017): 136.

11 See Edward Luce, *The Retreat of Western Liberalism* (New York: Atlantic Monthly Press, 2017), 92-93 for some telling examples.

12 See for one discussion of this Ezra Klein's article in Vox: https://www.vox.com/a/hillary-clinton-interview/the-gap-listener-leadership-quality.

13 The quote from this speech can be found on youtube: https://www.youtube.com/watch?v=GOmwVXDdKRM at 18:32.

14 See for example: Jared Yates Sexton, *The People Are Going to Rise Like the Waters Upon Your Shore: A Story of American Rage* (Berkeley, CA: Counterpoint, 2017), 94-95; and see interview with Martha Nussbaum in: Emma Green, "The Anger of the American People: A Philosopher Dissects the Outrage That Fueled Trump and More in U.S. Politics," *The Atlantic*, May 7, 2016, https://www.theatlantic.com/politics/archive/2016/05/martha-nussbaum-anger/481464/.

With his obsession about his image, Trump echoes Aristotle's famous statement that ethos can be considered the most effective form of persuasion.[15] Contrary to pathos or logos, ethos is not concerned with solid arguments or moving stories, but with making a favorable impression on the audience. Speakers that are judged to be trustworthy and knowledgeable have a much easier time convincing an audience than those who do not, Aristotle noted, because: "we believe fair-minded people to a greater extent and more quickly than we do others."[16]

Trump's persona, however, defies the Aristotelean notion of ethos based on expertise, benevolence, and virtue. He never reads books and boasts about his ruthlessness and promiscuity. Nevertheless, and in part as a result of the email scandal, candidate Trump was the more honest and trustworthy choice in the eyes of the electorate.[17] As Mark Thompson has pointed out, what matters in contemporary politics is not whether politicians are truly authentic, as long as they conform to the audience's given standard for authenticity. Thompson notes: "For anti-politicians like Trump, pure rhetorical 'authenticity' – their ability to reject the entire public discourse of the established political classes – is their central point of differentiation."[18]

Trump's perceived fake authenticity highlights an enduring problem with Aristotle's notion of ethos, namely that he fails to make a distinction between an actual and an artificially created persona. Aristotle maintains that we should focus solely on the character speakers create in their speeches and distinguishes this from prior reputation, fame, and other qualities they may possess independently of this.[19] He does not seem to worry about speakers who polish or lie about their true character and even feign who they are to persuade a given audience. As George Yoos already pointed out four decades ago, this position lays the "foundation of dissimulation," since it basically requires us to take the way the orator portrays him or herself at face value.[20]

---

15 In Aristotle's words: "character is almost, so to speak, the most authoritative form of persuasion," see: Aristotle, *On Rhetoric: A Theory of Civic Discourse*, trans. George Alexander Kennedy, 2nd ed. (New York: Oxford University Press, 2007), 39; 1356a4.

16 Aristotle, 38; 1356a4.

17 David Frum points to a Washington Post/ABC News poll that found Trump leading Clinton eight points in this regard on Election Day, see: *Trumpocracy: The Corruption of the American Republic* (New York: Harper, 2018), 20.

18 Mark Thompson, *Enough Said: What's Gone Wrong with the Language of Politics?* (London: Vintage, 2016), 156.

19 Aristotle, *On Rhetoric*, 38-39; 1356a4.

20 George E. Yoos, "A Revision of the Concept of Ethical Appeal," *Philosophy & Rhetoric* 12, no. 1 (1979): 45.

To characterize Trump's ethos, in other words, we need to move beyond classical theory. First, it is important to point out, as Eugene Garver has, that a feigned ethos is not inherently problematic. For example, we do not make inferences about the real personality of lawyers when they offer to defend suspects of the most horrible crimes. While this may hold for judicial and, to some extent, ceremonial speeches, it is certainly not true for political speech.[21] In politics, at least until recently, consistency is demanded of those seeking office.[22] Since voters in representative democracies can only hope that the officials they elect will actually carry out what they promise, a record of flip-flopping is detrimental to a candidate's credibility and electoral prospects. A good case in point is 2012 Republican nominee Mitt Romney, who had a hard time explaining how his professed objections to Obamacare could be reconciled with an identical healthcare system he enacted as governor of Massachusetts.

This political logic never got hold of Trump, a man who switched political parties at least seven times between 1999 and 2012, who supported partial-birth abortion before turning pro-life overnight, and who donated to Hillary Clinton and invited her to his wedding (to his third wife, Melania) before calling to lock her up. Such behavior defied the laws of politics that journalists and pundits had relied on for decades.[23] During the campaign, candidate Trump's inconsistency was pointed out time and again by the Clinton campaign and each time he would brush this off without any apparent damage to his popularity with his base. One reason why Trump is able to move on unscathed where others fell is his slippery and ambiguous persona. Whereas other presidential hopefuls 'act' the role of candidate on the campaign trail, weighing how their words and actions will affect their time in office, Trump just seemed to act in the moment, unbothered by how he would make good on his word once in office. Time and again, he would promise his supporters to solve a problem – illegal immigration, ISIS – with an outrageous plan – the wall, bomb their families – without considering the legality and feasibility of what he proposed. All the while it seems likely, as Michael Wolff suggests without offering proof, that Trump did not actually expect to win the election, but instead hoped to boost his brand and reboot his TV-career. "I don't think about losing," Wolff has him say, "because it's not losing. We've totally won."[24]

21 Eugene Garver, *Aristotle's Rhetoric: An Art of Character* (Chicago: University Of Chicago Press, 1994), 197.

22 For the conventional view, see for example: Thompson, *Enough Said*, 356-357.

23 Kranish and Fisher, *Trump Revealed*, 290, 286, 288.

24 Michael Wolff, *Fire and Fury: Inside the Trump White House* (London: Little, Brown, 2018), 11.

To make sense of Trump's ethos, Aristotle's theory should be supplemented with more modern rhetorical thinking about persona. Scholars of rhetoric have long realized that orators play a role when they are speaking and that this assumed character exists alongside their individual personality. The term they use for this is *persona*, which in ancient Roman theater used to refer to the masks that actors wore to assume a certain character. In a classic article on Marcus Garvey, B.L. Ware and Wil Linkugel explain that, like the Roman actors of old, speakers often assume the ethos of the charismatic leader – and the accompanying credibility. "Rhetorical *personae*," Ware and Linkugel write, "reflect the aspirations and cultural visions of audiences from which stems the symbolic construction of archetypal figures," by which they mean figures in history, myth or literature that reinforce the role the orator wants to assume.[25] Trump's ethos is in fact a modern version of this mask: an assumed artificial image that is carefully maintained. His 'archetype' is that of a 'modern Midas,' as Johnston notes, inspired by the mythical Greek king whose touch turned everything into gold.[26]

The rhetorical concept of persona offers a way out of the Aristotelian predicament because it places the possibility and likelihood of dissimulation front and center. As Edwin Black pointed out in a seminal essay, the very term 'persona' addresses the shortcoming of Aristotle's concept of ethos because it assumes a distinction between the real speaker and the one implied in the speech. Modern audiences, he argues, have learned to suspect that "the author implied by the discourse is an artificial creation: a persona, but not necessarily a person."[27] The type of persona the orator assumes – the choice of 'archetype' in other words – is telling of the kind of personality he or she believes will persuade the particular audience that is addressed. In Black's terms, this assumed persona of the speaker signifies the existence of a "second persona," the implied auditor, that in turn allows students of the speech to make "a model of what the rhetor would have his real auditor become."[28] In Trump's case, the audience is clearly assumed to care more about him being 'authentic' than correct and consistent.

As a theoretical concept, however, persona has its limits as well. Unlike the Roman actors of antiquity, it is often hard to see where Trump's mask ends and the man begins. Ware and Linkugel distinguish between the orator's per-

25 B.l. Ware and Wil A. Linkugel, "The Rhetorical Persona: Marcus Garvey as a Black Moses," *Communication Monographs* 49, no. 1 (March 1982): 50.

26 David Cay Johnston, *The Making of Donald Trump* (New York: Melville House, 2016), 78.

27 Edwin Black, "The Second Persona," *The Quarterly Journal of Speech* 55, no. 2 (1970): 596.

28 Black, "The Second Persona," 598.

sonal ethos and the ethos of the persona assumed and seem to suggest that a speaker can always be told apart from the role he or she assumes: "*persona* does not refer to the personality of the actor *qua* person but to the character assumed by the actor when he dons the mythical mask."[29] In Trump, however, persona and person – mask and reality – seem to melt into one. He seamlessly switches between the presidential ethos of his first State of the Union – when, as Wolff noted, "the president really did seem presidential"[30] – and the politically incorrect ethos of the twitter-troll. Trump dons the persona that seems most appropriate (or controversial) to him at that moment, without considering whether he is being consistent. He is able to pull this off, in large part, because of his long experience of carefully fashioning his public persona, which goes back to the early days of his professional career in the late 1960s.

2 Trump's Self-Fashioning

From the day Trump started to work fulltime at his father's business, his talents for self-fashioning helped him establish himself as a Manhattan mogul. Stephen Greenblatt, who coined the term, explains that 'self-fashioning' refers to the process of creating and recreating a public persona, which became increasingly central to image building in the 16th century. It is premised on the postmodern notion that, as Greenblatt puts it: "the fashioning of human identity [is] a manipulable artful process" and embraces the postmodern notion of the self as malleable. Greenblatt notes that "hypocrisy or deception" is inherent to self-fashioning and how it favors "mere outward ceremony" over substance. He argues that this type of self-promotion became increasingly accepted in the early modern period.[31]

Trump, by his own account, is a habitual and talented self-fashioner. Over the years he has succeeded in building a reputation on the basis of bluff, rather than performance, and his image is his prized possession. His method has not changed over the years and is explained in full in his ultimate piece of self-fashioning, *The Art of the Deal*. This bestselling book offers a glimpse into the mind of Trump, even if – or rather, exactly because – Trump's only contri-

---

29 Ware and Linkugel, "The Rhetorical Persona," 50-51.

30 Wolff, *Fire and Fury*, 148. Wolff adds that: "the hours following the speech were Trump's best in the White House."

31 Stephen Greenblatt, *Renaissance Self-Fashioning: From More to Shakespeare* (Chicago: University Of Chicago Press, 1980), 2, 3.

bution, according to co-author Tony Schwartz, was to insist that his name be printed larger on the cover.[32] In *The Art of the Deal*, Trump famously states:

> The way I promote is bravado. I play to people's fantasies. People may not always think big themselves, but they can still get very excited by those who do. That's why a little hyperbole never hurts. People want to believe that something is the biggest and the greatest and the most spectacular. I call it truthful hyperbole. It's an innocent form of exaggeration – and a very effective form of promotion.[33]

Trump's argument here rests on an oxymoron – hyperboles by definition distort the truth – that demonstrates his preference for form over substance. He does not hide his disdain for academia in the book, explaining that his Ivy League education at Penn's Wharton Business School taught him not to be impressed with academic credentials, since the "academic thing [is] only a preliminary to the main event."[34] In Trump's view, it does not matter whether you are truly successful, as long as you appear to be. He follows Machiavelli's famous dictum that it is not necessary for a prince to possess the qualities of a good ruler, as long as he gives people the impression he does. In short, for Trump exaggeration literally – considering the title of the book – is a form of art.

There is more to this than mere boasting; Trump is the living proof of the power of bluff. In the early 1990s, when Trump had run his Atlantic City casino enterprises into the ground, he managed to save his company by convincing his creditors that he was too big to fail and that it was worth more with his name on it.[35] As he recounts in *The Art of the Deal*, he learned the art of being a con-man at an early age. While working on an early investment in Cincinnati, Trump encounters a certain Irving, who he describes as a lying, stealing, lazy smooth-talker. Irving, according to Trump, is "one of the greatest bullshit artists I've ever met," and his admiration for him jumps off the page.[36] Men like Irving, Trump explains, are like lion tamers; the only thing keeping them alive is their big mouth and utter lack of fear. "If that animal sensed any

---

32 "Donald Trump's Ghostwriter Tells All," *The New Yorker*, July 25, 2016, http://www.newyorker.com/magazine/2016/07/25/donald-trumps-ghostwriter-tells-all.

33 Donald J. Trump and Tony Schwartz, *The Art of the Deal* (New York: Ballatine Books, 1987), 58.

34 Trump and Schwartz, *The Art of the Deal*, 77. 74.

35 Johnston, *The Making of Donald Trump*, 93; Kranish and Fisher, *Trump Revealed*, 199, 202.

36 Trump and Schwartz, *The Art of the Deal*, 85, 89.

weakness or any fear," Trump details, "he'd destroy the trainer in a second. But instead the trainer cracks his whip, walks with authority and, amazingly, the lion listens."[37] 'Irving,' whether he ever existed or not, allows Trump to share his view that the world belongs to those who bluff.

The Art of the Deal is full of anecdotes which feature Trump employing showmanship and bluff to trick others into giving him what he wants. When, for example, Trump needs to impress a group of local board members, he orders construction workers in Atlantic City to turn his vacant property into "the most attractive construction site in the history of the world," and, in his own words, leaves them stunned.[38] While the book sheds light on Trump's early practices of self-promotion, journalists have uncovered disturbing new techniques employed by Trump to craft his persona since the publication of the book in 1987.

First, at the core of Trump's ethos is his supposedly fabled wealth. As Johnston notes, "Trump's net worth is central to his public persona as a kind of modern Midas."[39] In *The Art of the Deal*, he brags how he craves money not for the wealth it brings but as a way to "keep score."[40] By his own account, he has done quite well. During the 2016 campaign, Trump's boasts about his net worth would fluctuate daily, from 8.7 billion one day to 10 billion another, and even at one point 11 billion dollars. His unprecedented refusal to hand over his tax returns, however, make it hard to check these numbers; in fact, it only helped fuel speculations about Trump's real wealth that started a decade earlier. In 2005, when journalist Timothy O'Brien concluded after lengthy research that Trump's net worth was closer to 200 million dollars, Trump exploded.[41] In Trumpian fashion, he immediately sued O'Brien for defamation and ordered that the story not be published.

In his testimonies for the ensuing court case *Donald J. Trump v. Timothy L. O'Brien*, Trump demonstrated his blatant disregard for consistency and awareness of the power of bluff. When asked whether he had ever lied about his net worth, Trump replied: "my net worth fluctuates, and it goes up and down with markets and with attitudes and with feelings, even my own feelings, but I try [to be truthful]."[42] After being presented with several official

37 Ibid., 88.

38 Ibid., 214-215.

39 Johnston, *The Making of Donald Trump*, 78.

40 Trump and Schwartz, *The Art of the Deal*, 63.

41 Timothy O'Brien, *TrumpNation: The Art of Being the Donald* (New York: Warner Books, 2005), 153-154.

42 "Donald J. Trump vs. Timothy L. O'Brien," Superior Court of New Jersey (2007), 10, https://assets.documentcloud.org/documents/2430267/trumps-lawsuit-on-net-worth.pdf.

bank records that showed his wealth to be as much as 788 million dollars, Trump's response exemplifies the kind of circular reasoning that would characterize his behavior on the campaign trail: "this [the bank records] doesn't include the value of branding… the value of my brand is very valuable."[43] Despite its self-referential character, this reasoning makes perfect sense from Trump's point of view. If all that matters is appearance and reality cannot be known, there is no objective net worth; the only thing that matters is how intangible assets make it much higher than the records suggests. Trump's wealth, in this sense, is just as elusive as his entire persona and becomes the object of speculation and controversy without any solid basis.

Furthermore, Trump not only tries to keep up appearances when it comes to his wealth, he also literally assumes the role of someone else. In the 1980s and 1990s, Trump would call reporters claiming to be 'John Barron' or 'John Miller,' posing as a vice-executive of the Trump Organization to brag about the business acumen and even sexual prowess of 'his' boss.[44] Though he later admitted under oath to posing as someone else, Trump continues to deny publicly that it was him. At the root of this lies Trump's assessment that that the press is always eager for a juicy story and hardly checks it sources. In *The Art of the Deal* he states that few reporters care for substance: "one thing I've learned about the press is that they're always hungry for a good story, and the more sensational the better."[45] Trump subscribes to the idea that there is no such thing as bad press and actively cultivates an aura of controversy and outrageousness to draw attention away from the very lack of substance that underlies his image as a successful entrepreneur. This same instinct for controversy helped him dominate the news during the 2016 campaign by personally calling in on shows like MSNBC's *Morning Joe* and *Fox and Friends* to share his latest thoughts. While the ensuing ratings left the networks spellbound, some of them admitted to having been played in the aftermath of the election.[46]

Finally, Trump is also literally an actor. According to the International Movie Database, Trump featured in over 20 productions – including the movie *Home Alone 2* (1992) and the TV-series *Sex and the City* (1999) – always playing 'himself.' Trump's first role in the 1989 movie *Ghosts Can't Do It* even earned him a Golden Raspberry for worst supporting actor. His ability to make light of this and himself, however, was what made him a frequent guest on (talk)shows.

43 Donald J. Trump vs. Timothy L. O'Brien, 66.
44 See Johnston, *The Making of Donald Trump*, chapters 17 and 18.
45 Trump and Schwartz, *The Art of the Deal*, 56.
46 See for this the post-election discussion at Harvard University: http://iop.harvard.edu/get-inspired/campaign-managers-conference/campaign-president-managers-look-2016.

When he appeared on *Saturday Night Live* in 2004, Trump impressed the producers with his willingness to make fun of himself.[47] When NBC starred Trump in *The Apprentice* in 2004, his talent as a performer immediately became clear to the production team. "Trump used no teleprompters, no cues," one contestant remembers, and he improvised all his lines – including the famous tag line "you're fired."[48] Hosting the show for fourteen seasons gave Trump ample opportunity to refine his public persona to a generation of viewers who were too young to remember his notoriety as Manhattan businessman. Trump soon started appearing on other shows, including *American Idol* and the WWE wrestling match this chapter started off with, which one critic noted, completed the "transition from business tycoon to pop-culture oddity."[49]

To sum up, Trump carefully and deliberately crafted a public persona of a wealthy, successful business mogul from the very start of his public career. This persona (more than his accomplishments) sustained his continuous presence in the limelight for over four decades. Ever the true con man, he managed to make others believe in his success by bluffing about it. Like Hans Christian Anderson's fairy tale emperor, Trump's unabashed boasting has convinced others of his new clothes, while there is a stark-naked history of bankruptcy and bluff. Unlike the emperor though, Trump seems acutely aware of his own nakedness. He likely understands that he is playing a part while denying it at the same time. Trump likes to boast, for example, that Michael Douglas once called him the best actor on television, but then vehemently denies this: "I'm not acting. This is who I really am."[50] This confusion about who the 'real' Donald Trump is only increased during the 2016 campaign. As a candidate, Trump retracted, contradicted, and outright denied his own statements or those of his campaign and he continued to do so as president.

As a result of his elusiveness, scholars and journalists struggle how to make sense of Trump's ambiguous persona. One compelling piece of evidence of Trump's success as self-fashioner is *Washington Post* journalists Mark Fisher and Michael Kranish (who supervised a team of two dozen reporters that spent months studying every aspect of Trump's life) regretfully recognizing that they remain in the dark about him, an admission they made the epilogue of their 451-page book *Trump Revealed.* "Trump seems not quite real," they write, "a character he had built to enhance his business empire, a construct designed to be at once an everyman and an impossibly high-flying king of

47 Kranish and Fisher, *Trump Revealed*, 265-266.
48 Ibid., 214.
49 Diane Werts quoted in: Ibid., 266.
50 Quoted in: Ibid., 217.

Manhattan."[51] While honest, this statement is at the same time deeply unsatisfying and even troubling. If we cannot truly know our leaders, after all, how can we hold them accountable? This problem is acute for the U.S. presidency, because personality greatly matters for how the office is executed.

3 Danger of Ambiguity?

Politics is a very personal affair; nowhere is this more evident than in the case of the U.S. presidency. Under the Constitution, the executive is an entire branch of government organized around one person. Naturally, the health and character of the person occupying that office has always been a major concern in American politics. In light of the dominating role of the president in today's politics, the relatively general terms in which Article II of the Constitution – dealing with the executive – discusses the powers of the Presidency comes as a surprise to many modern students of American government. The broad strokes the Constitution applies to paint the powers of the president to "take Care that the Laws be faithfully executed" and "recommend to their [Congress'] Consideration such Measures as he shall judge necessary and expedient" have allowed modern presidents to dominate policy-making today. Even though few framers of the Constitution would recognize their intentions in the contemporary presidency, the potential for this development was clearly there.

The need for a strong, single executive officer was a point of contention among the framers of the U.S. Constitution in Philadelphia. Pennsylvania delegate James Wilson considered "unity in the Executive" crucial for an independent and single-minded execution of the laws. However, Virginia delegate Edmund Randolph – who in the end refused to sign the Constitution – strongly objected to a single person executive which, to him, smacked of the British system of government and contained the "fœtus of monarchy." Americans would never stand for this, since "the permanent temper of the people [is] adverse to the very semblance of Monarchy."[52]

The ratification debates in the states largely proved Randolph right. The Presidency was one of the most compelling objections the opponents of the Constitution succeeded in leveling against it. This was especially true for the

51 Ibid., 334.

52 Max Farrand, ed., *The Records of the Federal Convention of 1787*, Revised Edition, vol. 1 (New Haven and London: Yale University Press, 1966), 65-66, 88.

older generation of revolutionaries who still remembered the supposed yoke of British tyranny, such as Virginia firebrand Patrick Henry. Fabled for his incendiary rhetoric, Henry set out to prove that the Constitution "squints toward monarchy." "Your President may easily become a king," Henry insisted, and with complete control over the military, there was nothing that the other branches of government could do to stop "a man of ambition and abilities… to render himself absolute."[53] The idea of a royal Presidency resonated then and ever since.[54] When a decade later President John Adams signed and invoked the Sedition Act to quell protest against his administration, he was branded King John I. More recently, when Massachusetts Representative Joe Kennedy was picked to deliver the response to Trump's first official State of the Union, his family name alone seemed to qualify him for the presidency in the eyes of some.[55]

In response to Anti-Federalist criticism, Alexander Hamilton wrote a ringing defense of the single person executive in Federalist 70. Hamilton, who at one point during the debates in Philadelphia envisaged the presidency as an "elected monarch,"[56] outlined the reasons why a strong unitary executive could be consistent with a republican form of government. First, he argued, one person would literally be more single-minded and thus more effective and determined in executing the laws than a group. One person, Hamilton maintained, will not have a difference of opinion with him or herself – apparently ruling out the possibility of being undecided – whereas there would be no end to a discussion if left up to a group. Second, and more important for the purposes of this chapter, Hamilton realized that a single person would be easier to hold accountable than a group. A body of people, he explained, "tends to conceal faults, and destroy responsibility"[57] by pointing to each other so that:

> it often becomes impossible, amidst mutual accusations, to determine on whom the blame or the punishment of a pernicious measure, or series of

53 John P. Kaminski and Gaspare J. Saladino, eds., *The Documentary History of the Ratification of the Constitution*, vol. 9 (Madison: State Historical Society of Wisconsin, 1990), 963-964 The secretary of the convention notes how: "Mr. Henry strongly and pathetically expatiated on the probability of the President's enslaving America, and the horrid consequences that must result."

54 Saul Cornell, *The Other Founders: Anti-Federalism and the Dissenting Tradition in America, 1788-1828* (Chapel Hill: University of North Carolina Press, 1999), 31.

55 See for example *The Guardian* on January 31: https://www.theguardian.com/us-news/2018/jan/31/joe-kennedy-response-state-of-the-union.

56 Richard R. Beeman, *Plain, Honest Men: The Making of the American Constitution* (New York: Random House, 2009), 169.

57 Jacob E. Cooke, ed., *The Federalist* (Middletown, CT: Wesleyan University Press, 1961), 476.

> pernicious measures, ought really to fall. It is shifted from one to another with so much dexterity, and under such plausible appearances, that the public opinion is left in suspense about the real author.[58]

As this quote demonstrates, Hamilton worried that both the qualities of individuals and their sense of responsibility would diminish in a group, which forced them to cooperate and compromise to arrive at decisions. Institutionalized groups, in other words, would bring out the worst – vanity, conceit, "self-love" – by allowing them to dodge responsibility for misconduct and blame others.[59] In his view, a unified executive was in fact a greater security for the faithful execution of the laws and the rights of the people, since it would always be clear who should be held accountable when mistakes were made or misconduct was detected. As a result, Hamilton portrayed the framers' choice for a potentially autocratic position as the product of Enlightenment attachment to "the dictates of reason and good sense."[60]

While Hamilton's distrust of the ambitions of his fellow citizens was typical for his time,[61] his trust in their ability to pursue misconduct and hold the culpable accountable has since proved unfounded. Past presidents have not turned out to be the honorable men Hamilton hoped they would be and proved unwilling to submit their record and actions to public scrutiny, especially in the case of Nixon and Clinton. In the end, however, Hamilton's confidence that the presidency was compatible with a republican form of government rested not so much on those holding the office, but the willingness and ability of the electorate and the other branches of government to closely scrutinize the president's every move and reign them in when necessary.

It is obvious that President Trump's elusive persona poses a clear problem. By virtue of deliberately spreading confusion about where he stands on issues and whether, in fact, he means what he says, Trump complicates the job of the electorate to hold the president accountable. If we accept the postmodern notion that the distinction between 'reality' and 'appearance' no longer holds in our so-called 'post-truth' society, then it becomes nearly impossible to hold our leaders accountable. Instead of pointing to someone else – as Hamilton feared – they can, as Trump so often does, deny they ever claimed the opposite of whatever position they hold at that point. In the waning days of the election,

---

58 Cooke ed., *The Federalist*, 476.

59 Ibid., 475, 477.

60 Ibid., 474.

61 Richard K. Matthews, *If Men Were Angels: James Madison and the Heartless Empire of Reason* (Lawrence: University Press of Kansas, 1995).

the Clinton campaign issued an attack ad that simply listed all the statements Trump denied having made in the presidential debates followed by footage of him making those exact same statements.[62]

The fact that Trump was elected despite – or perhaps because of – these inconsistencies has led some, including the president, to argue that contemporary American society tolerates and even approves such behavior. In this sense, Trump has a better grasp of the voting public's attitudes than his opponents, who kept ridiculing him for being dishonest and inconsistent. Trump, in short, is a mirror of society and he knows it. In *The Art of the Deal*, Trump not only blatantly admits to using bluff and deceit, he also implies that most people agree with him this behavior is justified as long as one can get away with it. Commenting on the 1980 controversy over the demolition of the Bonwitt Building's historic art deco friezes Trump tore down in order to build Trump Tower, he notes that the negative publicity that ensued only increased the sale of Trump Tower condos. "I'm not saying that's a good thing," Trump notes, "and in truth it probably says something perverse about the culture we live in."[63] In Trump's view, he is only doing what the people allow him to get away with. As his White House never failed to point out, Trump's showmanship and liberal attitude toward the truth were publicly known long before he ran for office and by electing him president voters signaled they were not bothered by this.[64]

This line of reasoning is problematic, however. First of all, many American voters *were* outraged by Trump and a majority of them in fact *did* vote for the other candidate. Secondly, it made Trump's problematic worldview official policy. Bret Stephens summarized this policy as "*truth is what you can get away with*."[65] Even though few will dispute Hannah Arendt's point that the relationship between truth and politics has always been strained, as a moral compass 'truth is what you can get away with' is unlikely to breed the type of trust necessary for a healthy democratic culture. The problem is not just Trump's status as a notorious liar, but that his continued lying created (in Arendt's words) "a peculiar kind of cynicism – an absolute refusal to believe the truth of anything, no matter how well this truth may be established." As a result, the very distinction between truth and falsehood has been destroyed. According to Arendt,

---

62 The ad, "Never Said That: The Briefing" can be found here: https://www.youtube.com/watch?v=EHclppeLdio.

63 Trump and Schwartz, *The Art of the Deal*, 175-176.

64 Frum, *Trumpocracy*, 198. As Frum points out: "No Trump supporter could fairly complain that he or she had not been amply warned."

65 Bret Stephens, "Don't Dismiss Trump's Attacks on the Media as Mere Stupidity," *Time*, February 18, 2017, http://time.com/4675860/donald-trump-fake-news-attacks/.

exactly this distinction forms "the sense by which we take our bearings in the real world."[66] Needless to say, such cynicism creates a political universe where the public no longer is interested in who the real Donald Trump is, let alone whether he can be held accountable for what he says and does. This state of affairs is still far off, but the Trump presidency certainly constitutes a constant stress test of the U.S. media's and electorate's commitment to separating between truth and falsehood, between person and persona.

66 Hannah Arendt, "Truth and Politics," in *The Portable Hannah Arendt*, ed. Peter Baehr (London: Penguin Classics, 2003), 568.

Bibliography

Abramowitz, Mildred W., *Eleanor Roosevelt and Federal Responsibility and Responsiveness to Youth, the Negro, and Others in Time of Depression*. Ph.D. Dissertation, New York University, 1971.

Allen, Craig, *Eisenhower and the Mass Media: Peace, Prosperity, and Prime-time TV*. Chapel Hill: University of North Carolina Press, 1993.

Allen, Craig, "Eisenhower's Congressional Defeat of 1956: Limitations of Television and the GOP." *Presidential Studies Quarterly* 22 (1992): 57-71.

Ambrose, Stephen, *Eisenhower: Soldier, General of the Army, President-Elect President*. New York: Simon & Schuster, 1983.

Ambrose, Stephen, *Eisenhower: The President*. New York: Simon & Schuster, 1985.

Anderson, Patrick, *Electing Jimmy Carter: The Campaign of 1976*. Baton Rouge and London: Louisiana State University Press, 1994.

Aristotle, *On Rhetoric: A Theory of Civic Discourse*, trans. George Alexander Kennedy, 2nd ed. New York: Oxford University Press, 2007.

Austin, Allan W., *Quaker Brotherhood: Interracial Activism and the American Friends Service Committee, 1917-1950*. Champaign: University of Illinois Press, 2012.

Baehr, Peter, ed., *The Portable Hannah Arendt*. London: Penguin Classics, 2003.

Balogh, Brian, and Bruce Schulman, *Recapturing the Oval Office: New Historical Approaches to the American Presidency*. Ithaca: Cornell University Press, 2015.

Barrett, David M., "The Mythology Surrounding Lyndon Johnson, His Advisers, and the 1965 Decision to Escalate the Vietnam War." *Political Science Quarterly* 103, no. 4 (1988): 637-663.

Barzun, Jacques, *Clio and the Doctors: Psycho-history, Quanto-history, & History*. Chicago: University of Chicago Press, 1974.

Baughman, James, *Television's Guardians: The FCC and the Politics of Programming, 1958-1967*. Knoxville: University of Tennessee Press, 1985.

Beale, Howard K., *The Critical Year: A Study of Andrew Johnson and Reconstruction*. New York: Hartcourt, Brace and Company, 1930.

Beasley, Maurine Hoffman, Holly Cowan Shulman and Henry R. Beasley, eds., *The Eleanor Roosevelt Encyclopedia*. Westport: Greenwood Press, 2001.

Beasley, Maurine Hoffman *Eleanor Roosevelt. Transformative First Lady*. Lawrence: University Press of Kansas, 2010.

Beeman, Richard R., *Plain, Honest Men: The Making of the American Constitution*. New York: Random House, 2009.

Bell, David, "Donald Trump Is Making the Great Man Theory of History Great Again," *Foreign Policy*, January 12, 2017.

Bell, Jonathan, *California Crucible: The Forging of Modern American Liberalism*. Philadelphia: University of Pennsylvania Press, 2012.

Benedict, Michael Les, *The Impeachment and Trial of Andrew Johnson*. New York: W.W. Norton & Co., 1973.

Benedict, Michael Les, "Preserving the Constitution: The Conservative Basis of Radical Reconstruction." *The Journal of American History* 61, no. 1 (1974): 65-90.

Benedict, Michael Les, *A Compromise of Principle: Congressional Republicans and Reconstruction, 1863-1869*. New York: W.W. Norton & Co., 1974.

Bennett Jr., Lerone, *Forced into Glory: Abraham Lincoln's White Dream*. Chicago: Johnson Publishing, 2000.

Bensel, Richard Franklin, *Yankee Leviathan: The Origins of Central State Authority in America, 1859-1877*. Cambridge: Cambridge University Press, 1991.

Berger, Jason, *A New Deal for the World: Eleanor Roosevelt and American Foreign Policy*. New York: Columbia University Press, 1981.

Bergeron, Paul H., ed., *The Papers of Andrew Johnson* 16 vols. Knoxville: University of Tennessee Press, 1991.

Bergeron, Paul H., *Andrew Johnson's Civil War and Reconstruction*. Knoxville: University of Tennessee Press, 2011.

Berlin, Ira, *Many Thousands Gone: The First Two Centuries of Slavery in North America*. Cambridge, Mass.: Harvard University Press, 1998.

Berlin, Ira, Joseph P. Reidy and Leslie S. Rowland, eds., *Freedom: A Documentary History of Emancipation, 1861-1867 – Series II: The Black Military Experience*. Cambridge: Cambridge University Press, 1982.

Berman, Larry, *Lyndon Johnson's War: The Road to Stalemate in Vietnam*. New York: W.W. Norton and Company, 1989.

Bernstein, Irving, *Guns or Butter: The Presidency of Lyndon Johnson*. New York: Oxford University Press, 1996.

Beschloss, Michael, *Reaching for Glory: Lyndon Johnson's Secret White House Tapes, 1964-1965*. New York: Simon and Schuster, 2001.

Birkner, Michael J., "What Was Modern Republicanism? A Review." *Register of the Kentucky Historical Society* 105, no. 3 (2007): 461-464.

Black, Allida M., *Casting Her Own Shadow. Eleanor Roosevelt and the Shaping of Postwar Liberalism*. New York: Columbia University Press, 1996.

Black, Allida M., ed., *The Eleanor Roosevelt Papers: The Human Rights Years, 1945-1948*. New York: Thomson Gale, 2007.

Black, Edwin, "The Second Persona." *The Quarterly Journal of Speech* 55, no. 2 (1970): 109-119.

Blake, David Haven, *Liking Ike: Eisenhower, Advertising, and the Rise of Celebrity Politics*. New York: Oxford University Press, 2016.

Blight, David W., *Race and Reunion: The Civil War in American Memory*. Cambridge: Belknap Press, 2002.

Bloodworth, Jeffrey, "Jimmy Carter's 1976 Presidential Campaign." In Scott Kaufman ed. *A Companion to Gerald R. Ford and Jimmy Carter*. Chichester: John Wiley & Sons, 2016.

Blumenthal, Sidney, *The Political Life of Abraham Lincoln: Wrestling with His Angel, 1849-1856*. New York: Simon and Schuster, 2017.

Borgwardt, Elizabeth, *A New Deal for the World: America's Vision for Human Rights*. Cambridge: Harvard University Press, 2005.

Bornet, Vaughn Davis, "Reappraising the Presidency of Lyndon B. Johnson." *Presidential Studies Quarterly* 20, no. 3 (1990): 591-602.

Bourne, Peter G., *Jimmy Carter: A Comprehensive Biography from Plains to Postpresidency*. New York: Scribner, 1997.

Bowen, David W., *Andrew Johnson and the Negro*. Knoxville: University of Tennessee Press, 2005.

Brands, H.W., *The General vs. the President: MacArthur and Truman at the Brink of Nuclear War*. New York: Doubleday, 2016.

Branyan, Robert L. and R. Alton Lee, "Lyndon B. Johnson and the Art of the Possible." *The Southwestern Social Science Quarterly* 45, no. 3 (1964): 213-225.

Brauer, Carl M., "Kennedy, Johnson, and the War on Poverty." *The Journal of American History*, 69, no. 1 (June 1982): 98-119.

Brinkley, Alan, "A President for Certain Seasons." *Wilson Quarterly* 14, no. 2 (Spring 1990): 110-119.

Brownell, Kathryn Cramer, "'Ideological Plugola,' 'Elitist Gossip,' and the Need for Cable Television." In Bruce Schulman and Julian Zelizer eds., *Media Nation: A Political History of the News*. Philadelphia: University of Pennsylvania Press, 2017.

Brownell, Kathryn Cramer, *Showbiz Politics: Hollywood in American Political Life*. Chapel Hill; University of North Carolina Press, 2014.

Burlingame, Michael, *The Inner World of Abraham Lincoln*. Urbana and Chicago: University of Illinois Press, 1994.

Burlingame, Michael, *Abraham Lincoln: A Life*. Baltimore: Johns Hopkins University Press, 2008.

Burns, James MacGregor and Susan Dunn, *The Three Roosevelts: Patrician Leaders Who Transformed America*. New York: Groove Press, 2001.

Califano, Joseph A. Jr., *The Triumph and Tragedy of Lyndon Johnson: The White House Years*. New York: Simon and Schuster, 1991.

Campbell, Angus, Philip E. Converse, Warren E. Miller, and Donald E. Stokes, *The American Voter*. New York: Wiley, 1960.

Campbell, Angus, Gerald Gurin, and Warren Miller, *The Voter Decides*. Evanston, Ill.: Row, Peterson, 1954.

Cannon, Lou, *Governor Reagan: His Rise to Power*. New York: PublicAffairs, 2003.

Cannon, Lou, *President Reagan: The Role of a Lifetime*. New York: PublicAffairs, 1991.

Caro, Robert A., *The Years of Lyndon Johnson: The Path to Power*. New York: Alfred A. Knopf, 1982.

Caro, Robert A., *The Years of Lyndon Johnson: Means of Ascent*. New York: Alfred A. Knopf, 1990.

Caro, Robert A., *The Years of Lyndon Johnson: The Master of the Senate*. New York: Alfred A. Knopf, 2002.

Caro, Robert A., *The Years of Lyndon Johnson: The Passage of Power*. New York: Vintage Press, 2013.

Carter, Dan T., *The Politics of Rage: George Wallace, the Origins of the New Conservatism, and the Transformation of American Politics*. 2nd ed., Baton Rouge: Louisiana State University Press, 2000.

Carter, Jimmy, *Why Not the Best? The First Fifty Years*. 1st edition 1975, Fayetteville: The University of Arkansas Press, 1996.

Carter, Jimmy, *An Hour Before Daylight: Memories of a Rural Boyhood*. New York etc.: Simon & Schuster, 2001.

Castel, Albert, *The Presidency of Andrew Johnson*. Lawrence: University of Kansas Press, 1979.

Chafe, William H., "Biographical Sketch." In Joan Hoff-Wilson and Marjorie Lightman eds., *Without Precedent: The Life and Career of Eleanor Roosevelt*. Bloomington: Indiana University Press, 1984.

Churchill, Winston, *The Second World War*. 6 vols. Boston, MA: Houghton Mifflin, 1949-1953.

Classen, Steven D. *Watching Jim Crow: The Struggles over Mississippi TV, 1955-1969*. Durham: Duke University Press, 2004.

Clifford, Clark, *Counsel to the President: A Memoir*. New York: Random House, 1991.

Cohen, Warren I., and Nancy Bernkopf Tucker, eds., *Lyndon Johnson Confronts the World: American Foreign Policy, 1963-1968*. New York: Cambridge University Press, 1994.

Conkin, Paul K., *Big Daddy from the Pedernales: Lyndon Baines Johnson*. Boston: Twayne Publishers, 1968.

Conway, Thomas W., *The Freedmen of Louisiana. Final Report of the Bureau of Free Labor, Department of the Gulf, to Major General E.R.S. Canby, Commanding*. New Orleans: New Orleans Times Book and Job Office, 1865.

Cook, Blanche Wiesen, *Eleanor Roosevelt: The Early Years, 1884-1933*. New York: Penguin, 1992.

Cook, Blanche Wiesen, *Eleanor Roosevelt: The Defining Years, 1933-1938*. New York: Penguin Books, 1999.

Cooke, Jacob E., ed., *The Federalist*. Middletown, CT: Wesleyan University Press, 1961.

Cormier, Frank, *LBJ: The Way He Was*. New York: Doubleday and Company, 1977.

Cornell, Saul, *The Other Founders: Anti-Federalism and the Dissenting Tradition in America, 1788-1828*. Chapel Hill: University of North Carolina Press, 1999.

Cornog, Evan, *The Power and the Story: How the Crafted Presidential Narrative Has Determined Political Success from George Washington to George W. Bush*. New York: Penguin, 2004.

Costigliola, Frank, *Roosevelt's Lost Alliances: How Personal Politics Helped Start the Cold War*. Princeton: Princeton University Press, 2012.

Costigliola, Frank, "'I React Intensely to Everything': Russia and the Frustrated Emotions of George F. Kennan, 1933-1958." *Journal of American History* 102, no. 4 (March 2016): 1075-1106.

Costigliola, Frank, "Personal Dynamics and Presidential Transition: The Case of Roosevelt and Truman." In Brian Balogh and Bruce Schulman eds., *Recapturing the Oval Office: New Historical Approaches to the American Presidency*. Ithaca: Cornell University Press, 2015.

Cox, LaWanda, and John H. Cox, *Politics, Principle, and Prejudice, 1865-1866: Dilemma of Reconstruction America*. New York: Free Press of Glencoe, 1963.

Culbert, David, "Television's Visual Impact on Decision-Making in the USA, 1968: The Tet Offensive and Chicago's Democratic National Convention." *Journal of Contemporary History* 33, no. 3 (1998): 419-449.

D'Antonio, Michael, *Never Enough: Donald Trump and the Pursuit of Success*. New York: St. Martin's Press, 2015.

D'Este, Carlo, *Warlord: A Life of Winston Churchill at War, 1874-1945*. New York: HarperCollins, 2008.

Dallek, Robert, *Lone Star Rising: Lyndon Johnson and His Times, 1908-1960*. New York: Oxford University Press, 1991.

Dallek, Robert, *Flawed Giant: Lyndon Johnson and his Times, 1961-1973*. New York: Oxford University Press, 1999.

Davis, David Brion, "Slavery and the Post-World War II Historians." *Daedalus* 103 (1974): 1-16.

Dawson, Joseph G., *Army Generals and Reconstruction: Louisiana, 1862-1877*. Baton Rouge: Louisiana State University Press, 1982.

Dirck, Brian R., *Lincoln the Lawyer*. Urbana and Chicago: University of Illinois Press, 2007.

Dow, Bonnie J., "Taking Trump Seriously: Persona and Presidential Politics in 2016." *Women's Studies in Communication* 40, no. 2 (2017): 136-139.

Downs, Gregory P., "The Mexicanization of American Politics: The United States' Transnational Path from Civil War to Stabilization." *The American Historical Review* 117, no. 2 (2012): 387-409.

Downs, Gregory, and Kate Masur, eds., *The World the Civil War Made*. Chapel Hill: University of North Carolina Press, 2015.
Duberman, Martin B., *The Antislavery Vanguard: New Essays on the Abolitionists*. Princeton: Princeton University Press, 1965.
Dufresne, Todd, *Freud Under Analysis: History, Theory, Practice: Essays in Honor of Paul Roazen*. London: Jaron Aronson Inc., 1997.
Dugger, Ronnie, *The Politician: The Drive For Power from the Frontier to Master of the Senate*. New York: Norton, 1982.
Eisner, Marc Allen, *From Warfare State to Welfare State: World War I, Compensatory State Building, and the Limits of the Modern Order*. University Park: Pennsylvania University Press, 2000.
Eizenstat, Stuart E., *President Carter: The White House Years*. New York: St. Martin's Press, 2018.
Ellis, Sylvia, *Freedom's Pragmatist: Lyndon Johnson and Civil Rights*. Gainesville: University Press of Florida, 2013.
Elovitz, Paul, *The Making of Psychohistory*. London: Routledge, 2018.
Erikson, Erik H., "The Strange Case of Freud, Bullitt, and Woodrow Wilson: I," *The New York Review of Books*, February 9, 1967: 3-6.
Eshet, Dan, *Fundamental Freedoms. Eleanor Roosevelt and the Universal Declaration of Human Rights*. Brookline: Facing History and Ourselves National Foundation, 2010.
Evans, Roland, and Robert Novak, *Lyndon Johnson: The Exercise of Power*. New York: New American Library, 1966.
Farrand, Max ed., *The Records of the Federal Convention of 1787*, Revised Edition, 3 vols. New Haven and London: Yale University Press, 1966.
Farrell, John, *Richard Nixon: The Life*. New York: Doubleday, 2017.
Fazzi, Dario, "Eleanor Roosevelt's Peculiar Pacifism: Activism, Pragmatism, and Political Efficacy in Interwar America," *European Journal of American Studies* 12, No. 1 (Spring 2017) 1-18.
Fehrenbacher, Don E., "The Making of a Myth: Lincoln and the Vice-Presidential Nomination in 1864." *Civil War History* 41, no. 4 (January 2012): 273-290.
Feldstein, Mark, *Poisoning the Press: Richard Nixon, Jack Anderson, and the Rise of Washington's Scandal Culture*. New York: Picor, 2011.
Fenster, Julie M., *FDR's Shadow: Louis Howe, The Force that Shaped Franklin and Eleanor Roosevelt*. New York: St. Martin's Griffin, 2009.
Ferrell, Robert, *The Dying President: Franklin D. Roosevelt, 1944-1945*. Columbia, MI: University of Missouri Press, 1998.
Fertel, Rien, *Southern Rock Opera*. New York: Bloomsbury Academic, 2019.
Finley, Keith M., *Delaying the Dream: Southern Senators and the Fight Against Civil Rights, 1938-1965*. Baton Rouge: Louisiana State University Press, 2008.

Fite, Gilbert C., *Richard B. Russell, Jr., Senator From Georgia*. Chapel Hill: The University of North Carolina Press, 1991.

Fitzgerald, Michael W., *Splendid Failure: Postwar Reconstruction in the American South*. Chicago: Ivan R. Dee, 2007.

Foner, Eric, *Reconstruction: America's Unfinished Revolution, 1863-1877*. New York: Perennial Classics, 2002.

Forgie, George B., *Patricide in the House Divided*. New York: W.W. Norton, 1979.

Freud, Sigmund, and William C. Bullitt, *Thomas Woodrow Wilson, Twenty-eighth President of the United States: A Psychological Study*. Boston: Houghton Mifflin, 1967.

Frum, David, *Trumpocracy: The Corruption of the American Republic*. New York: Harper, 2018.

Galambos, Louis, *Eisenhower: Becoming the Leader of the Free World*. Baltimore: Johns Hopkins University Press, 2018.

Garver, Eugene, *Aristotle's Rhetoric: An Art of Character*. Chicago: University Of Chicago Press, 1994.

Gay, Peter, *Freud for Historians*. Oxford: Oxford University Press, 1985.

Geertz, Clifford, *After the Fact: Two Countries, Four Decades, One Anthropologist*. Cambridge, MA: Harvard University Press, 1995.

Gellman, Irwin F., *The President and the Apprentice: Eisenhower and Nixon, 1952-1961*. New Haven: Yale University Press, 2015.

Gerstle, Gary, "Race and Nation in the Thought and Politics of Woodrow Wilson." In John Milton Cooper ed. *Reconsidering Woodrow Wilson: Progressivism, Internationalism, War, and Peace*. Washington, D.C.: Johns Hopkins University Press, 2008.

Gerstle, Gary, *Liberty and Coercion: The Paradox of American Government from the Founding to the Present*. Princeton: Princeton University Press, 2015.

Giap, Vo Nguyen, *How We Won the War*. Philadelphia: Recon Publishers, 1976.

Gilbert, Robert E., "The Eisenhower Campaign of 1952: War Hero as Television Candidate." *Political Communication* 3, no. 3 (1986): 293-311.

Gillette, William, *The Right to Vote: Politics and the Passage of the Fifteenth Amendment*. Baltimore: Johns Hopkins University Press, 1965.

Glad, Betty, *Jimmy Carter: In Search of the Great White House*. New York and London: W.W. Norton & Company, 1980.

Glendon, Mary Ann, *A World Made New. Eleanor Roosevelt and the Universal Declaration of Human Rights*. New York: Random House, 2001.

Goldman, Eric F., *The Tragedy of Lyndon Johnson*. New York: Alfred A. Knopf, 1969.

Goldman, Robert M., *Reconstruction and Black Suffrage: Losing the Vote in Reese and Cruikshank*. Lawrence: University Press of Kansas, 2001.

Goldsmith, Harry, *A Conspiracy of Silence: The Health and Death of Franklin D. Roosevelt*. New York: iUniverse, 2007.

Goldsmith, John A., *Colleagues: Richard B. Russell and his Apprentice, Lyndon B. Johnson*. Washington, D.C.: Seven Locks Press, 1993.

Goldwater, Barry, *The Conscience of a Conservative*. Shepardsville, KY: Victor Publishing, 1960.

Goodwin, Doris Kearns, *No Ordinary Time: Franklin and Eleanor Roosevelt: The Home Front in World War II*. New York: Simon and Schuster, 1994.

Graham, Hugh Davis, *Uncertain Triumph: Federal Education Policy in the Kennedy and Johnson Years*. Chapel Hill: The University of North Carolina Press, 1984.

Green, Anna, and Kathleen Troup, *The Houses of History: A Critical Reader in Twentieth-century History and Theory*. New York: New York University Press, 1999.

Greenberg, Kenneth S., "Why Masters Are Slaves." Review of *James Henry Hammond and the Old South: A Design for Mastery*, by Drew Gilpin Faust. *Reviews in American History* 11, no. 3 (1983): 386-389.

Greenberg, David, *Nixon's Shadow: The History of an Image*. New York: W.W. Norton, 2003.

Greenberg, David, *Republic of Spin: An Inside History of the American Presidency*. New York: W.W. Norton, 2016.

Greenblatt, Stephen, *Renaissance Self-Fashioning: From More to Shakespeare*. Chicago: University Of Chicago Press, 1980.

Greenstein, Fred I., *The Hidden-Hand Presidency: Eisenhower as Leader*. New York: Basic Books, 1982.

Greenstein, Fred I., "The Hidden-Hand Presidency: Eisenhower as Leader: A 1994 Perspective." *Presidential Studies Quarterly* 24, no. 2 (1994): 233-241.

Griffith, Robert, "Dwight D. Eisenhower and the Corporate Commonwealth." *American Historical Review* 87, no. 1 (1982): 87-122.

Guelzo, Allen C., *Lincoln's Emancipation Proclamation: The End of Slavery in America*. New York: Simon and Schuster, 2005.

Hackney, Sheldon, "Southern Violence," *The American Historical Review* 74, no. 3 (Feb. 1969): 906-925.

Hamilton, Nigel, *Monty*. 3 vols. New York: McGraw Hill, 1981, 1984 and 1987.

Hamilton, Nigel, *Biography: A Brief History*. Cambridge, MA: Harvard University Press, 2007.

Hamilton, Nigel, *American Caesars: Lives of the Presidents, From Franklin D. Roosevelt to George W. Bush*. New Haven: Yale University Press, 2010.

Hamilton, Nigel, *The Mantle of Command: FDR at War, 1941-1942*. Boston, MA: Houghton Mifflin Harcourt, 2014.

Hamilton, Nigel, "Biography as Corrective." In Hans Renders, Binne de Haan, and Jonne Harmsma, eds., *The Biographical Turn: Lives in History*. London: Routledge, 2017: 15-30.

Hamilton, Nigel, *Commander in Chief: FDR's Battle with Churchill, 1943*. Boston, MA: Houghton Mifflin, 2017.

Hamilton, Nigel, *War and Peace: FDR's Final Odyssey, 1943-1945*. Boston, MA: Houghton Mifflin, 2019.

Hardesty, Robert L., *The LBJ the Nation Seldom Saw*. San Marcos: Southwest Texas State University, 2003.

Hareven, Tamara K., *Eleanor Roosevelt. An American Conscience*. New York: Quadrangle Books, 1968.

Hastings, Max, *Winston's War: Churchill 1940-1945*. New York: Knopf, 2010.

Heinemann, Ronald L., *Harry Byrd of Virginia* (Charlottesville: University of Virginia Press, 1996).

Hemmer, Nicole, *Messengers of the Right: Conservative Media and the Transformation of American Politics*. Philadelphia: University of Pennsylvania Press, 2016.

Hennessey, Melinda Meek "Race and Violence in Reconstruction New Orleans: The 1868 Riot." *Louisiana History: The Journal of the Louisiana Historical Association* 20, no. 1 (1979): 77-91.

Herring, George C., *LBJ and Vietnam: A Different Kind of War*. Austin: University of Texas Press, 1994.

Herring, George C., *America's Longest War: The United States and Vietnam, 1950-1975*. New York: McGraw-Hill Higher Education, 2013.

Herring, George C., *The War Bells Have Rung: The LBJ Tapes and the Americanization of the Vietnam War*. Charlottesville: University of Virginia Press, 2015.

Hilmes, Michele, *Radio Voices: American Broadcasting, 1922-1952*. Minneapolis: University of Minnesota Press, 1997.

Hitchcock, William I., *The Age of Eisenhower: America and the World in the 1950s*. New York: Simon & Schuster, 2018.

Hoekstra, Douglas J., "The Politics of *Politics*: Skowronek and Presidential Research." *Presidential Studies Quarterly* 29, no. 3 (1999): 657-671.

Hoffman, Nancy, *Eleanor Roosevelt and the Arthurdale Experiment*. North Haven: Linnet Books, 2001.

Hofling, Charles K., *The Psychiatrist as Psychohistorian: Report of the Task Force on Psychohistory of the American Psychiatric Association*. Washington: APA, 1976.

Hofstadter, Richard, "The Paranoid Style in American Politics." *Harper's Magazine* (November 1964): 77-86.

Hofstadter, Richard, *The American Political Tradition and the Men Who Made It*. New York: Knopf, 1948.

Hogue, James K., *Uncivil War: Five New Orleans Street Battles And the Rise And Fall of Radical Reconstruction*. Baton Rouge: Louisiana State University Press, 2006.

Hood, Patterson, "The Southern Thing," recorded 2001, track 7 on *Southern Rock Opera*, Lost Highway Records, compact disc.

Horton, James Oliver and Lois E. Horton, *Slavery and the Making of America*. New York: Oxford University Press, 2004.

Houck, Davis and Amos Kiewe, *FDR's Body Politics: The Rhetoric of Disability*. Texas A&M University Press, 2003.

Hufbauer, Benjamin, *Presidential Temples: How Memorials and Libraries Shape Public Memory*. Lawrence: University Press of Kansas, 2005.

Hughes, Emmet John, *The Ordeal of Power: A Political Memoir of the Eisenhower Years*. New York: Atheneum, 1963.

Hyman, Herbert H., and Paul B. Sheatsley, "The Political Appeal of President Eisenhower." *Public Opinion Quarterly* 17, no. 4 (1953-1954): 443-460.

James, Scott C., "Historical Institutionalism, Political Development, and the Presidency." In George C. Edwards and William G. Howell eds., *The Oxford Handbook of the American Presidency*, eds. Oxford; Oxford University Press, 2009.

Janowitz, Morris, and Dwaine Marvick, *Competitive Pressure and Democratic Consent: An Interpretation of the 1952 Presidential Election*, 2nd edition. Chicago: Quadrangle, 1964.

John, Richard R., *Spreading the News: The American Postal System from Franklin to Morse*. Cambridge: Harvard University Pres, 1998.

John, Richard R., *Network Nation: Inventing American Telecommunications*. Cambridge: Belknap Press, 2015.

Johnson, Lyndon B., *A Time For Action: A Selection From the Speeches and Writings of Lyndon B. Johnson, 1953-1964*. New York: Atheneum Publishers, 1964.

Johnson, Lyndon B., *My Hope for America*. New York: Random House, 1964.

Johnson, Lyndon Baines, *The Vantage Point: Perspectives of the Presidency, 1963-1969*. New York: Holt, Rinehart, and Winston, 1971.

Johnson, Robert David, *All the Way with LBJ: The 1964 Presidential Election*. Cambridge: Cambridge University Press, 2009.

Johnston, David Cay, *The Making of Donald Trump*. New York: Melville House, 2016.

Jordan, David M., *FDR, Dewey, and the Election of 1944*. Bloomington: Indiana University Press, 2011.

Judis, John B., *William F. Buckley, Jr.: Patron Saint of the Conservatives*. New York: Simon and Schuster, 1988.

Kaczorowski, Robert J., *The Politics of Judicial Interpretation: The Federal Courts, Department of Justice and Civil Rights, 1866-1876*. New York: Fordham University Press, 2005.

Kaczorowski, Robert J., "Revolutionary Constitutionalism in the Era of the Civil War and Reconstruction." *N.Y.U. Law Review* 61, no. 5 (1986): 863-941.

Kaminski, John P., and Gaspare J. Saladino, eds., *The Documentary History of the Ratification of the Constitution*. 34 volumes. Madison: State Historical Society of Wisconsin, 1976-2019.

Kammen, Michael, *Mystic Chords of Memory: The Transformation of Tradition in American Culture*. New York: Random House, 1991.

Kaplan, Fred, *Lincoln and the Abolitionists: John Quincy Adams, Slavery, and the Civil War*. New York: HarperCollins, 2017.

Karnow, Stanley, *Vietnam: A History*. Middlesex, Penguin Books, 1984.

Kearns, Doris, *Lyndon Johnson and the American Dream*. New York: Harper and Row, 1968.

Kearns, Doris, "Lyndon Johnson's Political Personality." *Political Science Quarterly* 91, no. 3 (Autumn 1976): 385-409.

Keller, Morton, *Affairs of State: Public Life in Late Nineteenth Century America*. Cambridge: Belknap Press, 1977.

Kelly, Timothy, Margaret Power, and Michael Cary, *Hope in Hard Times: Norvelt and the Struggle for Community During the Great Depression*. University Park: Penn State University Press, 2016.

Keys, Barbara, "Henry Kissinger: The Emotional Statesman." *Diplomatic History* 35, no. 4 (September 2011): 587-609.

Klein, Naomi, *No Is Not Enough: Defeating the New Shock Politics*. London: Allen Lane, 2017.

Koncewicz, Michael, *They Said No to Nixon: Republicans Who Stood Up to the President's Abuses of Power*. Oakland: University of California Press, 2018.

Kotz, Nick, *Judgement Days: Lyndon Baines Johnson, Martin Luther King Jr., and the Laws that Changed America*. Boston: Houghton Mifflin Company, 2005.

Krabbendam, Hans, and John M. Thompson, *America's Transatlantic Turn: Theodore Roosevelt and the "Discovery" of Europe*. New York: Palgrave, 2012.

Kranish, Michael, and Marc Fisher, *Trump Revealed. The Definitive Biography of the 45th President*. London: Simon & Schuster, 2016.

Labbé, Ronald M., and Jonathan Lurie, *The Slaughterhouse Cases: Regulation, Reconstruction, and the Fourteenth Amendment*. Lawrence: University Press of Kansas, 2003.

Langer, William L., "Presidential Address Delivered at the Annual Dinner of the American Historical Association the Statler Hotel, New York City, December 29, 1957." *American Historical Review* 63, no. 2 (January 1958): 283-304.

Langer, Walter C., *The Mind of Adolf Hitler: The Secret Wartime Report*. New York: Basic Books, 1972.

Larrabee, Eric, *Commander in Chief: Franklin Delano Roosevelt, His Lieutenants & Their War*. New York: Harper & Row, 1987.

Lash, Joseph P., *Eleanor and Franklin*. New York: Norton & Company, 1971.

Lassiter, Matthew, *The Silent Majority: Suburban Politics in the Sunbelt South*. Princeton: Princeton University Press, 2007.

Lebeaux, Richard, *Young Man Thoreau*. Amherst: University of Massachusetts Press, 1989.

Lechner, Zachary J., *The South of the Mind: American Imaginings of White Southernness, 1960-1980*. Athens: The University of Georgia Press, 2018.

Lee, Bandy X., ed., *The Dangerous Case of Donald Trump*. New York: Thomas Dunne Books, 2017.

Lerner, Mitchell, "'Almost a Populist': Texas the South and the Rise of Lyndon Johnson." *Southwestern Historical Quarterly* 117, no. 3 (January 2014): 236-265.

Lesseig, Corey T., "Talmadge, Eugene," In John A. Garraty and Mark C. Carnes eds., *American National Biography*. New York and Oxford: Oxford University Press, 1999.

Leuchtenburg, William E., *The White House Looks South: Franklin D. Roosevelt, Harry S. Truman, Lyndon B. Johnson*. Baton Rouge: Louisiana State University Press, 2005.

Levi-Strauss, Claude, *Introduction to the Work of Marcel Mauss*. London: Routledge & Kegan Paul.

Lifton, Robert J., "On Psychohistory." In Robert Jay Lifton and Erik Olson eds., *Explorations in Psychohistory: The Wellfleet Papers*. New York: Simon and Schuster, 1974.

Lowrey, Walter M., "The Political Career of James Madison Wells." *Louisiana Historical Quarterly* 31 (1948): 1080-1083.

Lusane, Clarence, *The Black History of the White House*. San Francisco: City Light Books, 2011.

Macpherson, James, *Tried by War: Abraham Lincoln as Commander-in-Chief*. New York: Penguin Press, 2008.

Mandelbaum, Michael, "Vietnam: The Television War." *Daedalus* 111, no. 4 (1982): 157-169.

Mangione, Jerre, *The Dream and the Deal: The Federal Writers' Project, 1935-1943*. New York: Avon, 1972.

Marling, Karal Ann, *Wall-to-Wall America, A Cultural History of Post Office Murals in the Great Depression*. Minneapolis: University of Minnesota Press, 1982.

Mart, Michelle, "Eleanor Roosevelt, Liberalism and Israel." *Shofar: An Interdisciplinary Journal of Jewish Studies* 24, no. 3 (2006): 58-89.

Mason, Robert, "Citizens for Eisenhower and the Republican party, 1951-1965." *Historical Journal* 56, no. 2 (2013): 513-536.

Matthews, Richard K., *If Men Were Angels: James Madison and the Heartless Empire of Reason*. Lawrence: University Press of Kansas, 1995.

Matusow, Allen J., *The Unraveling of America: A History Of Liberalism in the 1960s*. New York: Harper and Row, 1984.

Maxwell, Angie, *The Indicted South: Public Criticism, Southern Inferiority, and the Politics of Whiteness*. Chapel Hill: The University of North Carolina Press, 2014.

Mazlish, Bruce, *Kissinger: The European Mind in American Policy*. New York: Basic Books, 1976.

Mazlish, Bruce, *In Search of Nixon: A Psychohistorical Inquiry*. Baltimore, MD: Penguin Books, 1974).

McCrary, Peyton, *Abraham Lincoln and Reconstruction: The Louisiana Experiment*. Princeton: Princeton University Press, 1978.

McFeely, William S., *Yankee Stepfather: General O.O. Howard and the Freedmen*. New Haven: Yale University Press, 1968.

McGinniss, Joe, *The Selling of the President, 1968*. New York: Trident Press, 1969.

McGirr, Lisa, *Suburban Warriors: The Origins of the New American Right*. Princeton: Princeton University Press, 2002.

McKitrick, Eric L., *Andrew Johnson and Reconstruction*. Chicago: University of Chicago Press, 1960.

McKitrick, Eric L., ed., *Andrew Johnson: A Profile*. New York: Hill and Wang, 1969.

McPherson, James M., *Drawn with the Sword: Reflections on the American Civil War*. New York: Oxford University Press, 1996.

Meringolo, Denise, *Museums, Monuments, and National Parks: Toward a New Genealogy of Public History*. Amherst: University of Massachusetts Press, 2012.

Miller, James, "The President's Advocate: OTP and Broadcast Issues." *Journal of Broadcasting & Electronic Media* 26, no. 3 (1982): 625-639.

Miller, Merle, *Lyndon: An Oral Biography*. New York: Putnam, 1980.

Miller, Warren E., and Santa A. Traugott, *American National Election Studies Data Sourcebook, 1952-1986*. Cambridge, Mass.: Harvard University Press, 1989.

Milton, George Fort, *The Age of Hate: Andrew Johnson and the Radicals*. New York: Coward-McCann, 1930.

Mitchell, Greg, *Tricky Dick and the Pink Lady: Richard Nixon vs. Helen Gahagan Douglan: Sexual Politics and the Red Scare*. New York: Random House, 1998.

Morison, Samuel E., *The Two Ocean War: A Short History of the United States Navy in the Second World War*. Boston, MA: Little Brown, 1963.

Morris, Kenneth E., and Barry Schwartz, "Why They Liked Ike: Tradition, Crisis, and Heroic Leadership." *Sociological Quarterly* 43, no. 1 (1993): 133-151.

Morris, Edmund, *The Rise of Theodore Roosevelt*. New York: Coward McCann, 1979.

Morris, Edmund, *Theodore Rex*. New York: Random House, 2001.

Morris, Edmund, *Colonel Roosevelt*. New York: Random House, 2010.

Morris, Kenneth E., *Jimmy Carter: American Moralist*. Athens and London: The University of Georgia Press, 1996.

Moss, George D., *Vietnam: An American Ordeal*, 6th Edition. New York: Routledge, 2010.

Mueller, John, *War, Presidents, and Public Opinion*. New York: Wiley, 1978.

Muslin, Hyman L., and Thomas H. Jobe, *Lyndon Johnson The Tragic Self: A Psychohistorical Portrait*. New York: Plenum Press, 1991.

Neal, Steve, *Harry and Ike: The Partnership That Remade the Postwar World*. New York: Scribner, 1991.

Neal, Steve, *Eleanor and Harry: The Correspondence of Eleanor Roosevelt and Harry S. Truman*. New York: Lisa Drew Book, 2002.

Neustadt, Richard E., *Presidential Power and the Modern Presidents: The Politics of Leadership from Roosevelt to Reagan*. New York: Free Press, 1990.

Newton, Jim, *Eisenhower: The White House Years*. New York: Doubleday, 2011.

Nichols, David A., *Ike and McCarthy: Eisenhower's Secret Campaign Against Joseph McCarthy*. New York: Simon & Schuster, 2017.

Nieman, Donald G., *To Set the Law in Motion: The Freedmen's Bureau and the Legal Rights of Blacks, 1865-1868*. New York: Millwood, 1979.

Nystrom, Justin A., *New Orleans after the Civil War*. Baltimore: John Hopkins University Press, 2010.

O'Brien, Timothy, *TrumpNation: The Art of Being the Donald*. New York: Warner Books, 2005.

O'Connor, Francis, "Federal Support for the Visual Arts: The New Deal Then and Now." *The New Deal Art Projects, An Anthology of Memoirs*. Washington, D.C.: Smithsonian Institution, 1972.

O'Farrell, Brigid, *She Was One of Us: Eleanor Roosevelt and the American Worker*. Ithaca: Cornell University Press, 2010.

Ownby, Ted, "Freedom, Manhood, and White Male Tradition in 1970s Southern Rock Music." In nne Goodwyn Jones and Susan V. Donaldson eds., *Haunted Bodies: Gender and Southern Texts*. Charlottesville: University Press of Virginia, 1997.

Parmet, Herbert S., *Eisenhower and the American Crusades*. New York: Macmillan, 1972.

Patel, Kiran, *The New Deal: A Global History*. Princeton: Princeton University Press, 2016.

Patterson, James T., *Grand Expectations: The United States, 1945-1974*. New York: Oxford University Press, 1996.

Patterson, James T., *The Eve of Destruction: How 1965 Transformed America*. New York: Basic Books, 2012.

Pawelec, Tomasz, "Bruce Mazlish: Pioneer Psychohistorian." *Clio's Psyche* 3, no. 3 (December 1996): 76-81.

Peirce, Charles Sanders, *Collected Papers of Charles Sanders Peirce*. Cambridge: Belknap Press, 1958.

Perlman, Allison, *Public Interests: Media Advocacy and the Struggles over U.S. Television*. New Brunswick: Rutgers University Press, 2016.

Perlstein, Rick, *Nixonland: The Rise of a President and the Fracturing of America*. New York: Scribner, 2009.

Perret, Geoffrey, *Eisenhower*. New York: Random House, 1999.

Peterson, Merrill D., *Lincoln in American Memory*. New York: Oxford University Press, 1974.

Phillips, Julieanne, "League of Women Voters." In Maurine Hoffman Beasley, Holly Cowan Shulman, and Henry R. Beasley eds., *The Eleanor Roosevelt Encyclopedia*. Westport: Greenwood Press, 2001.

Phillips, Kevin, *The Emerging Republican Majority*.New York: Arlington House, 1969.

Phillips, Kevin, *Mediacracy: American Parties and Politics in the Communications Age*. New York: Doubleday, 1974.

Pickett, William B., *Eisenhower Decides to Run: Presidential Politics and Cold War Strategy*. Chicago: Ivan R. Dee, 2000.

Pietikainen, Petteri, and Juhani Ihanus, "On the Origins of Psychoanalytic Psychohistory." *History of Psychology* 6, no. 2 (2003).

Pogue, Forrest, *The Supreme Command*. Washington: U.S. Department of the Army, 1954.

Ponce de Leon, Charles, *And That's The Way It Was: A History of Television News in America*. Chicago: University of Chicago Press, 2015.

Porter, William E., *Assault on the Media: The Nixon Years*. Ann Arbor: University of Michigan Press, 1976.

Quinn, Susan, *Eleanor and Hick: The Love Affair That Shaped a First Lady*. New York: Penguin, 2016.

Rable, George C., "Republican Albatross: The Louisiana Question, National Politics, and the Failure of Reconstruction." *Louisiana History* 23, no. 2 (1982): 109-130.

Reichard, Gary W., *The Reaffirmation of Republicanism: Eisenhower and the Eighty-third Congress*. Knoxville: University of Tennessee Press, 1975.

Remnick, David, *The Bridge: The Life and Rise of Barack Obama*. London: Picador, 2010.

Renders, Hans, and Binne de Haan, "The Challenges of Biography Studies." In Hans Renders and Binne de Haan eds., *Theoretical Discussions of Biography: Approaches From History, Microhistory, and Life Writing*. Leiden and Boston: Brill, 2014: 1-8.

Renshaw, Patrick, *Franklin D. Roosevelt: Profiles in Power*. Harlow: Pearson, 2004.

Reynolds, David, *In Command of History: Winston Churchill, Fighting and Writing the Second World War*. London: Allen Lane, 2004.

Reynolds, David, *In Command of History*. New York: Random House, 2005.

Reynolds, Donald E., "The New Orleans Riot of 1866, Reconsidered." *Louisiana History: The Journal of the Louisiana Historical Association* 5, no. 1 (1964): 5-27.

Ribuffo, Leo P., "God and Jimmy Carter." In M.L. Bradbury and James B. Gilbert, eds., *Transforming Faith: The Sacred and the Secular in Modern American History*. New York etc.: Greenwood Press, 1989.

Ricard, Serge, ed., *A Companion to Theodore Roosevelt*. Chichester: Blackwell Publishing, 2011.

Richards, Leonard L., *Who Freed the Slaves? The Fight Over the Thirteenth Amendment*. Chicago: University of Chicago Press, 2015.

Ripley, C. Peter, *Slaves and Freedmen in Civil War Louisiana*. Baton Rouge: Louisiana State University Press, 1976.

Robertson, David Brian, *Federalism and the Making of America*. New York: Routledge 2017.

Rodrigue, John C., "The Freedmen's Bureau and Wage Labor in the Louisiana Sugar Region." In Paul A. Cimbala and Randall M. Miller eds., *The Freedmen's Bureau and Reconstruction: Reconsiderations*. New York: Fordham University Press, 1999.

Rogin, Michael, *Fathers and Children: Andrew Jackson and the Subjugation of the American Indian*. New Jersey: Transaction Publishers, 1991.

Rollins, Peter C., "The Vietnam War: Perceptions Through Literature, Film, and Television." *American Quarterly* 36, no. 3 (1984): 419-432.

Roosevelt, Eleanor, "The Negro and Social Change." In Allida M. Black ed., *Courage in a Dangerous World: The Political Writings of Eleanor Roosevelt*. New York: Columbia University Press, 1999.

Roosevelt, Eleanor, "Keepers of Democracy." *The Virginia Quarterly Review* 15, no. 1 (1939): 1-5.

Rosenwald, Brian, *Talk Radio America: How an Industry Took Over a Political Party that Took Over the United States*. Cambridge: Harvard University Press, 2019.

Ross, Michael A., *Justice of Shattered Dreams: Samuel Freeman Miller and the Supreme Court during the Civil War Era*. Baton Rouge: Louisiana State University Press, 2003.

Rourke, Francis E., and Roger E. Brown, "Presidents, Professionals, and Telecommunications Policy Making in the White House." *Presidential Studies Quarterly* 25, no. 2 (Spring 1996): 539-549.

Runyan, William McKinley, *Psychology and Historical Interpretation*. New York: Oxford University Press, 1988.

Samuel, Lawrence R., *Shrink: A Cultural History of Psychoanalysis in America*. Lincoln: University of Nebraska Press, 2013.

Sandburg, Carl, *Abraham Lincoln: The Prairie Years*, 2 vols. New York, Harcourt, Brace, 1926.

Sandburg, Carl, *Abraham Lincoln: The War Years*, 4 vols. New York: Harcourt, Brace, 1939.

Sayer, Faye, *Public History: A Practical Guide*. New York: Bloomsbury, 2015.

Schandler, Herbert Y., *Lyndon Johnson and Vietnam: The Unmasking of a President*. Princeton: Princeton University Press, 1977.

Schlup, Leonard C., and Donald W. Whisenhunt, eds., *It Seems to Me: Selected Letters of Eleanor Roosevelt*. Lexington: The University Press of Kentucky, 2001.

Schulman, Bruce, *The Seventies: The Great Shift in American Culture, Society, and Politics*. Boston: Da Capo Press, 2001.

Schulman, Frances M. Seeber, "Eleanor Roosevelt and Women in the New Deal: A Network of Friends." *Presidential Studies Quarterly* 20, no. 4 (Fall 1990): 707-717.

Schwartz, Barry, *Abraham Lincoln and the Forge of National Memory*. Chicago: University of Chicago Press, 2000.

Schwartz, Barry, *Abraham Lincoln in the Post-Heroic Era*. Chicago: University of Chicago Press, 2008.

Sefton, James E., *Andrew Johnson and the Uses of Constitutional Power*. New York: Little, Brown, 1980.

Sexton, Jared Yates, *The People Are Going to Rise Like the Waters Upon Your Shore: A Story of American Rage*. Berkeley, CA: Counterpoint, 2017.

Shenk, Joshua Wolf, *Lincoln's Melancholy*. Boston: Houghton Mifflin, 2005.

Shermer, Elizabeth Tandy, *Sunbelt Capitalism: Phoenix and the Transformation of American Politics*. Philadelphia: University of Pennsylvania Press, 2015.

Simpson, Brooks D., *The Reconstruction Presidents*. Lawrence: University Press of Kansas, 1998.

Skidmore, Max J., "Introduction." In Max J. Skidmore ed., *Maligned Presidents: The Late 19th Century*. New York, NY: Palgrave Pivot, 2014.

Skowronek, Stephen, "Theory and History, Structure and Agency." *Presidential Studies Quarterly* 29, no. 3 (1999): 672-681.

Sloan, John W., "The Management and Decision-Making Style of President Eisenhower." *Presidential Studies Quarterly* 20, no. 2 (1990): 295-313.

Smith, Jean Edward, *FDR*. New York: Random House, 2007.

Smith, Jean Edward, *Eisenhower in War and Peace*. New York: Random House, 2012.

Stampp, Kenneth M., *The Era of Reconstruction, 1865-1877*. New York: Random House, 1965.

Starr, Paul, *The Creation of the Media: The Political Origins of Modern Communications*. New York: Basic Books, 2002.

Stein, Sally, "The President's Two Bodies: Staging and Restagings of FDR and the New Deal Body Politic." *American Art* 18, no. 1 (Spring 2004): 32-57.

Steinberg, Alfred, *Sam Johnson's Boy: A Close-Up of the President from Texas*. New York: MacMillan, 1968.

Stewart, David O., *Impeached: The Trial of President Andrew Johnson and the Fight for Lincoln's Legacy*. New York: Simon & Schuster, 2010.

Stroud, Kandy, *How Jimmy Won: The Victory Campaign from Plains to the White House*. New York: William Morrow and Company, Inc., 1977.

Strozier, Charles B., and Daniel Offer, *The Leader: Psychohistorical Essays*. New York: Plenum Press, 1985.

Stryker, Lloyd Paul, *Andrew Johnson: A Study in Courage*. New York: Macmillan, 1936.

Summers, Mark Wahlgren, *A Dangerous Stir: Fear, Paranoia, and the Making of Reconstruction*. Chapel Hill: University of North Carolina Press, 2009.

Summers, Mark Wahlgren, *The Ordeal of the Reunion: A New History of Reconstruction*. Chapel Hill: University of North Carolina Press, 2014.

Tananbaum, Duane, *The Bricker Amendment Controversy: A Test of Eisenhower's Political Leadership*. Ithaca: Cornell University Press, 1988.

Taylor, Joe Gray, *Louisiana Reconstructed, 1863-1877*. Baton Rouge: Louisiana State University Press, 1974.

Thomas, Benjamin P., *Abraham Lincoln: A Biography*. 1952; reprint Carbondale, Ill.: Southern Illinois University Press, 2008.

Thomas, Evan, *Being Nixon: A Man Divided*. New York: Random House, 2016.

Thompson, Kenneth W., ed., *The Eisenhower Presidency: Eleven Intimate Perspectives of Dwight D. Eisenhower*. Lanham, Md.: University Press of America, 1984.

Thompson, Mark, *Enough Said: What's Gone Wrong with the Language of Politics?* London: Vintage, 2016.

Thomson, Charles A.H., and Frances M. Shattuck, *The 1956 Presidential Campaign*. Washington, D.C.: Brookings Institution, 1960.

Trefousse, Hans L., *Andrew Johnson: A Biography*. New York: W.W. Norton & Co., 1989.

Tregle, Joseph G., "Thomas J. Durant, Utopian Socialism, and the Failure of Presidential Reconstruction in Louisiana." *The Journal of Southern History* 45, no. 4 (1979): 485-512.

Trump, Donald J. and Tony Schwartz, *The Art of the Deal*. New York: Ballatine Books, 1987.

Tunnell, Ted, *Crucible of Reconstruction: War, Radicalism and Race in Louisiana, 1862-1877*. Baton Rouge: Louisiana State University Press, 1992.

Tyrrel, Ian, *Transnational Nation: United States History in Global Perspective Since 1789*. New York: Palgrave Macmillan 2007.

Tyrrel, Ian, *Reforming the World: The Creation of America's Moral Empire*. Princeton: Princeton University Press, 2010.

Unger, Irwin, and Debi Unger, *LBJ: A Life*. New York: Wiley, 1999.

Vandal, Gilles, "The Origins of the New Orleans Riot of 1866, Revisited." *Louisiana History: The Journal of the Louisiana Historical Association* 22, no. 2 (1981): 135-165.

VanDeMark, Brian, *Into the Quagmire: Lyndon Johnson and the Escalation of the Vietnam War*. New York: Oxford University Press, 1995.

Vandiver, Frank E., *Shadows of Vietnam: Lyndon Johnson's Wars*. College Station: Texas A&M Press, 1997.

Waldrep, Christopher, *Roots of Disorder: Race and Criminal Justice in the American South, 1817-80*. Urbana: University of Illinois Press, 1998.

Waldrep, Christopher, and Donald G. Nieman eds., *Local Matters: Race, Crime, and Justice in the Nineteenth-Century South*. Athens: University of Georgia Press, 2001.

Ward, Geoffrey and Ken Burns, *The Roosevelts: An Intimate History*. New York: Alfred A. Knopf, 2014.

Ware, B.L., and Wil A. Linkugel, "The Rhetorical Persona: Marcus Garvey as Black Moses." *Communication Monographs* 49, no. 1 (1982): 50-62.

Westen, Drew, *The Political Brain: The Role of Emotions in Deciding the Fate of the Nation*. New York: PublicAffairs, 2008.

White, Howard A., *The Freedmen's Bureau in Louisiana*. Baton Rouge: Louisiana State University Press, 1970.

White Jr., Ronald C., *A. Lincoln: A Biography*. New York: Random House, 2009.

White, William S., *The Professional: Lyndon B. Johnson*. Boston: Houghton Mifflin Company, 1964.

Wicker, Tom, *Dwight D. Eisenhower*. New York: Times Books, 2002.

Wilkinson, Burke, *Young Louis Fourteenth: The Early Years of the Sun King*. Basingstoke: Macmillan, 1970.

Williams, Juan, *Eyes on the Prize: America's Civil Rights Years, 1954-1965*. New York: Penguin Books, 1987.

Wilson, Douglas L., *Lincoln Before Washington: New Perspectives on the Illinois Years*. Urbana and Chicago: University of Illinois Press, 1997.

Wilson, Robert H., Norman J. Glickman and Laurence E. Lynn Jr., eds., *LBJ's Neglected Legacy: How Lyndon Johnson Reshaped Domestic Policy and Government*. Austin: University of Texas Press, 2015.

Winston, Robert W., *Andrew Johnson, Plebeian and Patriot*. New York: H. Holt and Company, 1928.

Witcover, Jules, *Marathon: The Pursuit of the Presidency, 1972-1976*. New York: The Viking Press, 1977.

Witherspoon, Patricia D., "'Let Us Continue:' The Rhetorical Initiation of Lyndon Johnson's Presidency." *Presidential Studies Quarterly* 17, no. 3 (1987): 531-539.

Wolff, Michael, *Fire and Fury: Inside the Trump White House*. London: Little, Brown, 2018.

Woods, Michael E., *Emotional and Sectional Conflict in the Antebellum United States*. Cambridge: Cambridge University Press, 2014.

Woods, Randall B., *LBJ: Architect of American Ambition*. New York: Free Press, 2006.

Woods, Randall B., *Prisoners of Hope: Lyndon B. Johnson, the Great Society, and the Limits of Liberalism*. New York: Basic Books, 2016.

Yoos, George E., "A Revision of the Concept of Ethical Appeal." *Philosophy & Rhetoric* 12, no. 1 (1979): 41-58.

Zarefsky, David, "Lincoln's 1862 Annual Message: A Paradigm of Rhetorical Leadership." *Rhetoric & Public Affairs* 3, no. 1 (2000): 5-14.

Zarefsky, David, "Philosophy and Rhetoric in Lincoln's First Inaugural Address." *Philosophy and Rhetoric* 45, no. 2 (2012): 165-188.

Zelizer, Julian E., *Jimmy Carter*. New York: Times Books, 2010.

Zelizer, Julian E., *Lyndon Johnson, Congress, and the Battle for the Great Society*. New York: Penguin Books, 2015.

Zwiers, Maarten, "Good Cop, Bad Cop: Segregationist Strategies and Democratic Party Politics in Mississippi, 1948-1960." *The Southern Quarterly* 54, no. 1 (Fall 2016): 29-52.

Index